SOCIAL SECURITY LEGISLATION SUPPLEMENT 2017/18

General Editor
Nick Wikeley, M.A. (Cantab)

Commentary by
Ian Hooker, LL.B.
Formerly Lecturer in Law, University of Nottingham
Formerly Chairman, Social Security Appeal Tribunals

John Mesher, B.A., B.C.L. (Oxon), LL.M. (Yale)

Edward Mitchell, LL.B.
Judge of the Upper Tribunal

Richard Poynter B.C.L., M.A. (Oxon)
District Tribunal Judge,
Judge of the Upper Tribunal

Mark Rowland, LL.B.
Judge of the Upper Tribunal

Robin White, M.A., LL.M.
Emeritus Professor of Law, University of Leicester,
Formerly Judge of the Upper Tribunal

Nick Wikeley, M.A. (Cantab)
Judge of the Upper Tribunal,
Emeritus Professor of Law, University of Southampton

Consultant Editor
Child Poverty Action Group

GW00691213

SWEET & MAXWELL

THOMSON REUTERS

Published in 2018 by Thomson Reuters,
trading as Sweet & Maxwell.
Registered in England & Wales. Company No. 1679046.
Registered office 5 Canada Square, Canary Wharf, London E14 5AQ.

Typeset by Wright and Round Ltd., Gloucester
Printed and bound in Great Britain by
Ashford Colour Press, Gosport, Hants

For further information on our products and services,
visit www.sweetandmaxwell.co.uk

No natural forests were destroyed to make this product.
Only farmed timber was used and re-planted.

A CIP catalogue record for this book is
available from the British Library

ISBN 978–0–414–06721–9

PREFACE

This is the Supplement to the 2017/18 edition of the five volume work, *Social Security Legislation*, which was published in September 2017. Part I of this Supplement contains new legislation, presented in the same format as in the main volumes. Parts II, III, IV, V and VI contain the standard updating material—a separate Part for each volume of the main work—which amends the legislative text and key aspects of the commentary, drawing attention to important recent case law, so as to be up to date as at December 7, 2017. Part VII of this Supplement includes the relevant parts of the Scotland Act 1998 as now in force (and as amended by the Scotland Act 2016) in recognition of the importance of the impending devolution of certain social security functions and benefits. Finally, Part VIII gives some notice of changes forthcoming between December 2017 and the date to which the main work (2018/19 edition) will be up to date (mid-April 2018) along with the April 2018 benefit rates.

The many updating changes included in this Supplement describe and analyse important developments in the Upper Tribunal case law relating to the descriptors for both personal independence payment (PIP) and employment and support allowance (ESA). There has also been extensive significant case law in both the Upper Tribunal and the courts impacting on the right to reside. We also include the text of the Loans for Mortgage Interest Regulations 2017 (SI 2017/725), coming into force from April 2018, which will end the current provision of help with owner-occupier payments (commonly known as Support for Mortgage Interest or "SMI"). Instead, assistance will be provided to benefit claimants who are homeowners in respect of their liability to make payments (principally mortgage interest) in the form of interest-bearing loan payments. There are further Commencement Orders relating to the controversial phased roll-out of universal credit.

As always we welcome comments from those who use this Supplement. Please address these to the General Editor, Nick Wikeley, c/o School of Law, The University of Southampton, Highfield, Southampton SO17 1BJ (*njw@soton.ac.uk*).

Ian Hooker
John Mesher
Edward Mitchell
Richard Poynter

Mark Rowland
Robin White
Nick Wikeley

December 11, 2017

CONTENTS

USING THE UPDATING MATERIAL IN THIS SUPPLEMENT

The amendments and updating material contained in Parts II-VI of this Supplement are keyed in to the page numbers of the relevant main volume of *Social Security Legislation 2017/18*. Where there have been a significant number of changes to a provision, the whole section, subsection, paragraph or regulation, as amended will tend to be reproduced. Other changes may be noted by an instruction to insert or substitute new material or to delete part of the existing text. The date the change takes effect is also noted. Where explanation is needed of the change, or there is updating relating to existing annotations but no change to the legislation, you will also find commentary in this Supplement. The updating material explains new statutory material, takes on board Upper Tribunal or court decisions, or gives prominence to points which now seem to warrant more detailed attention.

For the most part any relevant new legislation since the main volumes were published is contained in Part I, while amendments to existing legislative provisions are contained in Parts II–VI respectively, together with commentary on new case law. This Supplement amends the text of the main volumes of *Social Security Legislation 2017/18* to be up to date as at December 7, 2017.

Nick Wikeley
General Editor

PAGES OF MAIN VOLUMES AFFECTED BY MATERIAL IN THIS SUPPLEMENT

Main volume page affected	Relevant paragraph in supplement
VOLUME I	
p.44	2.001
p.60	2.002
p.62	2.003
p.148	2.004
p.170	2.004.1
p.323	2.004.2
p.330	2.005
p.439	2.006
p.664	2.007
p.667	2.008
p.670	2.009
p.679	2.010
p.682	2.011
p.683	2.012
p.693	2.013
p.717	2.014
p.728	2.015
p.749	2.016
p.752	2.017
p.762	2.018
p.763	2.018.1
p.766	2.019
p.769	2.020
p.772	2.021
p.773	2.022
p.774	2.023
p.780	2.024
p.783	2.025
p.785	2.026
p.795	2.026.1
p.797	2.027
p.799	2.028
p.800	2.029
p.801	2.030
p.808	2.031
p.809	2.032
p.810	2.033
p.812	2.034
p.812	2.035
p.814	2.036
p.815	2.037

Pages of Main Volumes Affected by Material in this Supplement

VOLUME III

TABLE OF ABBREVIATIONS USED IN THIS SERIES

1978 Act	Employment Protection (Consolidation) Act 1978
1979 Act	Pneumoconiosis (Workers' Compensation) Act 1979
1995 Regulations	Social Security (Incapacity for Work) (General) Regulations 1995
1998 Act	Social Security Act 1998
1999 Regulations	Social Security and Child Support (Decisions and Appeals) Regulations 1999
2002 Act	Tax Credits Act 2002
2004 Act	Child Trust Funds Act 2004
AA	Attendance Allowance
AA Regulations	Social Security (Attendance Allowance) Regulations 1991
AAC	Administrative Appeal Chamber
AACR	Administrative Appeals Chamber Reports
AAW	Algemene Arbeidsongeschiktheidswet (Dutch General Act on Incapacity for Work)
A.C.	Law Reports Appeal Cases
A.C.D.	Administrative Court Digest
ADHD	Attention Deficit Hyperactivity Disorder
Admin	Administrative Court
Admin L.R.	Administrative Law Reports
Administration Act	Social Security Administration Act 1992
AIDS	Acquired Immune Deficiency Syndrome
AIIS	Analogous Industrial Injuries Scheme
AIP	assessed income period
All E.R.	All England Reports
All E.R. (E.C.)	All England Reports (European Cases)
AMA	American Medical Association
AO	Adjudication Officer
AO	Authorised Officer
AOG	*Adjudication Officers Guide*
art.	article
Art.	Article
ASD	Autistic Spectrum Disorder
ASP	Act of the Scottish Parliament
ASPP	Additional Statutory Paternity Pay

A.T.C.	Annotated Tax Cases
Attendance Allowance Regulations	Social Security (Attendance Allowance) Regulations 1991
AWT	All Work Test
BA	Benefits Agency
BAMS	Benefits Agency Medical Service
B.C.L.C.	Butterworths Company Law Cases
B.H.R.C.	Butterworths Human Rights Cases
B.L.G.R.	Butterworths Local Government Reports
Blue Books	*The Law Relating to Social Security*, Vols 1–11
BMI	body mass index
B.M.L.R.	Butterworths Medico Legal Reports
B.P.I.R.	Bankruptcy and Personal Insolvency Reports
B.T.C.	British Tax Cases
BTEC	Business and Technology Education Council
B.V.C.	British Value Added Tax Reporter
B.W.C.C.	Butterworths Workmen's Compensation Cases
C	Commissioner's decision
c.	chapter
C&BA 1992	Social Security Contributions and Benefits Act 1992
CAA 2001	Capital Allowances Act 2001
CAB	Citizens Advice Bureau
CAO	Chief Adjudication Officer
CBA 1975	Child Benefit Act 1975
CBJSA	Contribution-Based Jobseeker's Allowance
C.C.L. Rep.	Community Care Law Reports
CCM	HMRC New Tax Credits Claimant Compliance Manual
CCN	New Tax Credits Claimant Compliance Manual
C.E.C.	European Community Cases
CERA	cortical evoked response audiogram
CESA	Contribution-based Employment and Support Allowance
CFS	chronic fatigue syndrome
Ch.	Chancery Division Law Reports
Child Benefit Regulations	Child Benefit (General) Regulations 2006
CIR	Commissioners of Inland Revenue
Citizenship Directive	Directive 2004/38

Table of Abbreviations used in this Series

CJEC	Court of Justice of the European Communities
CJEU	Court of Justice of the European Union
Claims and Payments Regulations	Social Security (Claims and Payments) Regulations 1987
Claims and Payments Regulations 1979	Social Security (Claims and Payments) Regulations 1979
CMA	Chief Medical Adviser
CMEC	Child Maintenance and Enforcement Commission
C.M.L.R.	Common Market Law Reports
C.O.D.	Crown Office Digest
Com. L.R.	Commercial Law Reports
Commissioners Procedure Regulations	Social Security Commissioners (Procedure) Regulations 1999
Community treaties	EU treaties
Community institution	EU institution
Community instrument	EU instrument
Community law	EU law
Community legislation	EU legislation
Community obligation	EU obligation
Community provision	EU provision
Computation of Earnings Regulations	Social Security Benefit (Computation of Earnings) Regulations 1978
Computation of Earnings Regulations 1996	Social Security Benefit (Computation of Earnings) Regulations 1996
Con. L.R.	Construction Law Reports
Consequential Provisions Act	Social Security (Consequential Provisions) Act 1992
Const. L.J.	Construction Law Journal
Contributions and Benefits Act	Social Security Contributions and Benefits Act 1992
COPD	chronic obstructive pulmonary disease
Council Tax Benefit Regulations	Council Tax Benefit (General) Regulations 1992 (SI 1992/1814)
CP	Carer Premium
CP	Chamber President
CPAG	Child Poverty Action Group
C.P.L.R.	Civil Practice Law Reports
CPR	Civil Procedure Rules
C.P. Rep.	Civil Procedure Reports
Cr. App. R.	Criminal Appeal Reports
Cr. App. R. (S.)	Criminal Appeal Reports (Sentencing)
CRCA 2005	Commissioners for Revenue and Customs Act 2005

Table of Abbreviations used in this Series

Credits Regulations 1974	Social Security (Credits) Regulations 1974
Credits Regulations 1975	Social Security (Credits) Regulations 1975
Crim. L.R.	Criminal Law Review
CRU	Compensation Recovery Unit
CSA 1995	Child Support Act 1995
CSIH	Inner House of the Court of Session
CSOH	Outer House of the Court of Session
CS(NI)O	Child Support (Northern Ireland) Order 1995
CSO	Child Support Officer
CSPSSA 2000	Child Support, Pensions and Social Security Act 2000
CTA	Common Travel Area
CTB	Council Tax Benefit
CTC	Child Tax Credit
CTC Regulations	Child Tax Credit Regulations 2002
CTF	child trust fund
CTS	Carpal Tunnel Syndrome
CV	curriculum vitae
DCA	Department for Constitutional Affairs
DCP	Disabled Child Premium
Decisions and Appeals Regulations 1999	Social Security Contributions (Decisions and Appeals) Regulations 1999
Dependency Regulations	Social Security Benefit (Dependency) Regulations 1977
DfEE	Department for Education and Employment
DHSS	Department of Health and Social Security
DIY	do it yourself
Digital Service Regulations 2014	Universal Credit (Digital Service) Amendment Regulations 2014
Disability Living Allowance Regulations	Social Security (Disability Living Allowance) Regulations
DLA	Disability Living Allowance
DLA Regulations	Social Security (Disability Living Allowance) Regulations 1991
DLAAB Regs	Disability Living Allowance Advisory Board Regulations 1991
DLADWAA 1991	Disability Living Allowance and Disability Working Allowance Act 1991
DM	Decision Maker
DMA	Decision-making and Appeals
DMG	Decision Makers' Guidance
DMP	Delegated Medical Practitioner

DP	Disability Premium
DPTC	Disabled Person's Tax Credit
D.R.	European Commission of Human Rights Decisions and Reports
DRO	Debt Relief Order
DSD	Department for Social Development (Northern Ireland)
DSDNI	Department for Social Development, Northern Ireland
DSS	Department of Social Security
DTI	Department of Trade and Industry
DWA	Disability Working Allowance
DWP	Department for Work and Pensions
DWPMS	Department for Work and Pensions Medical Service
EAA	Extrinsic Allergic Alveolitis
EAT	Employment Appeal Tribunal
EC	Treaty establishing the European Economic Community
ECHR	European Convention on Human Rights
ECJ	European Court of Justice
ECSMA Agreement	European Convention on Social and Medical Assistance
E.C.R.	European Court Report
ECtHR	European Court of Human Rights
Ed.C.R.	Education Case Reports
EEA	European Economic Area
EEA Regulations	Immigration (European Economic Area) Regulations 2006
EEC	European Economic Community
EESSI	Electronic Exchange of Social Security Information
E.G.	Estates Gazette
E.G.L.R.	Estates Gazette Law Reports
EHIC	European Health Insurance Card
E.H.R.L.R.	European Human Rights Law Review
E.H.R.R.	European Human Rights Reports
E.L.R.	Education Law Reports
EMA	Education Maintenance Allowance
EMO	Examining Medical Officer
EMP	Examining Medical Practitioner
Employment and Support Allowance Regulations	Employment and Support Allowance Regulations 2008
Enforceable Community right	Enforceable EU right

English Regulations (eligible children)	Care Planning, Placement and Case Review (England) Regulations 2010
English Regulations (relevant children)	Care Leavers (England) Regulations 2010
Eq. L.R.	Equality Law Reports
ERA	Employment, Retention and Advancement Scheme
ERA	Evoked Response Audiometry
ERA 1996	Employment Rights Act 1996
ER(NI)O	Employers Rights (Northern Ireland) Order 1996
ES	Employment Service
ESA	Employment and Support Allowance
ESA Regulations 2008	Employment and Support Allowance Regulations 2008
ESA WCAt	Employment and Support Allowance Work Capability Assessment
ESC	Employer Supported Childcare
ETA 1973	Employment and Training Act 1973
ETA(NI) 1950	Employment and Training Act (Northern Ireland) 1950
EU	European Union
Eu.L.R.	European Law Reports
European Coal and Steel Communities	European Union
EWCA Civ	Civil Division of the Court of Appeal in England and Wales
EWHC Admin	Administrative Court division of the High Court (England and Wales)
F(No.2)A 2005	Finance (No.2) Act 2005
FA 1990	Finance Act 1990
FA 1993	Finance Act 1993
FA 1996	Finance Act 1996
FA 2000	Finance Act 2000
FA 2004	Finance Act 2004
Fam. Law	Family Law
FAS	Financial Assistance Scheme
F.C.R.	Family Court Reporter
FIS	Family Income Supplement
FISMA 2000	Financial Services and Markets Act 2000
Fixing and Adjustment of Rates Regulations 1976	Child Benefit and Social Security (Fixing and Adjustment of Rates) Regulations 1976
F.L.R.	Family Law Reports
Former Regulations	Employment and Support Allowance (Transitional Provisions, Housing Benefit and Council Tax Benefit) (Existing Awards) Regulations 2010

FME	further medical evidence
FOTRA	Free of Tax to Residents Abroad
FRAA	flat rate accrual amount
FSCS	Financial Services Compensation Scheme
FSMA 2000	Financial Services and Markets Act 2000
FSVG	Bundesgestez über die Sozialversicherung freiberuflich selbständig Erwerbstätiger (Austrian Federal Act of 30 November 1978 on social insurance for the self-employed in the liberal professions)
FTT	First-tier Tribunal
GA	Guardian's Allowance
GA Regulations	Social Security (Guardian's Allowance) Regulations 1975
General Benefit Regulations 1982	Social Security (General Benefit) Regulations 1982
General Regulations	Statutory Maternity Pay (General) Regulations 1986
GMP	Guaranteed Minimum Pension
G.P.	General Practitioner
GPoW	genuine prospects of work
GRA	Gender Recognition Act
GRB	Graduated Retirement Benefit
GRP	Graduated Retirement Pension
G.W.D.	Greens Weekly Digest
HASSASSA	Health and Social Services and Social Security Adjudication Act 1983
HB	Housing Benefit
HCD	House of Commons Debates
HCP	health care professional
HCWA	House of Commons Written Answer
HESC	Health, Education and Social Care
HIV	Human Immunodeficiency Virus
H.L.R.	Housing Law Reports
HMIT	Her Majesty's Inspector of Taxes
HMRC	Her Majesty's Revenue and Customs
HMSO	Her Majesty's Stationery Office
HNCIP	(Housewives') Non-Contributory Invalidity Pension
Hospital In-Patients Regulations 1975	Social Security (Hospital In-Patients) Regulations 1975
Housing Benefit Regulations	Housing Benefit Regulations 2006
HPP	Higher Pensioner Premium
HRA 1998	Human Rights Act 1998
H.R.L.R.	Human Rights Law Reports–UK Cases

HRR	High Risk Renewal
HSE	Health and Safety Executive
IAC	Immigration and Asylum Chamber
IAP	Intensive Activity Period
IB	Invalidity Benefit
IB/IS/SDA	Incapacity Benefits' Regime
IBJSA	Income-Based Jobseeker's Allowance
IB PCA	Incapacity Benefit Personal Capability Assessment
IB Regs	Social Security (Incapacity Benefit) Regulations 1994
IB Regulations	Social Security (Incapacity Benefit) Regulations 1994
IBS	Irritable Bowel Syndrome
ICA	Invalid Care Allowance
ICA Regulations	Social Security (Invalid Care Allowance) Regulations 1976
ICA Unit	Invalid Care Allowance Unit
I.C.R.	Industrial Cases Reports
ICTA 1988	Income and Corporation Taxes Act 1988
I(EEA) Regulations	Immigration (European Economic Area) Regulations 2006
IFW Regulations	Incapacity for Work (General) Regulations 1995
I.I.	Industrial Injuries
IIAC	Industrial Injuries Advisory Council
IIDB	Industrial Injuries Disablement Benefit
ILO	International Labour Organization
ILO Convention	International Labour Organization Convention
ILR	indefinite leave to remain
Imm. A.R.	Immigration Appeal Reports
Immigration and Asylum Regulations	Social Security (Immigration and Asylum) Consequential Amendments Regulations 2000
Incapacity for Work Regulations	Social Security (Incapacity for Work) (General) Regulations 1995
Income Support General Regulations	Income Support (General) Regulations 1987
Income Support Regulations	Income Support (General) Regulations 1987
Increases for Dependants Regulations	Social Security Benefit (Dependency) Regulations 1977
IND	Immigration and Nationality Directorate of the Home Office

Table of Abbreviations used in this Series

I.N.L.R.	Immigration and Nationality Law Reports
IO	Information Officer
I.O.	Insurance Officer
IPPR	Institute of Public Policy Research
IRC	Inland Revenue Commissioners
IRESA	Income-Related Employment and Support Allowance
I.R.L.R.	Industrial Relations Law Reports
IS Regs	Income Support Regulations
IS Regulations	Income Support (General) Regulations 1987
IS	Income Support
ISA	Individual Savings Account
ISA Regulations 1998	Individual Savings Account Regulations 1998
ITA 2007	Income Tax Act 2007
ITEPA	Income Tax (Earnings and Pensions) Act 2003
ITEPA 2003	Income Tax, Earnings and Pensions Act 2003
I.T.L. Rep.	International Tax Law Reports
ITS	Independent Tribunal Service
ITTOIA	Income Tax (Trading and Other Income) Act 2005
ITTOIA 2005	Income Tax (Trading and Other Income) Act 2005
IVB	Invalidity Benefit
IWA 1994	Social Security (Incapacity for Work) Act 1994
IW	Incapacity for Work
IW (Dependants) Regs	Social Security (Incapacity for Work) (Dependants) Regulations
IW (General) Regs	Social Security (Incapacity for Work) (General) Regulations 1995
IW (Transitional) Regs	Incapacity for Work (Transitional) Regulations
JD(NI)O 1995	Jobseekers (Northern Ireland) Order 1995
Jobseeker's Allowance Regulations	Jobseeker's Allowance Regulations 1996
Jobseeker's Regulations 1996	Jobseeker's Allowance Regulations 1996
J.P.	Justice of the Peace Reports
J.P.L.	Journal of Public Law
JSA	Jobseeker's Allowance
JSA 1995	Jobseekers Act 1995
JSA (NI) Regulations	Jobseeker's Allowance (Northern Ireland) Regulations 1996

Table of Abbreviations used in this Series

JSA (Transitional) Regulations	Jobseeker's Allowance (Transitional) Regulations 1996
JSA Regulations 1996	Jobseekers Allowance Regulations 1996
JSA Regulations	Jobseeker's Allowance Regulations 1996
JS(NI)O 1995	Jobseekers (Northern Ireland) Order 1995
J.S.S.L.	Journal of Social Security Law
J.S.W.F.L.	Journal of Social Welfare and Family Law
J.S.W.L.	Journal of Social Welfare Law
K.B.	Law Reports, King's Bench
K.I.R.	Knight's Industrial Law Reports
L.& T.R.	Landlord and Tenant Reports
LCW	limited capability for work
LCWA	Limited Capability for Work Assessment
LCWRA	Limited Capability for Work-Related Activity
LEA	local education authority
LEL	Lower Earnings Limit
LET	low earnings threshold
L.G.R.	Local Government Law Reports
L.G. Rev.	Local Government Review
L.J.R.	Law Journal Reports
Ll.L.Rep	Lloyd's List Law Report
Lloyd's Rep.	Lloyd's Law Reports
LRP	liable relative payment
L.S.G.	Law Society Gazette
LTAHAW	Living Together as Husband and Wife
Luxembourg Court	Court of Justice of the European Union (also referred to as CJEC and ECJ)
MA	Maternity Allowance
MAF	Medical Assessment Framework
MAT	Medical Appeal Tribunal
Maternity Allowance Regulations	Social Security (Maternity Allowance) Regulations 1987
Maternity Benefit Regulations	Social Security (Maternity Benefit) Regulations 1975
ME	myalgic encephalomyelitis
Medical Evidence Regulations	Social Security (Medical Evidence) Regulations 1976
M.H.L.R.	Mental Health Law Reports
MHP	mental health problems
MIG	minimum income guarantee
Migration Regulations	Employment and Support Allowance (Transitional Provisions, Housing Benefit and Council Tax Benefit (Existing Awards) (No.2) Regulations 2010

MIRAS	mortgage interest relief at source
MRI	Magnetic resonance imaging
MRSA	methicillin-resistant Staphylococcus aureus
MS	Medical Services
MWAS	Jobseeker's Allowance (Mandatory Work Activity Scheme) Regulations 2011
NACRO	National Association for the Care and Resettlement of Offenders
NCB	National Coal Board
NDPD	Notes on the Diagnosis of Prescribed Diseases
NHS	National Health Service
NI	National Insurance
N.I.	Northern Ireland Law Reports
NI Com	Northern Ireland Commissioner
NI	National Insurance
NICA	Northern Ireland Court of Appeal
NICs	National Insurance Contributions
NICom	Northern Ireland Commissioner
NINO	National Insurance Number
NIQB	Northern Ireland, Queen's Bench Division
NIRS 2	National Insurance Recording System
N.L.J.	New Law Journal
NMC	Nursing and Midwifery Council
Northern Ireland Contributions and Benefits Act	Social Security Contributions and Benefits (Northern Ireland) Act 1992
N.P.C.	New Property Cases
NS&I	National Savings and Investments
NTC Manual	Clerical procedures manual on tax credits
NUM	National Union of Mineworkers
OA	Osteoarthritis
OCD	Obsessive Compulsive Disorder
OGA	Agricultural Insurance Organisation
Ogus, Barendt and Wikeley	A. Ogus, E. Barendt and N. Wikeley, *The Law of Social Security* (4th edn, Butterworths, 1995)
O.J.	Official Journal
Old Cases Act	Industrial Injuries and Diseases (Old Cases) Act 1975
OPA	Overseas Pensions Act 1973
OPB	One Parent Benefit
O.P.L.R.	Occupational Pensions Law Reports

OPSSAT	Office of the President of Social Security Appeal Tribunals
Overlapping Benefits Regulations	Social Security (Overlapping Benefits) Regulations 1979
Overpayments Regulations	Social Security (Payments on account, Overpayments and Recovery) Regulations
P. & C.R.	Property and Compensation Reports
pa	per annum
para.	paragraph
PAYE	Pay As You Earn
Payments on Account Regulations	Social Security (Payments on account, Overpayments and Recovery) Regulations
PCA	Personal Capability Assessment
PD	prescribed disease
P.D.	Practice Direction
Pens. L.R.	Pensions Law Reports
Persons Abroad Regulations	Social Security Benefit (Persons Abroad) Regulations 1975
Persons Residing Together Regulations	Social Security Benefit (Persons Residing Together) Regulations 1977
PIE	Period of Interruption of Employment
PILON	pay in lieu of notice
PIP	personal independence payment
P.I.Q.R.	Personal Injuries and Quantum Reports
PIW	Period of Incapacity for Work
P.I.W.R.	Personal Injury and Quantum Reports
P.L.R.	Estates Gazette Planning Law Reports
Polygamous Marriages Regulations	Social Security and Family Allowances (Polygamous Marriages) Regulations 1975
PPF	Pension Protection Fund
Prescribed Diseases Regulations	Social Security (Industrial Injuries) (Prescribed Diseases) Regulations 1985
Present Regulations	Employment and Support Allowance (Transitional Provisions, Housing Benefit and Council Tax Benefit) (Existing Awards) (No.2) Regulations 2010
PSCS	Pension Service Computer System
Pt	Part
PTA	pure tone audiometry
P.T.S.R.	Public and Third Sector Law Reports
PTWR 2000	Part-time Workers (Prevention of Less Favourable Treatment) Regulations 2000
PVS	private or voluntary sectors
pw	per week
Q.B.	Queen's Bench Law Reports

Table of Abbreviations used in this Series

QBD (NI)	Queen's Bench Division (Northern Ireland)
QEF	qualifying earnings factor
QYP	qualifying young person
R	Reported Decision
r.	rule
RC	Rules of the Court of Session
REA	Reduced Earnings Allowance
Recoupment Regulations	Social Security (Recoupment) Regulations 1990
reg.	regulation
RIPA	Regulation of Investigatory Powers Act 2000
RMO	Responsible Medical Officer
rr.	rules
R.T.R.	Road Traffic Reports
S	Scottish Decision
s.	section
SAP	Statutory Adoption Pay
SAPOE	Schemes for Assisting Persons to Obtain Employment
SAYE	Save As You Earn
SB	Supplementary Benefit
SBAT	Supplementary Benefit Appeal Tribunal
SBC	Supplementary Benefits Commission
S.C.	Session Cases
S.C. (H.L.)	Session Cases (House of Lords)
S.C. (P.C.)	Session Cases (Privy Council)
S.C.C.R.	Scottish Criminal Case Reports
S.C.L.R.	Scottish Civil Law Reports
Sch.	Schedule
SDA	Severe Disablement Allowance
SDP	Severe Disability Premium
SEC	Social Entitlement Chamber
SERPS	State Earnings Related Pension Scheme
Severe Disablement Allowance Regulations	Social Security (Severe Disablement Regulations Allowance) Regulations 1984
SI	Statutory Instrument
SIP	Share Incentive Plan
S.J.	Solicitors Journal
S.J.L.B.	Solicitors Journal Law Brief
SLAN	Statement Like an Award Notice
S.L.T.	Scots Law Times
SMP	Statutory Maternity Pay

SMP (General) Regulations 1986	Statutory Maternity Pay (General) Regulations 1986
SP	Senior President
SPC	State Pension Credit
SPC Regulations	State Pension Credit Regulations 2002
SPCA	State Pension Credit Act 2002
SPCA 2002	State Pension Credit Act 2002
SPCA(NI) 2002	State Pension Credit Act (Northern Ireland) 2002
SPP	Statutory Paternity Pay
SPP and SAP (Administration) Regs 2002	Statutory Paternity Pay and Statutory Adoption Pay (Administration) Regulations 2002
SPP and SAP (General) Regulations 2002	Statutory Paternity Pay and Statutory Adoption Pay (General) Regulations 2002
SPP and SAP (National Health Service)	Statutory Paternity Pay and Statutory Adoption Pay (National Health Service Employees) Regulations 2002
SPP and SAP (Weekly Rates) Regulations	Statutory Paternity Pay and Statutory Adoption Pay (Weekly Rates) Regulations 2002
SS(MP)A 1977	Social Security (Miscellaneous Provisions) Act 1977
ss.	sections
SSA 1975	Social Security Act 1975
SSA 1977	Social Security Act 1977
SSA 1978	Social Security Act 1978
SSA 1979	Social Security Act 1979
SSA 1981	Social Security Act 1981
SSA 1986	Social Security Act 1986
SSA 1988	Social Security Act 1988
SSA 1989	Social Security Act 1989
SSA 1990	Social Security Act 1990
SSA 1998	Social Security Act 1998
SSAA 1992	Social Security Administration Act 1992★
SSAC	Social Security Advisory Committee
SSAT	Social Security Appeal Tribunal
SSCB(NI)A	Social Security Contributions and Benefits (Northern Ireland) Act 1992
SSCBA 1992	Social Security Contributions and Benefits Act 1992★
SSCPA 1992	Social Security (Consequential Provisions) Act 1992
SSHBA 1982	Social Security and Housing Benefits Act 1982
SSHD	Secretary of State for the Home Department

Table of Abbreviations used in this Series

SS(MP) A 1977	Social Security (Miscellaneous Provisions) Act 1977
SS (No.2) A 1980	Social Security (No.2) Act 1980
SSPP	statutory shared parental pay
SSP	Statutory Sick Pay
SSP (General) Regulations	Statutory Sick Pay (General) Regulations 1982
SSPA 1975	Social Security Pensions Act 1975
SSWP	Secretary of State for Work and Pensions
State Pension Credit Regulations	State Pension Credit Regulations 2002
S.T.C.	Simon's Tax Cases
S.T.C. (S.C.D.)	Simon's Tax Cases: Special Commissioners Decisions
S.T.I.	Simon's Tax Intelligence
STIB	Short-Term Incapacity Benefit
Strasbourg Court	European Court of Human Rights
Students Directive	Directive 93/96/EEC
subpara.	subparagraph
subs.	subsection
T	Tribunal of Commissioners' Decision
Taxes Act	Income and Corporation Taxes Act 1988
(TC)	Tax and Chancery
T.C.	Tax Cases
TC (Claims and Notifications) Regs 2002	Tax Credits (Claims and Notifications) Regulations 2002
TCA	Tax Credits Act
TCA 1999	Tax Credits Act 1999
TCA 2002	Tax Credits Act 2002
TCEA 2007	Tribunals, Courts and Enforcement Act 2007
TCGA	Taxation of Chargeable Gains Act 1992
TCGA 1992	Taxation of Chargeable Gains Act 2002
TCTM	Tax Credits Technical Manual
TEC	Treaty Establishing the European Community
TENS	transutaneous electrical nerve stimulation
TEU	Treaty on European Union
TFC	Tax-Free Childcare
TFEU	Treaty on the Functioning of the European Union
The Board	Commissioners for Revenue and Customs
TIOPA 2010	Taxation (International and Other Provisions) Act 2010
TMA 1970	Taxes Management Act 1970

Table of Abbreviations used in this Series

WIA	Wet Werk en inkomen naar arbeidsvermogen (Dutch Act on Work and Income according to Labour Capacity)
Widow's Benefit and Retirement Pensions Regs	Social Security (Widow's Benefit and Retirement Pensions) Regulations 1979
Wikeley, Annotations	N. Wikeley, "Annotations to Jobseekers Act 1995 (c.18)" in *Current Law Statutes Annotated* (1995)
Wikeley, Ogus and Barendt	Wikeley, Ogus and Barendt, *The Law of Social Security* (5th ed., Butterworths, 2002)
W.L.R.	Weekly Law Reports
Workmen's Compensation Acts	Workmen's Compensation Acts 1925 to 1945
WPS	War Pensions Scheme
W-RA Regs	Employment and Support Allowance (Work-Related Activity) Regulations 2011 (SI 2011/1349)
WRA 2007	Welfare Reform Act 2007
WRA 2009	Welfare Reform Act 2009
WRA 2012	Welfare Reform Act 2012
WRAAt	Work-Related Activity Assessment
WRPA 1999	Welfare Reform and Pensions Act 1999
WRP(NI)O 1999	Welfare Reform and Pensions (Northern Ireland) Order
WTC	Working Tax Credit
WTC (Entitlement and Maximum Rate) Regulations 2002	Working Tax Credit (Entitlement and Maximum Rate) Regulations 2002
WTC Regulations	Working Tax Credit (Entitlement and Maximum Rate) Regulations 2002
W.T.L.R.	Wills & Trusts Law Reports

TABLE OF CASES

TABLE OF SOCIAL SECURITY COMMISSIONERS' DECISIONS

TABLE OF EUROPEAN LEGISLATION

TABLE OF STATUTES

TABLE OF STATUTORY INSTRUMENTS

PART I

NEW LEGISLATION

NEW REGULATIONS

The Childcare Payments Act 2014 (Commencement No.3 and Transitional Provisions) Regulations 2017

SI 2017/578

Made: April 20, 2017

ARRANGEMENT OF REGULATIONS

1.001

The Treasury, in exercise of the powers conferred on them by sections 69(2)(n) and 75(2) and (3) of the Childcare Payments Act 2014, make the following Regulations:

Citation and interpretation

1.—(1) These Regulations may be cited as the Childcare Payments Act 2014 (Commencement No. 3 and Transitional Provisions) Regulations 2017.

1.002

(2) In these Regulations—

"the Act" means the Childcare Payments Act 2014;

"disabled child" is to be read in accordance with regulations made under section 14 of the Act (qualifying child);

"the relevant day" means the day specified by the Treasury for the purposes of sections 270AA and 318AZA of ITEPA 2003;

"the trial" has the meaning given by regulation 1(2) of the Childcare Payments Act 2014 (Commencement No. 2) Regulations 2016.

Commencement

2.—(1) The day appointed for the coming into force of the provisions of the Act set out in regulation 2(2) in respect of—

(a) a child born on or after 1st September 2013 and any sibling; and

1.003

(b) a disabled child and any sibling;

is 21st April 2017.

(2) (a) section 1;

(b) sections 3 and 4;

(c) sections 6 to 15;

(d) sections 17 to 25;

(e) section 62; and

(f) section 73(2) to (4).

(3) In this regulation "sibling" means any child normally living in the same household as a child referred to in paragraph 1 at the time the declaration of eligibility is made.

Commencement

1.004   **3.** The day appointed for the coming into force of the following provisions of the Act, as far as they are not already in force, is 21st April 2017—

(a) section 2;

(b) section 5;

(c) section 16;

(d) sections 30 to 42;

(c) sections 44 to 61;

(f) sections 63 and 64; and

(g) sections 66 and 67.

Commencement

1.005   **4.** The day appointed for the coming into force of all remaining provisions of the Act, as far as they are not already in force, in respect of those recruited to participate in the trial, is 16th May 2017.

Transitional provisions relating to the trial

1.006   **5.**—(1) Where a person recruited to participate in the trial makes their first reconfirming declaration on or after 16th May 2017, that declaration is to be treated, for the purposes of sections 12 and 39 of the Act, as if it were a declaration of eligibility for the purposes of opening a childcare account.

(2) In this regulation "reconfirming declaration" has the meaning given by regulation 6(3) of the Childcare Payments Regulations 2015.

Transitional provisions relating to section 12 of the Act and section 270AA of ITEPA 2003

1.007   **6.**—(1) Where the period of 52 tax weeks ending on or before the date a person makes a declaration of eligibility, does not include at least one qualifying week, that person is to be treated for the purposes of section 12(1)(a), (2)(a) and (3)(a) of the Act as not being an eligible employee in relation to a relevant childcare scheme.

(2) Paragraph (1) has effect until the end of the day before the relevant day.

(3) In this regulation "qualifying week" and "tax week" have the meanings given by section 270AA(5) of ITEPA 2003.

Transitional provisions relating to section 12 of the Act and section 318AZA of ITEPA 2003

7.—(1) Where the period of 52 tax weeks ending on or before the date a person makes a declaration of eligibility, does not include at least one qualifying week, that person is to be treated for the purposes of section 12(1)(a), (2)(b) and (3)(b) of the Act as not being an eligible employee in relation to a relevant childcare scheme.

(2) Paragraph (1) has effect until the end of the day before the relevant day.

(3) In this regulation "qualifying week" and "tax week" have the meanings given by section 318AZA(5) of ITEPA 2003.

Transitional provisions relating to sections 63 and 64 of the Act

8. At any time before the relevant day, sections 270AA and 318AZA of ITEPA 2003 have effect as if conditions A and B in both those sections, and any reference to them, were omitted.

1.008

1.009

The Welfare Reform Act 2012 (Commencement No.19, 22, 23 and 24 and Transitional and Transitory Provisions (Modification)) Order 2017

SI 2017/584

Made: April 24, 2017

The Secretary of State for Work and Pensions makes the following Order in exercise of the powers conferred by section 150(3) and (4)(a), (b)(i) and (c) of the Welfare Reform Act 2012:

ARRANGEMENT OF ARTICLES

Citation

1.011   **1.** This Order may be cited as the Welfare Reform Act 2012 (Commencement No.19, 22, 23 and 24 and Transitional and Transitory Provisions (Modification)) Order 2017.

Interpretation

1.012   **2.**—(1) In this Order—
"claimant"—
  (a) in relation to an employment and support allowance, has the same meaning as in Part 1 of the Welfare Reform Act 2007;
  (b) in relation to a jobseeker's allowance, has the same meaning as in the Jobseekers Act 1995 (as it applies apart from the amendments made by Part 1 of Schedule 14 to the Welfare Reform Act

6

2012 that remove references to an income-based jobseeker's allowance);

   (c) in relation to universal credit, has the same meaning as in Part 1 of the Welfare Reform Act 2012;

"the Claims and Payments Regulations 1987" means the Social Security (Claims and Payments) Regulations 1987;

"employment and support allowance" means an employment and support allowance under Part 1 of the Welfare Reform Act 2007;

"jobseeker's allowance" means a jobseeker's allowance under the Jobseekers Act 1995;

"the No.19 Order" means the Welfare Reform Act 2012 (Commencement No.19 and Transitional and Transitory Provisions and Commencement No.9 and Transitional and Transitory Provisions (Amendment)) Order 2014;

"the No.22 Order" means the Welfare Reform Act 2012 (Commencement No.22 and Transitional and Transitory Provisions) Order 2015;

"the No.23 Order" means the Welfare Reform Act 2012 (Commencement No.23 and Transitional and Transitory Provisions) Order 2015;

"the No.24 Order" means the Welfare Reform Act 2012 (Commencement No.24 and Transitional and Transitory Provisions and Commencement No.9 and Transitional and Transitory Provisions (Amendment)) Order 2015;

"the September 2016 Order" means the Welfare Reform Act 2012 (Commencement No.19, 22, 23 and 24 and Transitional and Transitory Provisions (Modification)) Order 2016.

(2) In this Order, references to "designated postcodes", by numbered "Part", are to any postcode district or part-district in the corresponding numbered Part of the Schedule to this Order.

(3) For the purposes of this Order, the Universal Credit, Personal Independence Payment, Jobseeker's Allowance and Employment and Support Allowance (Claims and Payments) Regulations 2013 apply for the purpose of deciding—

   (a) whether a claim for universal credit is made; and

   (b) the date on which the claim is made.

(4) For the purposes of this Order, the Claims and Payments Regulations 1987 apply, subject to paragraphs (5) and (6), for the purposes of deciding—

   (a) whether a claim for an employment and support allowance or a jobseeker's allowance is made; and

   (b) the date on which the claim is made or treated as made.

(5) Subject to paragraph (6), for the purposes of this Order—

   (a) a person makes a claim for an employment and support allowance or a jobseeker's allowance if that person takes any action which results in a decision on a claim being required under the Claims and Payments Regulations 1987; and

   (b) it is irrelevant that the effect of any provision of those Regulations is that, for the purposes of those Regulations, the claim is made or treated as made at a date that is earlier than the date on which that action is taken.

(6) Where, by virtue of—

(a) regulation 6(1F)(b) or (c) of the Claims and Payments Regulations 1987, in the case of a claim for an employment and support allowance; or

(b) regulation 6(4ZA) to (4ZD) and (4A)(a)(i) and (b) of those Regulations, in the case of a claim for a jobseeker's allowance,

a claim for an employment and support allowance or a jobseeker's allowance is treated as made at a date that is earlier than the date on which the action referred to in paragraph (5)(a) is taken, the claim is treated as made on that earlier date.

Modification of the No.22 and 24 Orders: removal of the gateway conditions from 3rd May 2017

1.013   **3.**—(1) This article applies in the case of a claim for universal credit that is made, or a claim for an employment and support allowance or a jobseeker's allowance that is made or treated as made, on or after 3rd May 2017.

(2) Where this article applies, the provisions referred to in sub-paragraphs (a) to (f) have effect, with respect to a claimant residing in the designated postcodes referred to in the sub-paragraph in question, as though the reference in those provisions to meeting the gateway conditions were omitted—

(a) articles 3(2)(c) and 4(2)(e) and (f) of the No.22 Order, in respect of the Part 1 designated postcodes;

(b) articles 3(2)(a) and 4(2)(a) and (b) of the No.24 Order, in respect of the Part 2 designated postcodes;

(c) articles 3(2)(i) and 4(2)(q) and (r) of the No.24 Order, in respect of the Part 3 designated postcodes;

(d) articles 3(2)(p) and 4(2)(ee) and (ff) of the No.24 Order, in respect of the Part 4 designated postcodes;

(e) articles 3(2)(t) and 4(2)(mm) and (nn) of the No.24 Order, in respect of the Part 5 designated postcodes;

(f) articles 3(2)(u) and 4(2)(oo) and (pp) of the No.24 Order, in respect of the Part 6 designated postcodes.

Modification of the No.22 and 24 Orders: removal of the gateway conditions from 10th May 2017

1.014   **4.**—(1) This article applies in the case of a claim for universal credit that is made, or a claim for an employment and support allowance or a jobseeker's allowance that is made or treated as made, on or after 10th May 2017.

(2) Where this article applies, the provisions referred to in sub-paragraphs (a) to (e) have effect, with respect to a claimant residing in the designated postcodes referred to in the sub-paragraph in question, as though the reference in those provisions to meeting the gateway conditions were omitted—

(a) articles 3(2)(b) and 4(2)(c) and (d) of the No.22 Order, in respect of the Part 7 designated postcodes;

(b) articles 3(2)(b) and 4(2)(c) and (d) of the No.24 Order, in respect of the Part 8 designated postcodes;

(c) articles 3(2)(f) and 4(2)(k) and (l) of the No.24 Order, in respect of the Part 9 designated postcodes;

(d) articles 3(2)(g) and 4(2)(m) and (n) of the No.24 Order, in respect of the Part 10 designated postcodes;

(e) articles 3(2)(p) and 4(2)(ee) and (ff) of the No.24 Order, in respect of the Part 11 designated postcodes.

Modification of the No.19 Order: removal of the gateway conditions from 17th May 2017

5.—(1) This article applies in the case of a claim for universal credit that is made, or a claim for an employment and support allowance or a jobseeker's allowance that is made or treated as made, on or after 17th May 2017. **1.015**

(2) Where this article applies, the provisions referred to in sub-paragraphs (a) and (b) have effect, with respect to a claimant residing in the designated postcodes referred to in the sub-paragraph in question, as though the reference in those provisions to meeting the gateway conditions were omitted—

(a) articles 3(2)(d) and 4(2)(d) of the No.19 Order, in respect of the Part 12 designated postcodes;

(b) articles 3(2)(k) and 4(2)(k) of the No.19 Order, in respect of the Part 13 designated postcodes.

Modification of the No.22 and 24 Orders: removal of the gateway conditions from 24th May 2017

6.—(1) This article applies in the case of a claim for universal credit that is made, or a claim for an employment and support allowance or a jobseeker's allowance that is made or treated as made, on or after 24th May 2017. **1.016**

(2) Where this article applies, the provisions referred to in sub-paragraphs (a) and (b) have effect, with respect to a claimant residing in the designated postcodes referred to in the sub-paragraph in question, as though the reference in those provisions to meeting the gateway conditions were omitted—

(a) articles 3(2)(e) and 4(2)(i) and (j) of the No.22 Order, in respect of the Part 14 designated postcodes;

(b) articles 3(2)(n) and 4(2)(aa) and (bb) of the No.24 Order, in respect of the Part 15 designated postcodes.

Modification of the No.22 and 24 Orders: removal of the gateway conditions from 7th June 2017

7.—(1) This article applies in the case of a claim for universal credit that is made, or a claim for an employment and support allowance or a jobseeker's allowance that is made or treated as made, on or after 7th June 2017. **1.017**

(2) Where this article applies, the provisions referred to in sub-paragraphs (a) to (d) have effect, with respect to a claimant residing in the designated postcodes referred to in the sub-paragraph in question, as though the reference in those provisions to meeting the gateway conditions were omitted—

    (a) articles 3(2)(a) and 4(2)(a) and (b) of the No.22 Order, in respect of the Part 16 designated postcodes;

    (b) articles 3(2)(e) and 4(2)(i) and (j) of the No.22 Order, in respect of the Part 17 designated postcodes;

    (c) articles 3(2)(a) and 4(2)(a) and (b) of the No.24 Order, in respect of the Part 18 designated postcodes;

    (d) articles 3(2)(l) and 4(2)(w) and (x) of the No.24 Order, in respect of the Part 19 designated postcodes.

Modification of the No.22 and 24 Orders: removal of the gateway conditions from 14th June 2017

1.018   **8.**—(1) This article applies in the case of a claim for universal credit that is made, or a claim for an employment and support allowance or a jobseeker's allowance that is made or treated as made, on or after 14th June 2017.

(2) Where this article applies, the provisions referred to in sub-paragraphs (a) to (d) have effect, with respect to a claimant residing in the designated postcodes referred to in the sub-paragraph in question, as though the reference in those provisions to meeting the gateway conditions were omitted—

    (a) articles 3(2)(i) and 4(2)(q) and (r) of the No.22 Order, in respect of the Part 20 designated postcodes;

    (b) articles 3(2)(r) and 4(2)(ii) and (jj) of the No.22 Order, in respect of the Part 21 designated postcodes;

    (c) articles 3(2)(a) and 4(2)(a) and (b) of the No.24 Order, in respect of the Part 22 designated postcodes;

    (d) articles 3(2)(k) and 4(2)(u) and (v) of the No.24 Order, in respect of the Part 23 designated postcodes.

Modification of the No.22 and 24 Orders: removal of the gateway conditions from 28th June 2017

1.019   **9.**—(1) This article applies in the case of a claim for universal credit that is made, or a claim for an employment and support allowance or a jobseeker's allowance that is made or treated as made, on or after 28th June 2017.

(2) Where this article applies, the provisions referred to in sub-paragraphs (a) to (d) have effect, with respect to a claimant residing in the designated postcodes referred to in the sub-paragraph in question, as though the reference in those provisions to meeting the gateway conditions were omitted—

    (a) articles 3(2)(m) and 4(2)(y) and (z) of the No.22 Order, in respect of the Part 24 designated postcodes;

    (b) articles 3(2)(v) and 4(2)(qq) and (rr) of the No.24 Order, in respect of the Part 25 designated postcodes;

(c) articles 3(2)(z) and 4(2)(yy) and (zz) of the No.24 Order, in respect of the Part 26 designated postcodes;

(d) articles 3(2)(bb) and 4(2)(ccc) and (ddd) of the No.24 Order, in respect of the Part 27 designated postcodes.

Modifications in consequence of removal of the gateway conditions: the No.19 Order

10.—(1) This article applies in the case of a claim in relation to which provisions of the No.19 Order are modified under articles 5(2)(a) or 5(2)(b).

(2) Where this article applies, the modifications to the No.19 Order made by article 13(2) of the September 2016 Order have effect.

1.020

Modifications in consequence of removal of the gateway conditions: the No.22 Order

11.—(1) This article applies in the case of a claim in relation to which provisions of the No.22 Order are modified under—

(a) article 3(2)(a);

(b) article 4(2)(a);

(c) article 6(2)(a);

(d) article 7(2)(a) or (b);

(e) article 8(2)(a) or (b); or

(f) article 9(2)(a).

(2) Where this article applies, the modifications to the No.22 Order made by article 14(2) of the September 2016 Order have effect.

1.021

Modifications in consequence of removal of the gateway conditions: the No.24 Order

12.—(1) This article applies in the case of a claim in relation to which provisions of the No.24 Order are modified under—

(a) article 3(2)(b), (c), (d), (e) or (f);

(b) article 4(2)(b), (c), (d) or (e);

(c) article 6(2)(b);

(d) article 7(2)(c) or (d);

(e) article 8(2)(c) or (d); or

(f) article 9(2)(b), (c) or (d).

(2) Where this article applies, the modifications to the No.24 Order made by article 15(2) of the September 2016 Order have effect.

1.022

Modification of the No.23 Order: claims for housing benefit, income support or a tax credit

13. Article 7 of the No.23 Order (prevention of claims for housing benefit, income support or a tax credit)(1) applies as though the reference in paragraph (1) of that article to article 3(1) and (2)(a) to (c) of that Order included—

(a) a reference to paragraph (1) and sub-paragraphs (d) and (k) of paragraph (2) of article 3 of the No.19 Order, in respect of claims

1.023

in relation to which those sub-paragraphs are modified respectively by article 5(2)(a) and 5(2)(b) of this Order;

(b) a reference to paragraph (1) and sub-paragraphs (a), (b), (c), (i), (m) and (r) of paragraph (2) of article 3 of the No.22 Order, in respect of claims in relation to which those sub-paragraphs are modified respectively by articles 7(2)(a), 4(2)(a), 3(2)(a), 8(2)(a), 9(2)(a) and 8(2)(b) of this Order;

(c) a reference to paragraph (1) and sub-paragraph (e) of paragraph (2) of article 3 of the No.22 Order, in respect of claims in relation to which that sub-paragraph is modified by articles 6(2)(a) and 7(2)(b) of this Order;

(d) a reference to paragraph (1) and sub-paragraphs (b), (f), (g), (i), (k), (l), (n), (t), (u), (v), (z) and (bb) of paragraph (2) of article 3 of the No.24 Order, in respect of claims in relation to which those sub-paragraphs are modified respectively by articles 4(2)(b), 4(2)(c), 4(2)(d), 3(2)(c), 8(2)(d), 7(2)(d), 6(2)(b), 3(2)(e), 3(2)(f), 9(2)(b), 9(2)(c) and 9(2)(d) of this Order; and

(e) a reference to paragraph (1) and sub-paragraphs (a) and (p) of paragraph (2) of article 3 of the No.24 Order, in respect of claims in relation to which those sub-paragraphs are modified respectively by articles 3(2)(b), 7(2)(c) and 8(2)(c), and articles 3(2)(d) and 4(2)(e) of this Order.

1.024

SCHEDULE

Article 2(2)

POSTCODE DISTRICTS AND PART-DISTRICTS

PART 1

MK40.
MK41.
MK42.
MK43 7.
MK44 1.

PART 2

MK43 6.

PART 3

MK43 8.

PART 4

CT3 3.
CT14.
CT15.
CT16.
CT17.

PART 5

MK43 0.
MK43 9.
MK44 3.
MK45.

PART 6

MK44 2.

PART 7

DE7 0.
DE7 4.
DE7 9.
NG10 2.
NG10 4.
NG10 9.

PART 8

NG10 3.

PART 9

DE7 6.
DE7 8.

PART 10

DE7 5.
NG10 1.
NG10 5.

PART 11

DE72 3.

PART 12

BB10.
BB11.
BB12 0.
BB12 6.
BB12 8.

PART 13

BB12 7.
BB12 9.

PART 14

SN11.
SN13.
SN14 0.
SN14 6.
SN15.
SN16.

PART 15

SN14 7.

PART 16

BS22.
BS23.
BS29.
BS40 5.

PART 17

BS24.
BS25 1.

BS25 5.
BS26.
SP1.
SP2.
SP3.
SP4 5 to SP4 9.
SP5 3 and SP5 4.

PART 18

SP4 0.
SP5 1.

PART 19

SP5 2.

PART 20

HD6 1 and HD6 2.
HD6 4.
HD6 9.
HX1.
HX2.
HX3 0.
HX3 5.
HX3 7 to HX3 9.
HX4 8 and HX4 9.
HX5.
HX6.
HX7.
OL14 5 and OL14 6.
OL14 9.

PART 21

HD6 3.
HX4 0.

PART 22

OL14 7 and OL14 8.

PART 23

HX3 6.

PART 24

FK7.
FK8.
FK9.
FK10 1 and FK10 2.
FK11.
FK12.
FK13.
FK15 5.
FK16.
FK17.
FK18.
G63 9.

PART 25

FK20.

PART 26

FK10 3.

PART 27

FK14.
FK15 0.
FK15 9.
FK19.
FK21.

The Welfare Reform Act 2012 (Commencement No.29 and Commencement No.17, 19, 22, 23 and 24 and Transitional and Transitory Provisions (Modification)) Order 2017

SI 2017/664

Made: May 19, 2017

The Secretary of State for Work and Pensions makes the following Order in exercise of the powers conferred by section 150(3) and (4)(a), (b)(i) and (c) of the Welfare Reform Act 2012:

ARRANGEMENT OF ARTICLES

Citation

1. This Order may be cited as the Welfare Reform Act 2012 (Commencement No.29 and Commencement No.17, 19, 22, 23 and 24 and Transitional and Transitory Provisions (Modification)) Order 2017. 1.026

Interpretation

2.—(1) In this Order— 1.027
"claimant"—
   (a) in relation to an employment and support allowance, has the same meaning as in Part 1 of the Welfare Reform Act 2007;

(b) in relation to a jobseeker's allowance, has the same meaning as in the Jobseekers Act 1995 (as it applies apart from the amendments made by Part 1 of Schedule 14 to the Welfare Reform Act 2012 that remove references to an income-based jobseeker's allowance);

(c) in relation to universal credit, has the same meaning as in Part 1 of the Welfare Reform Act 2012;

"the Claims and Payments Regulations 1987" means the Social Security (Claims and Payments) Regulations 1987;

"employment and support allowance" means an employment and support allowance under Part 1 of the Welfare Reform Act 2007;

"jobseeker's allowance" means a jobseeker's allowance under the Jobseekers Act 1995;

"the No.17 Order" means the Welfare Reform Act 2012 (Commencement No.17 and Transitional and Transitory Provisions) Order 2014;

"the No.19 Order" means the Welfare Reform Act 2012 (Commencement No.19 and Transitional and Transitory Provisions and Commencement No.9 and Transitional and Transitory Provisions (Amendment)) Order 2014;

"the No.22 Order" means the Welfare Reform Act 2012 (Commencement No.22 and Transitional and Transitory Provisions) Order 2015;

"the No.23 Order" means the Welfare Reform Act 2012 (Commencement No.23 and Transitional and Transitory Provisions) Order 2015;

"the No.24 Order" means the Welfare Reform Act 2012 (Commencement No.24 and Transitional and Transitory Provisions and Commencement No.9 and Transitional and Transitory Provisions (Amendment)) Order 2015;

"the September 2016 Order" means the Welfare Reform Act 2012 (Commencement No.19, 22, 23 and 24 and Transitional and Transitory Provisions (Modification)) Order 2016.

(2) In this Order, references to "designated postcodes", by numbered "Part", are to any postcode district or part-district in the corresponding numbered Part of the Schedule to this Order.

(3) For the purposes of this Order, the Universal Credit, Personal Independence Payment, Jobseeker's Allowance and Employment and Support Allowance (Claims and Payments) Regulations 2013 apply for the purpose of deciding—

(a) whether a claim for universal credit is made; and

(b) the date on which the claim is made.

(4) For the purposes of this Order, the Claims and Payments Regulations 1987 apply, subject to paragraphs (5) and (6), for the purposes of deciding—

(a) whether a claim for an employment and support allowance or a jobseeker's allowance is made; and

(b) the date on which the claim is made or treated as made.

(5) Subject to paragraph (6), for the purposes of this Order—

(a) a person makes a claim for an employment and support allowance or a jobseeker's allowance if that person takes any action which results in a decision on a claim being required under the Claims and Payments Regulations 1987; and

(b) it is irrelevant that the effect of any provision of those Regulations is that, for the purposes of those Regulations, the claim is made or treated as made at a date that is earlier than the date on which that action is taken.

(6) Where, by virtue of—

(a) regulation 6(1F)(b) or (c) of the Claims and Payments Regulations 1987, in the case of a claim for an employment and support allowance; or

(b) regulation 6(4ZA) to (4ZD) and (4A)(a)(i) and (b) of those Regulations, in the case of a claim for a jobseeker's allowance,

a claim for an employment and support allowance or a jobseeker's allowance is treated as made at a date that is earlier than the date on which the action referred to in paragraph (5)(a) is taken, the claim is treated as made on that earlier date.

Modification of the No.22 and 24 Orders: removal of the gateway conditions from 5th July 2017

3.—(1) This article applies in the case of a claim for universal credit that is made, or a claim for an employment and support allowance or a jobseeker's allowance that is made or treated as made, on or after 5th July 2017.   1.028

(2) Where this article applies, the provisions referred to in sub-paragraphs (a) to (l) have effect, with respect to a claimant residing in the relevant designated postcodes, as though the reference in those provisions to meeting the gateway conditions were omitted—

(a) articles 3(2)(a) and 4(2)(a) and (b) of the No.22 Order, in respect of the Part 1 designated postcodes;

(b) articles 3(2)(c) and 4(2)(e) and (f) of the No.22 Order, in respect of the Part 2 designated postcodes;

(c) articles 3(2)(f) and 4(2)(k) and (l) of the No.22 Order, in respect of the Part 3 designated postcodes;

(d) articles 3(2)(g) and 4(2)(m) and (n) of the No.22 Order, in respect of the Part 4 designated postcodes;

(e) articles 3(2)(l) and 4(2)(w) and (x) of the No.22 Order, in respect of the Part 5 designated postcodes;

(f) articles 3(2)(t) and 4(2)(mm) and (nn) of the No.22 Order, in respect of the Part 6 designated postcodes;

(g) articles 3(2)(a) and 4(2)(a) and (b) of the No.24 Order, in respect of the Part 7 designated postcodes;

(h) articles 3(2)(f) and 4(2)(k) and (l) of the No.24 Order, in respect of the Part 8 designated postcodes;

(i) articles 3(2)(i) and 4(2)(q) and (r) of the No.24 Order, in respect of the Part 9 designated postcodes;

(j) articles 3(2)(l) and 4(2)(w) and (x) of the No.24 Order, in respect of the Part 10 designated postcodes;

(k) articles 3(2)(aa) and 4(2)(aaa) and (bbb) of the No.24 Order, in respect of the Part 11 designated postcodes;

(l) articles 3(2)(bb) and 4(2)(ccc) and (ddd) of the No.24 Order, in respect of the Part 12 designated postcodes.

Modification of the No.22 and 24 Orders: removal of the gateway conditions from 12th July 2017

1.029   **4.**—(1) This article applies in the case of a claim for universal credit that is made, or a claim for an employment and support allowance or a jobseeker's allowance that is made or treated as made, on or after 12th July 2017.

(2) Where this article applies, the provisions referred to in sub-paragraphs (a) to (i) have effect, with respect to a claimant residing in the relevant designated postcodes, as though the reference in those provisions to meeting the gateway conditions were omitted—

(a) articles 3(2)(a) and 4(2)(a) and (b) of the No.22 Order, in respect of the Part 13 designated postcodes;

(b) articles 3(2)(e) and 4(2)(i) and (j) of the No.22 Order, in respect of the Part 14 designated postcodes;

(c) articles 3(2)(g) and 4(2)(m) and (n) of the No.22 Order, in respect of the Part 15 designated postcodes;

(d) articles 3(2)(h) and 4(2)(o) and (p) of the No.22 Order, in respect of the Part 16 designated postcodes;

(e) articles 3(2)(j) and 4(2)(s) and (t) of the No.22 Order, in respect of the Part 17 designated postcodes;

(f) articles 3(2)(n) and 4(2)(aa) and (bb) of the No.22 Order, in respect of the Part 18 designated postcodes;

(g) articles 3(2)(s) and 4(2)(kk) and (ll) of the No.22 Order, in respect of the Part 19 designated postcodes;

(h) articles 3(2)(a) and 4(2)(a) and (b) of the No.24 Order, in respect of the Part 20 designated postcodes;

(i) articles 3(2)(l) and 4(2)(w) and (x) of the No.24 Order, in respect of the Part 21 designated postcodes.

Modification of the No.17, 19, 22 and 24 Orders: removal of the gateway conditions from 19th July 2017

1.030   **5.**—(1) This article applies in the case of a claim for universal credit that is made, or a claim for an employment and support allowance or a jobseeker's allowance that is made or treated as made, on or after 19th July 2017.

(2) Where this article applies, the provisions referred to in sub-paragraphs (a) to (j) have effect, with respect to a claimant residing in the relevant designated postcodes, as though the reference in those provisions to meeting the gateway conditions were omitted—

(a) articles 3(2)(a) and 4(2)(a) of the No.17 Order, in respect of the Part 22 designated postcodes;

(b) articles 3(2)(i) and 4(2)(i) of the No.17 Order, in respect of the Part 23 designated postcodes;

(c) articles 3(2)(k) and 4(2)(k) of the No.17 Order, in respect of the Part 24 designated postcodes;

(d) articles 3(2)(b) and 4(2)(b) of the No.19 Order, in respect of the Part 25 designated postcodes;

(e) articles 3(2)(g) and 4(2)(m) and (n) of the No.22 Order, in respect of the Part 26 designated postcodes;

(f) articles 3(2)(h) and 4(2)(o) and (p) of the No.22 Order, in respect of the Part 27 designated postcodes;

(g) articles 3(2)(d) and 4(2)(g) and (h) of the No.24 Order, in respect of the Part 28 designated postcodes;

(h) articles 3(2)(h) and 4(2)(o) and (p) of the No.24 Order, in respect of the Part 29 designated postcodes;

(i) articles 3(2)(p) and 4(2)(ee) and (ff) of the No.24 Order, in respect of the Part 30 designated postcodes;

(j) articles 3(2)(q) and 4(2)(gg) and (hh) of the No.24 Order, in respect of the Part 31 designated postcodes.

Modification of the No.24 Order: removal of the gateway conditions from 6th September 2017

6.—(1) This article applies in the case of a claim for universal credit   1.031
that is made, or a claim for an employment and support allowance or a jobseeker's allowance that is made or treated as made, on or after 6th September 2017.

(2) Where this article applies, the provisions referred to in sub-paragraphs (a) and (b) have effect, with respect to a claimant residing in the relevant designated postcodes, as though the reference in those provisions to meeting the gateway conditions were omitted—

(a) articles 3(2)(d) and 4(2)(g) and (h) of the No.24 Order, in respect of the Part 32 designated postcodes;

(b) articles 3(2)(p) and 4(2)(ee) and (ff) of the No.24 Order, in respect of the Part 33 designated postcodes.

Modification of the No.22 and 24 Orders: removal of the gateway conditions from 13th September 2017

7.—(1) This article applies in the case of a claim for universal credit   1.032
that is made, or a claim for an employment and support allowance or a jobseeker's allowance that is made or treated as made, on or after 13th September 2017.

(2) Where this article applies, the provisions referred to in sub-paragraphs (a) to (e) have effect, with respect to a claimant residing in the relevant designated postcodes, as though the reference in those provisions to meeting the gateway conditions were omitted—

(a) articles 3(2)(a) and 4(2)(a) and (b) of the No.22 Order, in respect of the Part 34 designated postcodes;

(b) articles 3(2)(c) and 4(2)(e) and (f) of the No.22 Order, in respect of the Part 35 designated postcodes;

(c) articles 3(2)(h) and 4(2)(o) and (p) of the No.24 Order, in respect of the Part 36 designated postcodes;

   (d) articles 3(2)(o) and 4(2)(cc) and (dd) of the No.24 Order, in respect of the Part 37 designated postcodes;

   (e) articles 3(2)(aa) and 4(2)(aaa) and (bbb) of the No.24 Order, in respect of the Part 38 designated postcodes.

Modification of the No.22 and 24 Orders: removal of the gateway conditions from 20th September 2017

1.033   **8.**—(1) This article applies in the case of a claim for universal credit that is made, or a claim for an employment and support allowance or a jobseeker's allowance that is made or treated as made, on or after 20th September 2017.

(2) Where this article applies, the provisions referred to in sub-paragraphs (a) to (c) have effect, with respect to a claimant residing in the relevant designated postcodes, as though the reference in those provisions to meeting the gateway conditions were omitted—

   (a) articles 3(2)(l) and 4(2)(w) and (x) of the No.22 Order, in respect of the Part 39 designated postcodes;

   (b) articles 3(2)(a) and 4(2)(a) and (b) of the No.24 Order, in respect of the Part 40 designated postcodes;

   (c) articles 3(2)(q) and 4(2)(gg) and (hh) of the No.24 Order, in respect of the Part 41 designated postcodes.

Modification of the No.22 and 24 Orders: removal of the gateway conditions from 27th September 2017

1.034   **9.**—(1) This article applies in the case of a claim for universal credit that is made, or a claim for an employment and support allowance or a jobseeker's allowance that is made or treated as made, on or after 27th September 2017.

(2) Where this article applies, the provisions referred to in sub-paragraphs (a) to (e) have effect, with respect to a claimant residing in the relevant designated postcodes, as though the reference in those provisions to meeting the gateway conditions were omitted—

   (a) articles 3(2)(f) and 4(2)(k) and (l) of the No.22 Order, in respect of the Part 42 designated postcodes;

   (b) articles 3(2)(l) and 4(2)(w) and (x) of the No.22 Order, in respect of the Part 43 designated postcodes;

   (c) articles 3(2)(c) and 4(2)(e) and (f) of the No.24 Order, in respect of the Part 44 designated postcodes;

   (d) articles 3(2)(l) and 4(2)(w) and (x) of the No.24 Order, in respect of the Part 45 designated postcodes;

   (e) articles 3(2)(r) and 4(2)(ii) and (jj) of the No.24 Order, in respect of the Part 46 designated postcodes.

Modifications in consequence of removal of the gateway conditions: the No.17 Order

1.035   **10.**—(1) This article applies in the case of a claim in relation to which provisions of the No.17 Order are modified under article 5(2)(a), (b) or (c).

(2) Where this article applies, the No.17 Order has effect as though—

(a) in article 2(1) (interpretation), the definition of "gateway conditions" were omitted;

(b) in article 3(2)(b), (d), (f), (h), (j) and (l) (coming into force of the universal credit provisions and incorrect information)—

    (i) in paragraph (i), "or meeting the gateway conditions" and "or does not meet the gateway conditions" were omitted;

    (ii) in paragraph (ii), "or meeting the gateway conditions" and "or does not or do not meet those conditions" were omitted;

    (iii) in paragraph (iii), "or meeting the gateway conditions" were omitted;

(c) in article 3(5) (article 3A of the No.9 Order and incorrect information)—

    (i) for the text from "No.8" to "No.13 relevant district" there were substituted "numbered relevant district referred to in paragraph (2)";

    (ii) "or meeting the gateway conditions" were omitted in both places it occurs;

(d) in article 4(2)(b), (d), (f), (h), (j) and (l) (abolition of income-related employment and support allowance and income-based jobseeker's allowance and incorrect information)—

    (i) in paragraph (i), "or meeting the gateway conditions" and "or does not meet the gateway conditions" were omitted;

    (ii) in paragraph (ii), "or meeting the gateway conditions" and "or does not or do not meet those conditions" were omitted;

    (iii) in paragraph (iii), "or meeting the gateway conditions" were omitted; and

(e) for article 4(7) (claims by couples) there were substituted—

"(7) Paragraphs (1A) and (1B) of article 5 of the No.9 Order apply for the purposes of paragraph (2)(a), (c), (e), (g), (i) and (k) as they apply for the purposes of article 4(2)(a) of the No.9 Order (but as if the references in paragraph (1A) to Schedule 5 to the No.9 Order were omitted).".

Modifications in consequence of removal of the gateway conditions: the No.19 Order

11.—(1) This article applies in the case of a claim in relation to which provisions of the No.19 Order are modified under article 5(2)(d).   1.036

(2) Where this article applies, the modifications to the No.19 Order made by article 13(2) of the September 2016 Order have effect.

Modifications in consequence of removal of the gateway conditions: the No.22 Order

12.—(1) This article applies in the case of a claim in relation to which provisions of the No.22 Order are modified under—   1.037

(a) article 3(2)(a), (b), (c), (d), (e) or (f);

(b) article 4(2)(a), (b), (c), (d), (e), (f) or (g);

(c) article 5(2)(e) or (f);

(d) article 7(2)(a) or (b);

(e) article 8(2)(a); or

(f) article 9(2)(a) or (b).

(2) Where this article applies, the modifications to the No.22 Order made by article 14(2) of the September 2016 Order have effect.

Modifications in consequence of removal of the gateway conditions: the No.24 Order

1.038   **13.**—(1) This article applies in the case of a claim in relation to which provisions of the No.24 Order are modified under—

(a) article 3(2)(g), (h), (i), (j), (k) or (l);

(b) article 4(2)(h) or (i);

(c) article 5(2)(g), (h), (i) or (j);

(d) article 6(2);

(e) article 7(2)(c), (d) or (c);

(f) article 8(2)(b) or (c); or

(g) article 9(2)(c), (d) or (e).

(2) Where this article applies, the modifications to the No.24 Order made by article 15(2) of the September 2016 Order have effect.

Modification of the No.23 Order: claims for housing benefit, income support or a tax credit

1.039   **14.** Article 7 of the No.23 Order (prevention of claims for housing benefit, income support or a tax credit) applies as though the reference in paragraph (1) of that article to article 3(1) and (2)(a) to (c) of that Order included—

(a) a reference to paragraph (1) and sub-paragraphs (a), (i) and (k) of paragraph (2) of article 3 of the No.17 Order, in respect of claims in relation to which those sub-paragraphs are modified respectively by article 5(2)(a), 5(2)(b) and 5(2)(c) of this Order;

(b) a reference to paragraph (1) and sub-paragraph (b) of paragraph (2) of article 3 of the No.19 Order, in respect of claims in relation to which that sub-paragraph is modified by article 5(2)(d) of this Order;

(c) a reference to paragraph (1) and sub-paragraphs (e), (j), (n), (s) and (t) of paragraph (2) of article 3 of the No.22 Order, in respect of claims in relation to which those sub-paragraphs are modified respectively by articles 4(2)(b), 4(2)(e), 4(2)(f), 4(2)(g) and 3(2)(f) of this Order;

(d) a reference to paragraph (1) and sub-paragraphs (a), (c), (f), (g), (h) and (l) of paragraph (2) of article 3 of the No.22 Order, in respect of claims in relation to which those sub-paragraphs are modified respectively by articles 3(2)(a), 4(2)(a) and 7(2)(a), articles 3(2)(b) and 7(2)(b), articles 3(2)(c) and 9(2)(a), articles 3(2)(d), 4(2)(c) and 5(2)(e), articles 4(2)(d) and 5(2)(f), and articles 3(2)(e), 8(2)(a) and 9(2)(b) of this Order;

(e) a reference to paragraph (1) and sub-paragraphs (c), (f), (i), (o), (r) and (bb) of paragraph (2) of article 3 of the No.24 Order, in respect of claims in relation to which those sub-paragraphs are modified respectively by articles 9(2)(c), 3(2)(h), 3(2)(i), 7(2)(d), 9(2)(e) and 3(2)(l) of this Order; and

(f) a reference to paragraph (1) and sub-paragraphs (a), (d), (h), (l), (p), (q) and (aa) of paragraph (2) of article 3 of the No.24 Order, in respect of claims in relation to which those sub-paragraphs are modified respectively by articles 3(2)(g), 4(2)(h) and 8(2)(b), articles 5(2)(g) and 6(2)(a), articles 5(2)(h) and 7(2)(c), articles 3(2)(j), 4(2)(i) and 9(2)(d), articles 5(2)(i) and 6(2)(b), articles 5(2)(j) and 8(2)(c), and articles 3(2)(k) and 7(2)(e) of this Order.

Appointed day

15. 19th June 2017 is the day appointed for the coming into force of 1.040 section 46(1) (sanctions) of the Welfare Reform Act 2012 for the purpose of the substitution of section 19C (hardship payments) of the Jobseekers Act 1995.

SCHEDULE 1.041

Article 2(2)

POSTCODE DISTRICTS AND PART-DISTRICTS

PART 1

IV6.
IV7.
IV14.
IV15.
IV16.
IV17.
IV18.
IV19.
IV20.
IV23.
IV24.
IV25.
IV27.
IV28.
IV40.
IV41.
IV42.
IV43.

IV44.
IV45.
IV46.
IV47.
IV48.
IV49.
IV51.
IV52.
IV53.
IV55.
IV56.
KW1.
KW3.
KW5.
KW6.
KW7.
KW8.
KW9.
KW10.
KW11.
KW12.
KW13.
KW14.
PH30.
PH31.
PH33 6 and PH33 7.
PH34.
PH35.
PH36.
PH37.
PH38.
PH39.
PH40.
PH41.
PH42.
PH43.
PH44.
PH49.
PH50.

PART 2

S63 0.
S63 8.
S70.
S72 0.
S72 7 and S72 8.
S73 3.
S73 8 and S73 9.

PART 3

DY1.
DY2.

PART 4

B62 2.
B62 9.
B63.
DY5 2 to DY5 4.
DY6 7 to DY6 9.
DY8 1.
DY8 3 to DY8 5.
DY8 9.
DY9 7 and DY9 8.

PART 5

B36.
B37.
B46 1 and B46 2.
B90 2 to B90 4.
B90 8 and B90 9.
B91.

PART 6

CH8 7.

PART 7

DY6 6.
PA80.

PART 8

B46 3.
B62 0.
B90 1.
DY9 0.
DY9 9.

PART 9

B62 8.
B64.
B65 0.
B65 8.

PART 10

1.042 DY6 0.
DY7.
DY8 2.
S63 3.
S63 5.
S63 9.
S73 0.
S74.

PART 11

S72 9.

PART 12

PH33 9.

PART 13

BS21.
BS48.
YO1.
YO10.
YO23 1.
YO24.
YO26 0.
YO26 4 to YO26 6.
YO30 4 to YO30 7.
YO31.
YO32 2 to YO32 4.
YO32 9.

PART 14

BA12.
BA13.

BA14.
BA15.
SN8 1.
SN8 3 and SN8 4.
SN8 9.
SN9.
SN10.
SN12.

PART 15

NP4.
NP44.

PART 16

TN39 3.
TN40.

PART 17

SO50 0.
SO50 4 and SO50 5.
SO50 8.
SO53 1 and SO53 2.

PART 18

TN39 4 and TN39 5.

PART 19

SN8 2.

PART 20

SO32 1 and SO32 2.   **1.043**
SO50 6 and SO50 7.
SO50 9.
SO51 0 and SO51 1.

SO51 5.
SO51 7 to SO51 9.
SO52.
SO53 3 to SO53 5.

PART 21

SO51 6.

PART 22

M31.
M32.
M33 2.
M33 4 to M33 7.
M41.
WA14 1 and WA14 2.
WA14 5.
WA15 5 and WA15 6.
WA15 9.

PART 23

M17 1.
M17 8.

PART 24

CH1.
CH2.
CH3.
CH4 7 and CH4 8.
CW1.
CW2 6 to CW2 8.
CW3 0.
CW4.
CW5.
CW10.
CW11.
WA6.
WA14 3 and WA14 4.

PART 25

M33 3.
WA15 0.
WA15 7 and WA15 8.

PART 26

SS0.
SS1.
SS2 4.
SS9 0 and SS9 1.

PART 27

ST7 2.
SY14 8.

PART 28

CT9.
CT11 0.
CT11 7 to CT11 9.

PART 29

W8.
W10 5 and W10 6.
W10 9.
W11.

PART 30

1.044

CT13 0.
CT13 9.

PART 31

CM18 6.
CM19 4.
CM20 1.

CM20 3.
CM20 9.

PART 32

CT7 9.
CT8.
CT10.
CT11 1.
CT12.

PART 33

CT7 0.
CT13 3.

PART 34

YO19 4 and YO19 5.
YO26 7 to YO26 9.
YO30 1 and YO30 2.
YO32 5.
YO61.
YO90.
YO91.

PART 35

S36 6 to S36 9.
S71 1 to S71 3.
S71 5.
S75 1 to S75 3.
S75 6.

PART 36

LS24 0.
YO19 6.
YO23 2 and YO23 3.
YO23 7.

PART 37

S35 5.
S35 7.
YO41.
YO42.

PART 38

S71 4.
S75 4 and S75 5.

PART 39

SS9 2 to SS9 4.

PART 40

SS3 8.   1.045

PART 41

CM17.
CM18 7.
CM19 5.
CM20 2.
CM21 9.
SS2 5 and SS2 6.
SS3 0.
SS3 9.
SS9 5.

PART 42

DY3 2 and DY3 3.
DY5 1.

PART 43

B92.
B93 3.
B93 9.

PART 44

B93 0.
B93 8.

PART 45

DY3 4.

PART 46

DY3 1.

The Loans for Mortgage Interest Regulations 2017

SI 2017/725

[In force, see reg.1(2)]

ARRANGEMENT OF REGULATIONS

1.046

Made on July 5, 2017 by the Secretary of State, in exercise of the powers conferred by sections 4(5), 35(1), 36(2) and (4) of the Jobseekers Act 1995, sections 2(3)(b) and sections 17(1) and 19(1) of the State Pension Credit Act 2002, sections 123(1)(a), 135(1), 137(1) and (2)(d) and 175(1), (3) and (4) of the Social Security Contributions and Benefits Act 1992, sections 4(2)(a), 24(1) and 25(2), (3) and (5)(a) of the Welfare Reform Act 2007, sections 11(3) and (4) and 42(1), (2) and (3)(a) of, and paragraph 1(1) of Schedule 6 to, the Welfare Reform Act 2012 and sections 18, 19 and 21 of the Welfare Reform and Work Act 2016.

This instrument contains only regulations made under, by virtue of, or consequential upon, sections 18, 19 and 21 of the Welfare Reform and Work Act 2016 and is made before the end of the period of 6 months beginning with the coming into force of those sections. Therefore, in accordance with section 173(5) of the Social Security Administration Act 1992, these Regulations are not required to be referred to the Social Security Advisory Committee.

GENERAL NOTE

At present, it is possible for some owner-occupiers who are entitled to IS, IBJSA, IRESA, SPC and universal credit to receive benefit to cover some of their housing costs. Such housing costs are paid as part of the applicable amount (IS, IBJSA and IRESA): see reg.17(1)(e) of, and Sch.3 to, the IS Regulations; reg.83(f) of, and Sch.2 to, the JSA Regulations 1996; reg.67(1)(c) of, and Sch.6 to, the ESA Regulations; or of the guarantee credit (SPC): see reg.6(6)(c) of, and Sch.2 to, the SPC Regulations; or as the housing costs element of universal credit: see s.11 of the WRA 2012 and regs 25 and 26 of, and Schs 1-3 and 5 to, the UC Regs 2013.

1.047

These Regulations, which are made under ss.18, 19 and 21 of the Welfare Reform and Work Act 2016 ("WRWA 2016") (see paras 1.201–1.206 of Vol.V of the main work), provide for (most) such housing costs to be replaced by repayable, interest-bearing, loans secured on the claimants' homes by way of a legal charge.

The bulk of the Regulations have been in force since July 27, 2017. It is therefore already theoretically possible for the Secretary of State to make an offer of a loan for mortgage interest. However, anyone eligible to receive such an offer would still be entitled to receive payment of their housing costs as part of their benefit under the provisions listed above. The new rules will commence for practical purposes on April 6, 2018, when regs 18-21 and Sch.5, which repeal most of those provisions as they relate to owner-occupiers, come into force.

Also on July 2017, ss.20(2)-(7) and (10) of the WRWA 2016 were brought into force by reg.2 of the Welfare Reform and Work Act 2016 (Commencement No. 5) Regulations 2017 (SI 2017/802). Among other things, these amend s.8 SSA 1998 to empower the Secretary of State to make decisions about loans under s.18 WRWA 2016. The consequence is that an appeal lies to the First-tier Tribunal against such a decision under s.12 SSA 1998 and thence to the Upper Tribunal under s.11 TCEA 2007.

It is expected that the remaining parts of s.20 WRWA 2016, which amend the substantive statute law relating to entitlement to housing costs as part of a means-tested benefit will be brought into force on April 6, 2018.

It must be stressed that the changes brought about by these Regulations relate exclusively to owner-occupiers. Renters will continue to be entitled to the housing costs element of universal credit under either s.11 of the WRA 2012 and regs 25 and 26 of, and Schs 1-4 to, the UC Regs 2013 or the Housing Benefit Regulations or the Housing Benefit (Persons who have attained the qualifying age for state pension credit) Regulations 2006.

Citation and commencement

1.048   **1.**—(1) These Regulations may be cited as the Loans for Mortgage Interest Regulations 2017.

(2) These Regulations come into force—

(a) for the purposes of regulations 18 to 21, on 6th April 2018;

(b) for all other purposes, on 27th July 2017.

Interpretation

1.049   **2.**—(1) In these Regulations—

"the Act" means the Welfare Reform and Work Act 2016;

"alternative finance payments" has the meaning given in paragraph 5(3) of Schedule 1 to these Regulations;

"applicable amount" means—

(a) in the case of employment and support allowance, the claimant's weekly applicable amount under regulations 67 to 70 of the ESA Regulations;

(b) in the case of income support, the claimant's weekly applicable amount under regulations 17 to 21AA of the IS Regulations;

(c) in the case of jobseeker's allowance, the claimant's weekly applicable amount under regulations 83 to 86C of the JSA Regulations;

(d) in the case of an SPC claimant, the claimant's weekly appropriate minimum guarantee under section 2 of the State Pension Credit Act 2002;

(e) in the case of a UC claimant, the maximum amount of a claimant's award of universal credit under regulation 23(1) of the UC Regulations;

"assessment period" has the meaning given in regulation 21 of the UC Regulations;

"benefit unit" means a single claimant and his or her partner (if any) or joint claimants;

"benefit week" has the meaning given—

(a) in the case of employment and support allowance, in regulation 2 of the ESA Regulations;

(b) the case of income support, in paragraph 4 of Schedule 7 to the Claims and Payment Regulations;

(c) in the case of jobseeker's allowance, in regulation 1 of the JSA Regulations;

(d) in the case of state pension credit, in regulation 1 of the SPC Regulations;

"charge by way of legal mortgage" has the meaning given in section 132(1) of the Land Registration Act 2002;

"child" means a person under the age of 16;

"claimant" means a single claimant or each of joint claimants;

"Claims and Payment Regulations" means the Social Security (Claims and Payments) Regulations 1987;

"close relative" means a parent, parent-in-law, son, son-in-law, daughter, daughter-in-law, step-parent, step-son, step-daughter, brother, sister, or, if any of the preceding persons is one member of a couple, the other member of that couple;

"couple" means—

(a) two people who are married to, or civil partners of, each other and are members of the same household;

(b) two people who are not married to, or civil partners of, each other but are living together as a married couple or civil partners;

"disabled person" has the meaning given—

(a) in the case of employment and support allowance, in paragraph 1(3) of Schedule 6 to the ESA Regulations,

(b) in the case of income support, in paragraph 1(3) of Schedule 3 to the IS Regulations;

(c) in the case of jobseeker's allowance, in paragraph 1(3) of Schedule 2 to the JSA Regulations;

(d) in the case of state pension credit, in paragraph 1(2)(a) of Schedule 2 to the SPC Regulations;

(e) in the case of universal credit, in paragraph 14(3) of Schedule 3 to these Regulations;

"dwelling"—

(a) in England and Wales, means a dwelling within the meaning of Part 1 of the Local Government Finance Act 1992;

    (b) in Scotland, means a dwelling within the meaning of Part 2 of that Act;

"earned income" has the meaning given in Chapter 2 of Part 6 of the UC Regulations;

"ESA Regulations" means the Employment and Support Allowance Regulations 2008;

"existing claimant" means a claimant who is entitled to a qualifying benefit, including an amount for owner-occupier payments, on 5th April 2018;

"financial year" has the meaning given in section 25(2) of the Budget Responsibility and National Audit Act 2011;

"income" means any income which is, or which is treated as, an individual's, including payments which are treated as earnings, and which is not disregarded, under—

    (a) in the case of employment and support allowance, Part 10 of the ESA Regulations;

    (b) in the case of income support, Part 5 of the IS Regulations;

    (c) in the case of jobseeker's allowance, Part 8 of the JSA Regulations;

    (d) in the case of state pension credit, Part 3 of the SPC Regulations;

"IS Regulations" means the Income Support (General) Regulations 1987;

"joint claimants"—

    (a) in the case of jobseeker's allowance means—

        (i) members of a joint-claim couple who have jointly made a claim for, and are entitled to, income-based jobseeker's allowance; or

        (ii) where Schedule 5 applies, members of a joint-claim couple who have made a claim for, but are not entitled to, such a benefit by reason only that they have income equal to or exceeding the applicable amount but less than the sum of that applicable amount and the amount of a loan payment they would receive under regulation 10 if they were so entitled;

    (b) in the case of universal credit m. ᵒ

        (i) members of a couple who   a claim for, and are entitled to, univeʳ

        (ii) where Schedule 5 applies, .   ɹ couple who have made a claim for, but are not entitled to, such a benefit by reason only that they have unearned income equal to or exceeding the applicable amount but less than the sum of that applicable amount and the amount of a loan payment they would receive under regulation 10 if they were so entitled;

"joint-claim couple" has the meaning in section 1(4) of the Jobseekers Act 1995;

"JSA Regulations" means the Jobseeker's Allowance Regulations 1996;

"legacy benefit" means income-related employment and support allowance, income support or income-based jobseeker's allowance;

"legacy benefit claimant" means a claimant who is entitled to a legacy benefit;

"legal estate" means any of the legal estates set out in section 1(1) of the Law of Property Act 1925;

"legal owner" means the owner, whether alone or with others, of a legal estate or, in Scotland, a heritable or registered interest, in the relevant accommodation;

"loan agreement" means an agreement entered into by a single claimant and his or her partner (if any), or each joint claimant, and the Secretary of State, which sets out the terms and conditions upon which the loan payments are made to the claimant;

"loan payments" means one or more payments, calculated under regulation 10, in respect of a claimant's liability to make owner-occupier payments in respect of the relevant accommodation;

"loan payments offer date" means the day on which the Secretary of State sends the loan agreement to a claimant;

"Modified Rules" means the Social Security (Housing Costs Special Arrangements) (Amendment and Modification) Regulations 2008;

"new claimant partner" has the meaning given in regulation 7 of the Transitional Provisions Regulations;

"non-dependant" has the meaning given—

  (a) in the case of employment and support allowance, in regulation 71 of the ESA Regulations;

  (b) in the case of income support, in regulation 3 of the IS Regulations;

  (c) in the case of jobseeker's allowance, in regulation 2 of the JSA Regulations;

  (d) in the case of state pension credit, in paragraph 1(4) of Schedule 2 to the SPC Regulations;

"owner-occupier payments" has the meaning given in regulation 3(2)(a);

"partner" means—

  (a) where a claimant is a member of a couple, the other member of that couple;

  (b) where a claimant is married polygamously to two or more members of the claimant's household, all such members;

"person who lacks capacity"—

  (a) in England and Wales, has the meaning given in section 2 of the Mental Capacity Act 2005;

  (b) in Scotland, means a person who is incapable under section 1(6) of the Adults with Incapacity (Scotland) Act 2000;

"polygamous marriage" means a marriage during which a party to it is married to more than one person and which took place under the laws of a country which permits polygamy;

"qualifying benefit" means income-related employment and support allowance, income support, income-based jobseeker's allowance, state pension credit or universal credit;

"qualifying lender" has the meaning given in section 19(7) of the Act;

"qualifying loan" means—

(a) in the case of a legacy benefit or state pension credit, a loan which qualifies under paragraph 2(2) or (4) of Schedule 1 to these Regulations;

(b) in the case of universal credit, a loan which qualifies under paragraph 5(2) of Schedule 1 to these Regulations;

"qualifying period" means a period of—

(a) nine consecutive assessment periods in which a claimant has been entitled to universal credit;

(b) 39 consecutive weeks in which a claimant—

(i) has been entitled to a legacy benefit; or

(ii) is treated as having been entitled to such a benefit under—

(aa) paragraph 14 of Schedule 3 to the IS Regulations;

(bb) paragraph 13 of Schedule 2 to the JSA Regulations; or

(cc) paragraph 15 of Schedule 6 to the ESA Regulations;

"qualifying young person" has the meaning given—

(a) in the case of a legacy benefit, in section 142 of the Social Security Contributions and Benefits Act 1992;

(b) in the case of state pension credit, in regulation 4A of the SPC Regulations;

(c) in the case of universal credit, in regulation 5 of the UC Regulations;

"relevant accommodation" means the accommodation which the claimant occupies, or is treated as occupying, as the claimant's home under Schedule 3;

"relevant date", apart from in regulation 21, means the first day with respect to which a claimant's liability to make owner-occupier payments is met by a loan payment;

"single claimant" means—

(a) an individual who has made a claim for, and is entitled to, a qualifying benefit as a single person; or

(b) where Schedule 5 applies, an individual who has made a claim for, but is not entitled to, a qualifying benefit as a single person by reason only that the individual has income or, in the case of universal credit, unearned income, equal to or exceeding the applicable amount but less than the sum of that applicable amount and the amount of a loan payment he or she would receive under regulation 10 if he or she were so entitled;

"single person" means an individual who is not a member of a couple;

"SPC claimant" means a claimant who is entitled to state pension credit;

"SPC Regulations" means the State Pension Credit Regulations 2002;

"standard security" has the meaning in Part 2 of the Conveyancing and Feudal Reform (Scotland) Act 1970;

"transitional end day" has the meaning given in regulations 19(1) and 20(2);

"Transitional Provisions Regulations" means the Universal Credit (Transitional Provisions) Regulations 2014;

"UC claimant" means a claimant who is entitled to universal credit;

"UC Regulations" means the Universal Credit Regulations 2013; and

"unearned income" has the meaning given in Chapter 3 of Part 6 of the UC Regulations.

(2) For the purposes of these Regulations, a reference to—

(a) entitlement to a qualifying benefit is to be read as a reference to entitlement as determined under the ESA Regulations, IS Regulations, JSA Regulations, SPC Regulations and UC Regulations;

(b) the claimant's family or to being a member of the claimant's family means a reference to the claimant's partner and any child or qualifying young person who is the responsibility of the claimant or the claimant's partner, where that child or qualifying young person is a member of the claimant's household;

(c) a person being responsible for a child or qualifying young person is to be read as a reference to a person being treated as responsible for a child or qualifying young person in the circumstances specified in—

(i) in the case of employment and support allowance, regulation 156(10) of the ESA Regulations;

(ii) in the case of income support, regulation 15 of the IS Regulations;

(iii) in the case of jobseeker's allowance, regulation 77 of the JSA Regulations;

(iv) in the case of state pension credit and universal credit, regulation 4 of the UC Regulations;

(d) a person being a member of a household is to be read as a reference to a person being treated as a member of the household in the circumstances specified in—

(i) in the case of employment and support allowance, in regulation 156 of the ESA Regulations;

(ii) in the case of income support, in regulation 16 of the IS Regulations;

(iii) in the case of jobseeker's allowance, in regulation 78 of the JSA Regulations;

(iv) in the case of state pension credit and universal credit, in regulation 5 of the SPC Regulations;

(e) a person being engaged in remunerative work is to be read as a reference to a person being treated as engaged in remunerative work—

(i) in the case of employment and support allowance, in regulations 41 to 43 of the ESA Regulations;

(ii) in the case of income support, in regulations 5 and 6 of the IS Regulations;

     (iii) in the case of jobseeker's allowance, in regulations 51 to 53 of the JSA Regulations;

     (iv) in the case of state pension credit, in paragraph 2 of Schedule 2 to the SPC Regulations.

The offer of loan payments

1.050   **3.**—(1) The Secretary of State may make an offer of loan payments to a claimant in respect of any owner-occupier payments the claimant is, or is to be treated as, being liable to make in respect of the accommodation which the claimant is, or is to be treated as, occupying as the claimant's home, unless paragraph (4) applies.

(2) For the purposes of paragraph (1)—

(a) owner-occupier payments are—

     (i) in the case of a legacy benefit claimant or SPC claimant, payments within the meaning of Part 1 of Schedule 1;

     (ii) in the case of a UC claimant, payments within the meaning of Part 2 of Schedule 1;

(b) the circumstances in which a claimant is, or is to be treated as, being liable to make owner-occupier payments are—

     (i) in the case of a legacy benefit claimant or SPC claimant, the circumstances specified in Part 1 of Schedule 2;

     (ii) in the case of a UC claimant, the circumstances specified in Part 2 of Schedule 2;

(c) the circumstances in which a claimant is, or is to be treated as, occupying accommodation as the claimant's home are—

     (i) in the case of a legacy benefit claimant or SPC claimant, the circumstances specified in Part 2 of Schedule 3;

     (ii) in the case of a UC claimant, the circumstances specified in Part 3 of Schedule 3.

(3) Where the liability for owner-occupier payments is shared with a person not in the benefit unit, the claimant shall be, or shall be treated as, liable to make owner-occupier payments by reference to the appropriate proportion of the payments for which the claimant is responsible.

(4) A UC claimant shall not be eligible for the offer of loan payments if—

(a) where the claimant is a single person, the claimant has any earned income; or

(b) where the claimant is a member of a couple, either member of the couple has any earned income.

Definitions

1.051   "benefit unit"—reg.2(1).
"claimant"—*ibid.*
"couple"—*ibid.*
"earned income"—*ibid.*
"legacy benefit claimant"—*ibid.*
"loan payments"—*ibid.*
"owner-occupier payments"—regs 2(1) and 3(2)(a).
"single person"—reg.2(1).

"SPC claimant"—*ibid.*
"UC claimant"—*ibid.*

Acceptance of loan payments offer

4. The offer of loan payments is accepted where the Secretary of State **1.052** has received the loan agreement signed by, in the case of a single claimant, the claimant and his or her partner (if any), or, in the case of joint claimants, each member of the couple, and the documents referred to in regulation 5(2).

DEFINITIONS

"claimant"—reg.2(1).
"couple"—*ibid.*
"joint claimants"—*ibid.*
"loan agreement"—*ibid.*
"loan payments"—*ibid.*
"partner"—*ibid.*
"single claimant"—*ibid.*

Conditions to meet before the loan payments can be made

5.—(1) The Secretary of State may make the loan payments if— **1.053**
 (a) the loan payments offer is accepted in accordance with regulation 4; and
 (b) the conditions in paragraph (2) are met.
 (2) The conditions are—
 (a) in England and Wales—
  (i) where all of the legal owners are within the benefit unit, each legal owner has executed a charge by way of legal mortgage in favour of the Secretary of State in respect of the relevant accommodation;
  (ii) where one or more legal owners are not within the benefit unit, each legal owner within the benefit unit (if any) has executed an equitable charge in respect of their beneficial interest in the relevant accommodation;
 (b) in Scotland, each legal owner within the benefit unit has executed a standard security in respect of his or her interest in the relevant accommodation;
 (c) the Secretary of State has obtained the written consent referred to in paragraph (3); and
 (d) the information condition in regulation 6 is met within the period of 6 months ending with the day on which the loan payments offer is accepted.
 (3) The consent required by paragraph (2)(c) is consent given in writing to the creation of the charge or, in Scotland, the standard security by any person in the benefit unit in occupation of the relevant accommodation, who is not a legal owner.

DEFINITIONS

"benefit unit"—reg.2(1).
"charge by way of legal mortgage"—*ibid.*

"legal owner"—*ibid.*
"loan payments"—*ibid.*
"relevant accommodation"—*ibid.*
"standard security"—*ibid.*

Information condition

1.054   **6.**—(1) The information condition is that the Secretary of State has provided relevant information about the loan payments to a single claimant and his or her partner (if any) or each joint claimant.

(2) For the purposes of this regulation, "relevant information" is information about the loan payments which must include—

  (a) a summary of the terms and conditions included within the loan agreement;

  (b) where the circumstances in regulation 5(2)(a)(i) or (b) apply, an explanation that the Secretary of State will seek to obtain a charge or, in Scotland, a standard security in respect of the relevant accommodation;

  (c) an explanation of the consent referred to in regulation 5(3); and

  (d) information as to where a single claimant and his or her partner (if any) or each joint claimant can obtain further information and independent legal and financial advice regarding loan payments.

DEFINITIONS

  "claimant"—reg.2(1).
  "loan agreement"—*ibid.*
  "loan payments"—*ibid.*
  "partner"—*ibid.*
  "relevant accommodation"—*ibid.*
  "single claimant"—*ibid.*
  "standard security"—*ibid.*

Time of each loan payment

1.055   **7.** Each loan payment shall be made—

  (a) in the case of a UC claimant, at monthly intervals in arrears; and

  (b) in the case of a legacy benefit claimant or SPC claimant—

    (i) where direct payments are made to a qualifying lender under regulation 17(1), at 4 weekly intervals in arrears; or

    (ii) where payments are made to the claimant under regulation 17(3), at the same intervals as the qualifying benefit is paid.

DEFINITIONS

  "claimant"—reg.2(1).
  "legacy benefit claimant"—*ibid.*
  "qualifying benefit"—*ibid.*
  "qualifying lender"—*ibid.*
  "SPC claimant"—*ibid.*
  "UC claimant"—*ibid.*

Period covered by loan payments

8.—(1) The period in respect of which the loan payments shall be 1.056
made shall begin on the later of—

(a) 6th April 2018;

(b) in the case of a UC claimant or legacy benefit claimant, the day
after the day on which the qualifying period ends;

(c) in the case of an SPC claimant, the date of claim in respect of the
claimant's award of state pension credit;

(d) the transitional end day.

(2) For the purposes of paragraph (1)(c), "date of claim" has the
meaning given by whichever is applicable of regulation 4F or regulation
19(2) and (3) of the Claims and Payments Regulations.

DEFINITIONS

"claimant"—reg.2(1).
"legacy benefit claimant"—*ibid.*
"loan payments"—*ibid*
"qualifying period"—*ibid.*
"SPC claimant"—*ibid.*
"transitional end day"—*ibid.*
"UC claimant"—*ibid.*

Duration of loan payments

9.—(1) Subject to paragraph (2), loan payments shall continue to be 1.057
made indefinitely at the intervals specified in regulation 7.

(2) If one of the circumstances in paragraph (3) occurs, the Secretary
of State shall terminate the loan payments immediately but subject to
paragraph (4).

(3) The circumstances are that—

(a) the claimant ceases to be entitled to a qualifying benefit;

(b) the claimant ceases to be, or to be treated as, liable to make
owner-occupier payments under Schedule 2;

(c) the claimant ceases to be, or to be treated as, occupying the
relevant accommodation under Schedule 3;

(d) the loan agreement is terminated in accordance with its terms;

(e) in the case of a UC claimant only, regulation 3(4) applies.

(4) The Secretary of State shall make the loan payments direct to the
claimant for the period specified in paragraph (6) if—

(a) a claimant ceases to be entitled to a legacy benefit by reason that,
in the case of a single claimant, the claimant or his or her partner
(if any), or, in the case of joint claimants, either member of the
couple, is engaged in remunerative work; and

(b) the conditions in paragraph (5) are met.

(5) The conditions are that, in the case of a single claimant, the
claimant or his or her partner (if any), or, in the case of joint claimants,
either member of the couple—

(a) is engaged in remunerative work which is expected to last for a
period of no less than 5 weeks;

(b) is still liable or treated as liable to make owner-occupier payments
under Schedule 2;

(c) has, for a continuous period of 26 weeks ending with the day on which he or she commences the work referred to in sub-paragraph (a), been entitled to a legacy benefit; and

(d) was, on the day before the day on which he or she commenced the work referred to in sub-paragraph (a), receiving loan payments under these Regulations.

(6) The period specified is the period of 4 weeks commencing with the day on which the relevant person is first engaged in remunerative work.

(7) If a legacy benefit claimant ceases to be entitled to a legacy benefit but becomes entitled again to the legacy benefit within the period of 52 weeks beginning with the day the claimant ceased to be entitled to it, the claimant shall not be required to satisfy the qualifying period if the claimant wishes to receive loan payments on the basis of the new entitlement.

DEFINITIONS

"claimant"—reg.2(1).
"couple"—*ibid.*
"entitlement"—reg.2(2)(a).
"joint claimants"—reg.2(1).
"legacy benefit"—*ibid.*
"legacy benefit claimant"—*ibid.*
"loan agreement"—*ibid.*
"loan payments"—*ibid.*
"owner-occupier payments"—regs 2(1) and 3(2)(a).
"partner"—reg.2(1).
"qualifying benefit"—*ibid.*
"qualifying period"—*ibid.*
"relevant accommodation"—*ibid.*
"remunerative work"—reg.2(2)(e).
"single claimant"—reg.2(1).
"UC claimant"—*ibid.*

Calculation of each loan payment

1.058   **10.** Subject to any deduction under regulation 14, each loan payment shall be the aggregate of the amounts resulting from regulations 11 and 12.

Calculation in respect of qualifying loans

1.059   **11.**—(1) Subject to paragraphs (3) and (4), the amount to be included in each loan payment for owner-occupier payments which are payments of interest on qualifying loans is determined as follows.

Step 1

Determine the amount of capital for the time being owing in connection with each qualifying loan to which the owner-occupier payments relate.

Step 2

If there is more than one qualifying loan, add together the amounts determined in step 1.

Step 3

Determine the identified amount which is the lower of—
(a) the amount resulting from step 1 or 2; and
(b) the capital limit specified in paragraph (2)(a) or (b).
If both amounts in (a) and (b) are the same, that is the identified amount.

Step 4

In respect of a legacy benefit claimant or SPC claimant, apply the following formula to achieve a weekly sum—

$$\frac{A \times SR}{52} - I$$

In respect of a UC claimant, apply the following formula to achieve a monthly sum—

$$\frac{A \times SR}{12} - I$$

In either case—
"A" is the identified amount in step 3,
"SR" is the standard rate that applies at the end of the calculation (see regulation 13), and
"I" is the amount of any income, in the case of a legacy benefit or SPC claimant, or unearned income, in the case of a UC claimant, above the claimant's applicable amount.
The result is the amount to be included in each loan payment for owner-occupier payments which are payments of interest on qualifying loans.
(2) The capital limit is—
(a) £200,000—
    (i) in the case of a legacy benefit claimant or SPC claimant where the Modified Rules apply;
    (ii) in the case of a UC claimant;
(b) £100,000 in all other cases.
(3) In the application of paragraph (2) to a qualifying loan (or any part of a qualifying loan) which was taken out for the purpose of making necessary adaptations to the accommodation to meet the needs of a disabled person—
(a) the qualifying loan (or the part of the qualifying loan) is to be disregarded for the purposes of steps 2 and 3; and
(b) "A" in step 4 is to be read as the amount resulting from step 1 in respect of the qualifying loan (or the sum of those amounts if there

47

is more than one qualifying loan taken out for the purpose of making such adaptations) plus the amount (if any) resulting from step 3 in relation to any other qualifying loan or loans.

(4) Subject to paragraph (5), any variation in the amount of capital for the time being owing in connection with a qualifying loan is not to be taken into account after the relevant date until such time as the Secretary of State recalculates the amount which shall occur—

(a) on the first anniversary of the relevant date; and

(b) in respect of any variation after the first anniversary, on the next anniversary which follows the date of the variation.

(5) In respect of an existing claimant, the Secretary of State shall recalculate the amount of capital owing in connection with a qualifying loan on the anniversary of the date on which the claimant's qualifying benefit first included an amount for owner-occupier payments.

DEFINITIONS

"applicable amount"—reg.2(1).
"claimant"—*ibid.*
"disabled person"—*ibid.*
"existing claimant"—*ibid.*
"income"—*ibid.*
"legacy benefit claimant"—*ibid.*
"Modified Rules"—*ibid.*
"owner-occupier payments"—regs 2(1) and 3(2)(a).
"qualifying benefit"—*ibid.*
"qualifying loan"—*ibid.*
"relevant date"—*ibid.*
"SPC claimant"—*ibid.*
"UC claimant"—*ibid.*
"unearned income"—*ibid.*

Calculation in respect of alternative finance payments

1.060   12.—(1) The amount to be included in each loan payment for owner-occupier payments which are alternative finance payments is determined as follows.

Step 1

Determine the purchase price of the accommodation to which the alternative finance payments relate.

Step 2

Determine the identified amount which is the lower of—

(a) the amount resulting from step 1; and

(b) the capital limit specified in paragraph (2)(a) or (b).

If both amounts are the same, that is the identified amount.

Step 3

In respect of an SPC claimant, apply the following formula to achieve a weekly sum—

$$\frac{A \times SR}{52} - I$$

In respect of a UC claimant, apply the following formula to achieve a monthly sum—

$$\frac{A \times SR}{12} - I$$

In either case—
"A" is the identified amount in step 2,
"SR" is the standard rate that applies at the date of the calculation (see regulation 13), and
"I" is the amount of any income, in the case of an SPC claimant, or unearned income, in the case of a UC claimant, above the claimant's applicable amount.

The result is the amount to be included in each loan payment for owner-occupier payments which are alternative finance payments.

(2) The capital limit is—

(a) £200,000 in the case of an SPC claimant where the Modified Rules apply or a UC claimant;

(b) £100,000 in all other cases.

(3) For the purposes of paragraph (1), "purchase price" means the price paid by a party to the alternative finance arrangements other than the claimant in order to acquire the interest in the accommodation to which those arrangements relate less—

(a) the amount of any initial payment made by the claimant in connection with the acquisition of that interest; and

(b) the amount of any subsequent payments made by the claimant or any partner to another party to the alternative finance arrangements before—

(i) the relevant date; or

(ii) in the case of an existing claimant, the date on which the claimant's qualifying benefit first included an amount for owner-occupier payments,

which reduce the amount owed by the claimant under the alternative finance arrangements.

(4) Subject to paragraph (5), any variation in the amount for the time being owing in connection with alternative finance arrangements is not to be taken into account after the relevant date until such time as the Secretary of State recalculates the amount which shall occur—

(a) on the first anniversary of the relevant date; and

(b) in respect of any variation after the first anniversary, on the next anniversary which follows the date of the variation.

(5) In respect of an existing claimant, the Secretary of State shall recalculate the amount for the time being owing in connection with a qualifying loan on the anniversary of the date on which the claimant's

qualifying benefit first included an amount for owner-occupier payments.

DEFINITIONS

"alternative finance payments"—reg.2(1).
"applicable amount"—*ibid.*
"claimant"—*ibid.*
"existing claimant"—*ibid.*
"income"—*ibid.*
"Modified Rules"—*ibid.*
"owner-occupier payments"—regs 2(1) and 3(2)(a).
"partner"—reg.2(1).
"qualifying benefit"—*ibid.*
"qualifying loan"—*ibid.*
"relevant date"—*ibid.*
"SPC claimant"—*ibid.*
"UC claimant"—*ibid.*
"unearned income"—*ibid.*

Standard rate to be applied under regulations 11 and 12

1.061   **13.**—(1) The standard rate is the average mortgage rate published by the Bank of England which has effect on the 5th April 2018.

(2) The standard rate is to be varied each time that paragraph (3) applies.

(3) This paragraph applies when, on any reference day, the Bank of England publishes an average mortgage rate which differs by 0.5 percentage points or more from the standard rate that applies on that reference day (whether it applies by virtue of paragraph (1) or by virtue of a previous application of this paragraph).

(4) The average mortgage rate published on that reference day then becomes the new standard rate in accordance with paragraph (5).

(5) Any variation in the standard rate by virtue of paragraphs (2) to (4) shall come into effect at the end of the period of 6 weeks beginning with the day referred to in paragraph (3).

(6) At least 7 days before a variation of the standard rate comes into effect under paragraph (5), the Secretary of State must arrange for notice to be published on a publicly accessible website of—

(a) the new standard rate; and

(b) the day on which the new standard rate comes into effect under paragraph (5).

(7) For the purposes of this Regulation—

"average mortgage rate" means the effective interest rate (non-seasonally adjusted) of United Kingdom resident banks and building societies for loans to households secured on dwellings, published by the Bank of England in respect of the most recent period specified for that rate at the time of publication; and

"reference day" means any day falling on or after 6th April 2018.

DEFINITIONS

"dwelling"—reg.2(1).

Non-dependant deductions

14.—(1) In the case of a legacy benefit claimant or SPC claimant, a   1.062
deduction from each loan payment shall be made in respect of any non-
dependant in accordance with paragraph (2).

(2) The amount to be deducted is calculated as follows.

Step 1

Identify the amount which is the sum of the loan payment calculated
under regulation 10 and the amount of housing costs (if any) paid to a
claimant under—
  (a) paragraph 17 of Schedule 3 to the IS Regulations;
  (b) paragraph 16 of Schedule 2 to the JSA Regulations;
  (c) paragraph 18 of Schedule 6 to the ESA Regulations; or
  (d) paragraph 13 of Schedule 2 to the SPC Regulations.

Step 2

Identify the total amount of the non-dependant deductions applicable
to the claimant under—
  (a) paragraph 18 of Schedule 3 to the IS Regulations;
  (b) paragraph 17 of Schedule 2 to the JSA Regulations;
  (c) paragraph 19 of Schedule 6 to the ESA Regulations; or
  (d) paragraph 14 of Schedule 2 to the SPC Regulations.

Step 3

Identify the proportion of the non-dependant deductions applicable to
the loan payment and housing costs (if any) in Step 1 by applying the
formula—

$$A \times (B \div C)$$

where—
  "A" is the total amount of the non-dependant deductions identified in
  Step 2,
  "B" is the amount of the loan payment calculated under regulation 10,
  and
  "C" is the amount identified in Step 1.

The result is the amount of the non-dependant deduction to be made
from each loan payment in the case of a legacy benefit claimant or SPC
claimant.

Definitions

  "claimant"—reg.2(1).
  "ESA Regulations"—*ibid.*
  "IS Regulations"—*ibid.*
  "JSA Regulations"—*ibid.*
  "legacy benefit claimant"—*ibid.*
  "non-dependant"—*ibid.*
  "SPC claimant"—*ibid.*
  "SPC Regulations"—*ibid.*

Interest

1.063   **15.**—(1) The Secretary of State shall charge interest on the sum of the loan payments until the earlier of—

(a) the day on which the loan payments and accrued interest are repaid in full;

(b) the event referred to in regulation 16(1)(c).

(2) Interest at the relevant rate shall accrue daily, with effect from the first day a loan payment is made to a qualifying lender or the claimant under regulation 17, and shall be added to the outstanding amount at the end of each month (or part month).

(3) The relevant rate is the interest rate for the relevant period.

(4) For the purposes of this regulation and regulation 16, the outstanding amount is the sum of the loan payments and interest which has been charged under paragraph (1).

(5) The interest rate referred to in paragraph (3) is the weighted average interest rate on conventional gilts specified in the most recent report published before the start of the relevant period by the Office for Budget Responsibility under section 4(3) of the Budget Responsibility and National Audit Act 2011.

(6) The relevant period is the period starting on—

(a) 1st January and ending on 30th June in any year; or

(b) 1st July and ending on 31st December in any year.

DEFINITIONS

"claimant"—reg.2(1).
"loan payments"—*ibid.*
"qualifying lender"—*ibid.*

Repayment

1.064   **16.**—(1) The outstanding amount shall become immediately due and payable, together with any further interest which accrues on that amount under regulation 15, where one of the following events occurs—

(a) the relevant accommodation is sold;

(b) legal or beneficial title in, or in Scotland, heritable or registered title to, the relevant accommodation is transferred, assigned or otherwise disposed of, unless paragraph (3) applies;

(c) in the case of a claimant with no partner, the claimant's death, or, in the case of a claimant with a partner, the death of the last member of the benefit unit ("the relevant person").

(2) Subject to paragraphs (4) to (7), repayment shall occur—

(a) in the event described in paragraph (1)(a) or (b), from the proceeds of sale, transfer, assignment or disposition;

(b) in the event described in paragraph (1)(c), from the relevant person's estate.

(3) This paragraph applies where legal or beneficial title is transferred to—

(a) the claimant's partner, following the death of the claimant, where the partner is in occupation of the relevant accommodation; or

(b) the claimant, from a former spouse or civil partner, under a court order or an agreement for maintenance where the claimant is in occupation of the relevant accommodation.

(4) Where, in England and Wales—

(a) the Secretary of State has a charge by way of legal mortgage over the relevant accommodation; and

(b) there is insufficient equity available in the relevant accommodation to discharge the outstanding amount,

repayment shall be limited to the amount of available equity in the relevant accommodation after any prior ranking charges by way of legal mortgage have been repaid, and, in the event described in paragraph (1)(c), this shall be taken to be the amount of equity at the date of death of the relevant person.

(5) Where, in England and Wales—

(a) the Secretary of State has an equitable charge over one legal owner's equitable interest in the relevant accommodation, repayment shall be limited to the amount of that legal owner's equitable interest in the relevant accommodation and, in the event described in paragraph (1)(c), this shall be taken to be the value of that equitable interest at the date of death of the relevant person;

(b) the Secretary of State has an equitable charge over more than one legal owner's equitable interest in the relevant accommodation, repayment shall be limited to the sum of the equitable interests in the relevant accommodation of all legal owners within the benefit unit and, in the event described in paragraph (1)(c), this shall be taken to be the value of those equitable interests at the date of death of the relevant person.

(6) Where, in Scotland—

(a) the Secretary of State has a standard security over the whole or part of the relevant accommodation; and

(b) there is insufficient equity available in the whole or part of the relevant accommodation over which the standard security is held,

repayment shall be limited to the amount of available equity in the whole or part of the relevant accommodation over which the standard security is held after any prior ranking standard securities have been repaid, and, in the event described in paragraph (1)(c), this shall be taken to be the amount of equity at the date of death of the relevant person.

(7) In the event that the relevant accommodation is sold or legal or beneficial title in, or in Scotland, heritable or registered title to, the relevant accommodation is transferred, assigned or otherwise disposed of for less than market value, the disposal shall be treated as if it occurred at market value for the purposes of repayment.

(8) Subject to paragraph (9), a claimant shall be permitted to repay some or all of the outstanding amount before an event in paragraph (1) occurs if the amount of each repayment is equal to or more than £100.

(9) Where the outstanding amount is less than £100, a claimant shall be permitted to repay that sum in full in one repayment.

Definitions

"benefit unit"—reg.2(1).
"charge by way of legal mortgage"—*ibid.*
"claimant"—*ibid.*
"legal owner"—*ibid.*
"partner"—*ibid.*
"relevant accommodation"—*ibid.*
"standard security"—*ibid.*

Direct payments to qualifying lenders

1.065   **17.**—(1) Where the circumstances specified in paragraph (2) are met, the loan payments must be made by the Secretary of State direct to a claimant's lender.

(2) The circumstances referred to in paragraph (1) are that—

(a) money was lent to the claimant in respect of which owner-occupier payments in respect of the relevant accommodation are payable to a qualifying lender; and

(b) those owner-occupier payments are taken into account in calculating the amount of each loan payment under regulation 10.

(3) Where the circumstances in paragraph (2) are not met, the loan payments must be made to the claimant.

(4) Schedule 4 has effect in relation to payments made under paragraph (1).

Definitions

"claimant"—reg.2(1).
"loan payments"—*ibid.*
"owner-occupier payments"—regs 2(1) and 3(2)(a).
"qualifying lender"—*ibid.*
"relevant accommodation"—*ibid.*

Consequential amendments

1.066   **18.** The amendments in Schedule 5 have effect.

General Note

This regulation is not yet in force: see reg.1(2)(a) and the General Note to the Regulations (above)

Transitional provision: existing claimants

1.067   **19.**—(1) Subject to regulation 20, in relation to an existing claimant the amendments made by Schedule 5 shall be treated as though they were not in force until the day that is the earlier of ("the transitional end day")—

(a) the day referred to in paragraph (2); or

(b) the day immediately following the day on which entitlement to a qualifying benefit ends.

(2) The day referred to is the later of—

(a) the day immediately following the end of the first benefit week, in the case of a legacy benefit claimant or SPC claimant, or the end of the first assessment period, in the case of a UC claimant, that ends on or after 6th April 2018; or

(b) the day immediately following the day referred to in paragraph (3).

(3) The day referred to is the earliest of—

(a) the day on which the Secretary of State receives notification from the claimant that the claimant does not wish to accept the offer of loan payments;

(b) (i) where the Secretary of State has received both the loan agreement and the documents referred to in regulation 5 within the period of 6 weeks beginning with the loan payments offer date, the day referred to in paragraph (4); or

(ii) where the Secretary of State has not received both the loan agreement and the documents referred to in regulation 5 within the period of 6 weeks beginning with the loan payments offer date, the day on which that period ends.

(4) The day referred to is the last day of the period of 4 weeks beginning with the first day at the beginning of which the Secretary of State has received the loan agreement and documents referred to in regulation 5(2).

DEFINITIONS

"assessment period"—reg.2(1) and reg.21 UC Regs2013.
"benefit week"—reg.2(1).
"claimant"—*ibid.*
"entitlement"—reg.2(2)(a).
"existing claimant"—reg.2(1).
"legacy benefit claimant"—*ibid.*
"loan agreement"—*ibid.*
"loan payments"—*ibid.*
"loan payments offer date"—*ibid.*
"qualifying benefit"—*ibid.*
"SPC claimant"—*ibid.*
"transitional end day"—*ibid.*
"UC claimant"—*ibid.*

GENERAL NOTE

This regulation is not yet in force: see reg.1(2)(a) and the General Note to the Regulations (above).

Transitional provision: lack of capacity

20.—(1) Paragraph (2) applies where the following conditions are met   1.068
in relation to an existing claimant—

(a) the Secretary of State is satisfied on or before 5th April 2018, or later than that date but within 6 weeks beginning with the loan payments offer date, that the claimant is a person who lacks capacity to make some or all decisions about entering into the loan agreement;

(b) an application for a decision as referred to in paragraph (6) is made on or before 5th April 2018, or later than that date but within 6 weeks beginning with the loan payments offer date; and

(c) at the time the Secretary of State is satisfied as referred to in sub-paragraph (a), he has not received the loan agreement and the documents referred to in regulation 5 and has not received a notification from the claimant that the claimant does not wish to accept the offer of loan payments.

(2) Where this paragraph applies, the amendments made by Schedule 5 shall be treated as though they were not in force until the day that is the earlier of ("the transitional end day")—

(a) the day referred to in paragraph (3); or

(b) the day immediately following the day on which entitlement to a qualifying benefit ends.

(3) The day referred to is the later of—

(a) the day immediately following the end of the first benefit week, in the case of a legacy benefit claimant or SPC claimant, or the end of the first assessment period, in the case of a UC claimant, that ends on or after 6th April 2018; or

(b) the day immediately following the day referred to in paragraph (4).

(4) The day referred to is the earlier of—

(a) the last day of the period of 6 weeks beginning with the day on which the relevant person makes a determination as to whether to make a decision referred to in paragraph (6); or

(b) the last day of the period of 6 weeks beginning with the day on which the relevant person receives notification that the application for such a decision is withdrawn.

(5) In paragraph (4), a relevant person makes a determination where the person makes a determination that is not dependent on receiving more information about the claimant's circumstances.

(6) The decisions referred to in paragraph (4) are—

(a) in England and Wales—

(i) a decision by the Court of Protection under section 16(2) of the Mental Capacity Act 2005 to appoint a deputy with power to act on the claimant's behalf in respect of entering into a loan agreement;

(ii) the making of an order by the Court of Protection under section 16(2) of the Mental Capacity Act 2005 that embraces a decision on behalf of the claimant with respect to entering into a loan agreement; or

(iii) a decision by the Public Guardian to register a lasting power of attorney under the Mental Capacity Act 2005 where the power includes power to act on the claimant's behalf in respect of entering into a loan agreement; or

(b) in Scotland—

(i) the making of an intervention order by the sheriff under section 53 of the Adults with Incapacity (Scotland) Act 2000 that embraces a decision on behalf of the claimant with respect to entering into a loan agreement;

(ii) the making of an order by the sheriff under section 58 of the Adults with Incapacity (Scotland) Act 2000 to appoint a guardian with power to act on the claimant's behalf in respect of entering into a loan agreement; or

(iii) the making of an order by the sheriff or the Court of Session under the Judicial Factors Act 1849 to appoint a judicial factor with power to act on the claimant's behalf in respect of entering into a loan agreement.

Definitions

"assessment period"—reg.2(1) and reg.21 UC Regs 2013.
"benefit week"—reg.2(1).
"claimant"—*ibid.*
"entitlement"—reg.2(2)(a).
"existing claimant"—reg.2(1).
"legacy benefit claimant"—*ibid.*
"loan agreement"—*ibid.*
"loan payments"—*ibid.*
"loan payments offer date"—*ibid.*
"person who lacks capacity"—*ibid.*
"qualifying benefit"—*ibid.*
"SPC claimant"—*ibid.*
"transitional end day"—*ibid.*
"UC claimant"—*ibid.*

General Note

This regulation is not yet in force: see reg.1(2)(a) and the General Note to the Regulations (above).

Transition from legacy benefit to universal credit

21.—(1) Paragraph (3) applies where—   1.069
(a) an award of universal credit is made to a claimant who—
   (i) was entitled to a legacy benefit (a "relevant award") at any time during the period of one month ending with the day on which the claim for universal credit was made or treated as made (or would have been so entitled were it not for termination of that award by virtue of an order made under section 150(3) of the Welfare Reform Act 2012 or the effect of the Transitional Provisions Regulations); or
   (ii) was at any time during the period of one month ending with the day on which the claim for universal credit was made or treated as made, the partner of a person ("P") who was at that time entitled to a relevant award, where the award of universal credit is not a joint award to the claimant and P;
(b) on the relevant date—
   (i) the relevant award included an amount in respect of housing costs under—
      (aa) paragraphs 14 to 16 of Schedule 2 to the JSA Regulations;

> (bb) paragraphs 16 to 18 of Schedule 6 to the ESA Regulations; or
>
> (cc) paragraphs 15 to 17 of Schedule 3 to the IS Regulations; or

(ii) the claimant was entitled to loan payments under these Regulations; and

(c) the amendments made by Schedule 5 apply in relation to the award of universal credit.

(2) In this regulation, the "relevant date" means—

(a) where paragraph (1)(a)(i) applies and the claimant was not entitled to the relevant award on the date on which the claim for universal credit was made or treated as made, the date on which the relevant award terminated;

(b) where paragraph (1)(a)(i) applies, the claimant is not a new claimant partner and he or she was entitled to the relevant award on the date on which the claim for universal credit was made, that date;

(c) where paragraph (1)(a)(i) applies, the claimant is a new claimant partner and he or she was entitled to the relevant award on the date on which the claim for universal credit was treated as made, that date;

(d) where paragraph (1)(a)(ii) applies, the date on which the claimant ceased to be the partner of P or, if earlier, the date on which the relevant award terminated.

(3) Where this paragraph applies, regulation 8(1)(b) does not apply.

(4) Paragraph (5) applies where paragraph (1)(a) applies and the amendments made by Schedule 5 apply in relation to the award of universal credit, but—

(a) the relevant award did not include an amount in respect of housing costs because the claimant's entitlement (or, as the case may be, P's entitlement) was nil by virtue of—

(i) paragraph 7(1)(b) of Schedule 2 to the JSA Regulations;

(ii) paragraph 9(1)(b) of Schedule 6 to the ESA Regulations; or

(iii) paragraph 8(1)(b) of Schedule 3 to the IS Regulations; or

(b) the amendments made by Schedule 5 applied in relation to the relevant award but the claimant was not entitled to loan payments by virtue of regulation 8(1)(b).

(5) Where this paragraph applies—

(a) the definition of "qualifying period" in regulation 2(1) does not apply; and

(b) "qualifying period" means the period of 273 days starting with the first day on which the claimant (or, as the case may be, P) was entitled to the relevant award, taking into account any period which was treated as a period of continuing entitlement under—

(i) paragraph 13 of Schedule 2 to the JSA Regulations;

(ii) paragraph 15 of Schedule 6 to the ESA Regulations; or

(iii) paragraph 14 of Schedule 3 to the IS Regulations,

provided that, throughout that part of the qualifying period after the award of universal credit is made, receipt of universal credit is continuous and the claimant otherwise qualifies for loan payments under these Regulations.

(6) Paragraph (7) applies where—

(a) a claimant has an award of universal credit which becomes subject to the amendments made by Schedule 5; and

(b) regulation 29 of the Transitional Provisions Regulations applied in relation to the award.

(7) Where this paragraph applies—

(a) where paragraph (3) of regulation 29 of the Transitional Provisions Regulations applied in relation to the award, regulation 8(1)(b) does not apply; and

(b) where paragraph (5) of regulation 29 of the Transitional Provisions Regulations applied in relation to the award, paragraph (5) of this regulation applies in relation to the award.

DEFINITIONS

"claimant"—reg.2(1).
"entitlement"—reg.2(2)(a).
"ESA Regulations"—reg.2(1).
"IS Regulations"—*ibid.*
"JSA Regulations"—*ibid.*
"legacy benefit"—*ibid.*
"loan payments"—*ibid.*
"new claimant partner"—*ibid.*
"partner"—*ibid.*
"qualifying period"—*ibid.*
"relevant date"—*ibid.*
"Transitional Provisions Regulations"—*ibid.*

GENERAL NOTE

This regulation is not yet in force: see reg.1(2)(a) and the General Note to the Regulations (above).

Delegation

22. A function of the Secretary of State under these Regulations may be exercised by a person authorised for that purpose by the Secretary of State.

1.070

Regulation 3(2)(a)

SCHEDULE 1

MEANING OF OWNER-OCCUPIER PAYMENTS

PART 1

LEGACY BENEFIT CLAIMANTS AND SPC CLAIMANTS

Application of Part 1

1. This Part applies to legacy benefit claimants and SPC claimants.

1.071

Payments of interest on qualifying loans and alternative finance payments

1.072   **2.**—(1) "Owner-occupier payments" means—

(a) payments of interest on a loan which qualifies under sub-paragraph (2) or (4); and

(b) in respect of an SPC claimant only, alternative finance payments within the meaning of paragraph 5(3).

(2) A loan qualifies under this sub-paragraph where the loan was taken out to defray monies applied for any of the following purposes—

(a) acquiring an interest in the relevant accommodation; or

(b) paying off another loan which would have qualified under paragraph (a) had it not been paid off.

(3) For the purposes of sub-paragraph (2), references to a loan also include a reference to money borrowed under a hire purchase agreement, as defined in section 189 of the Consumer Credit Act 1974, for any purpose specified in paragraph (a) or (b) of sub-paragraph (2).

(4) A loan qualifies under this sub-paragraph if it was taken out, with or without security, for the purpose of—

(a) carrying out repairs and improvements to the relevant accommodation;

(b) paying any service charge imposed to meet the cost of repairs and improvements to the relevant accommodation;

(c) paying off another loan that would have qualified under paragraphs (a) and (b) had it not been paid off,

as long as the loan is used for that purpose within 6 months beginning with the date of receipt or as soon as reasonably practicable.

(5) In sub-paragraph (4), "repairs and improvements" means any of the following measures undertaken with a view to maintaining the fitness of the relevant accommodation, or any part of the building containing the relevant accommodation, for human habitation—

(a) provision of a fixed bath, shower, wash basin, sink or lavatory, and necessary associated plumbing, including the provision of hot water not connected to a central heating system;

(b) repairs to existing heating systems;

(c) damp proof measures;

(d) provision of ventilation and natural lighting;

(e) provision of drainage facilities;

(f) provision of facilities for preparing and cooking food;

(g) provision of insulation;

(h) provision of electric lighting and sockets;

(i) provision of storage facilities for fuel or refuse;

(j) repairs of unsafe structural defects;

(k) adapting the accommodation for the special needs of a disabled person; or

(l) provision of separate sleeping accommodation for persons of different sexes aged 10 or over but under the age of 20 who live with the claimant and for whom the claimant or the claimant's partner is responsible.

(6) Where a loan is applied only in part for the purposes specified in sub-paragraph (2) or (4), only that portion of the loan which is applied for that purpose shall qualify.

Loans incurred during relevant period

3.—(1) Subject to sub-paragraph (5), loans which, apart from this paragraph, qualify under paragraph 2(2) or (4) shall not so qualify where the loan was incurred during the relevant period.

1.073

(2) The "relevant period" for the purposes of this paragraph is any period during which the person to whom the loan was made—

(a) is entitled to, or is treated as entitled to, a legacy benefit or state pension credit; or

(b) is living as a member of a family one of whom is entitled to, or is treated as entitled to, a legacy benefit or state pension credit,

together with any period falling between two such periods of entitlement separated by not more than 26 weeks.

(3) For the purposes of sub-paragraph (2), a person shall be treated as entitled to either a legacy benefit or state pension credit during any period when the person, the person's partner, or, where that person is a member of a joint-claim couple, the other member of that couple was not so entitled because—

(a) that person, the person's partner or, where that person is a member of a joint-claim couple, the other member of that couple, was participating in an employment programme specified in regulation 75(1)(a) of the JSA Regulations; and

(b) in consequence of such participation that person, the person's partner, or, where that person is a member of a joint-claim couple, the other member of that couple, was a person engaged in remunerative work and had income equal to or in excess of the applicable amount.

(4) Where a loan which qualifies under paragraph 2(2) was incurred during the relevant period—

(a) for paying off an earlier loan, and that earlier loan qualified under paragraph 2(2) and was incurred during the relevant period; or

(b) to finance the purchase of a property where an earlier loan, which qualified under paragraph 2(2) or (4) and was incurred during the relevant period in respect of another property, is paid off (in whole or in part) with monies received from the sale of that property,

then the amount of the loan to which sub-paragraph (1) applies is the amount (if any) by which the new loan exceeds the earlier loan.

(5) Loans taken out during the relevant period shall qualify as loans under paragraph 2(2) or (4), where a claimant satisfies any of the conditions specified in sub-paragraphs (6), (8) and (9), but—

(a) where the claimant satisfies the condition in sub-paragraph (6), those loans shall be subject to the additional limitation imposed by sub-paragraph (7); and

(b) where the claimant satisfies the conditions in more than one of these sub-paragraphs, only one sub-paragraph shall apply in the claimant's case, which shall be the one most favourable to the claimant.

(6) The first condition is that—

(a) during the relevant period, the claimant or a member of the claimant's family acquires an interest ("the relevant interest") in the relevant accommodation; and

(b) in the week preceding the week in which the relevant interest was acquired, the claimant or a member of the claimant's family was entitled to housing benefit.

(7) Where the condition in sub-paragraph (6) is satisfied, the amount of the loans which qualify shall initially not exceed the aggregate of—

(a) the housing benefit entitlement referred to in sub-paragraph (6)(b); and

(b) any amount included in the applicable amount of the claimant or a member of the claimant's family in that week,

and shall be increased subsequently only to the extent that it is necessary to take account of any increase in the standard rate under regulation 13 arising after the date of acquisition.

(8) The second condition is that the loan was taken out, or an existing loan increased, to acquire alternative accommodation more suited to the needs of a disabled person than the relevant accommodation which was occupied before the acquisition by the claimant.

(9) The third condition is that—

(a) the loan commitment increased in consequence of the disposal of the relevant accommodation and the acquisition of alternative accommodation; and

(b) the change of accommodation was made solely by reason of the need to provide separate sleeping accommodation for persons of different sexes aged 10 or over but under the age of 20 who live with the claimant and for whom the claimant or the claimant's partner is responsible.

PART 2

UC CLAIMANTS

Application of Part 2

1.074   **4.** This Part applies to UC claimants.

Payments of interest on loans and alternative finance payments

1.075   **5.**—(1) "Owner-occupier payments" means—

(a) payments of interest on a loan which qualifies under sub-paragraph (2);

(b) alternative finance payments within the meaning of sub-paragraph (3).

(2) A loan qualifies under this sub-paragraph if it is secured on the relevant accommodation.

(3) "Alternative finance payments" means payments that are made under alternative finance arrangements which were entered into to enable a person to acquire an interest in the relevant accommodation.

(4) "Alternative finance arrangements" has the meaning given in Part 10A of the Income Tax Act 2007.

DEFINITIONS

"alternative finance payments"—reg.2(1) and para. 5(3).
"alternative finance arrangements"—para.5(4).
"applicable amount"—reg.2(1).
"couple"—*ibid.*
"disabled person"—*ibid.*
"entitlement"—reg.2(2)(a).
"family"—reg.2(2)(b).
"income"—reg.2(1).
"joint-claim couple"—*ibid.*
"JSA Regulations"—*ibid.*
"legacy benefit"—*ibid.*
"legacy benefit claimant"—*ibid.*
"owner-occupier payments"—regs 2(1) and 3(2)(a) and paras 2(1) and 5(1).
"partner"—reg.2(1).
"qualifying loan"—*ibid.*
"relevant accommodation"—*ibid.*
"relevant period"—para.3(2).
"repairs and improvements"—para.2(5).
"remunerative work"—reg.2(2)(e).
"SPC claimant"—reg.2(1).
"UC claimant"—*ibid.*

Regulation 3(2)(b)

SCHEDULE 2

CIRCUMSTANCES IN WHICH A CLAIMANT IS, OR IS TO BE TREATED AS, LIABLE TO MAKE OWNER-OCCUPIER PAYMENTS

PART 1

LEGACY BENEFIT CLAIMANTS AND SPC CLAIMANTS

Application of Part 1

1. This Part applies to legacy benefit claimants and SPC claimants. **1.076**

Liable or treated as liable to make payments

2.—(1) A claimant is liable to make owner-occupier payments **1.077** where—
  (a) in the case of a single claimant, the claimant or the claimant's partner (if any), or, in the case of joint claimants, either member of the couple, has a liability to make the payments;
(2) A claimant is to be treated as liable to make owner-occupier payments where—
  (a) all of the following conditions are met—
    (i) the person who is liable to make the payments is not doing so;

63

 (ii) the claimant has to make the payments in order to continue occupation of the relevant accommodation; and

 (iii) it is reasonable in all the circumstances to treat the claimant as liable to make the payments; or

(b) all of the following conditions are met—

 (i) the claimant in practice shares the responsibility for the owner-occupier payments with other members of the household, none of whom are close relatives of, in the case of a single claimant, the claimant or the claimant's partner (if any), or, in the case of joint claimants, either member of the couple;

 (ii) one or more of those members is liable to meet those payments; and

 (iii) it is reasonable in all the circumstances to treat that member as sharing responsibility.

(3) Where any one or more, but not all, members of the claimant's family are affected by a trade dispute, the owner-occupier payments shall be treated as wholly the responsibility of those members of the family not so affected.

(4) For the purposes of sub-paragraph (2), "trade dispute" has the meaning given in section 244 of the Trade Union and Labour Relations (Consolidation) Act 1992.

Treated as not liable to make payments

1.078   **3.** A claimant is to be treated as not liable to make owner-occupier payments where the liability to make the payments is owed to a person who is a member of the claimant's household.

PART 2

UC CLAIMANTS

Application of Part 2

1.079   **4.** This Part applies to UC claimants.

Liable or treated as liable to make payments

1.080   **5.**—(1) A claimant is liable to make owner-occupier payments where—

(a) in the case of a single claimant, the claimant or the claimant's partner (if any), or, in the case of joint claimants, either member of the couple, has a liability to make the payments;

(2) A claimant is to be treated as liable to make owner-occupier payments where—

(a) the person who is liable to make the payments is a child or qualifying young person for whom the claimant is responsible;

(b) all of the following conditions are met—

 (i) the person who is liable to make the payments is not doing so;

 (ii) the claimant has to make the payments in order to continue occupation of the relevant accommodation;

(iii) the claimant's circumstances are such that it would be unreasonable to expect them to make other arrangements; and

(iv) it is otherwise reasonable in all the circumstances to treat the claimant as liable to make the payments; or

(c) the claimant—

(i) has a liability to make the payments which is waived by the person ("P") to whom the liability is owed; and

(ii) the waiver of that liability is by way of reasonable compensation for reasonable repair or re-decoration works carried out by the claimant to the relevant accommodation which P would otherwise have carried out or been required to carry out.

(3) Sub-paragraph (1)(b)(ii) does not apply to a person in a polygamous marriage who is a single claimant by virtue of regulation 3(4) of the UC Regulations.

Treated as not liable to make payments

6 A claimant is to be treated as not liable to make owner-occupier 1.081 payments

(a) where the liability to make the payments is owed to a person who is a member of the claimant's household;

(b) in respect of any amount which represents an increase in the sum that would otherwise be payable and is the result of—

(i) outstanding arrears of any payment or charge in respect of the relevant accommodation;

(ii) outstanding arrears of any payment or charge in respect of other accommodation previously occupied by the claimant; or

(iii) any other unpaid liability to make a payment or charge; or

(c) where the Secretary of State is satisfied that the liability to make the owner-occupier payments was contrived in order to secure the offer of loan payments or increase the amount of each loan payment.

DEFINITIONS

"child"—reg.2(1).
"couple"—*ibid.*
"family"—reg.2(2)(b).
"joint claimants"—reg.2(1).
"legacy benefit claimant"—*ibid.*
"loan payments"—*ibid.*
"owner-occupier payments"—regs 2(1) and 3(2)(a).
"member of a household"—reg.2(2)(b).
"partner"—reg.2(1).
"polygamous marriage"—*ibid.*
"qualifying young person"—*ibid.*
"relevant accommodation"—*ibid.*
"single claimant"—*ibid.*
"SPC claimant"—*ibid.*
"trade dispute"—para.2(4).
"UC claimant"—*ibid.*
"UC Regulations"—*ibid.*

SCHEDULE 3

CIRCUMSTANCES IN WHICH A CLAIMANT IS, OR IS TO BE, TREATED AS
OCCUPYING ACCOMMODATION

PART 1

GENERAL

Interpretation

1.082 **1.**—(1) In this Schedule—

"Abbeyfield Home" means an establishment run by the Abbeyfield
Society including all bodies corporate or incorporate which are affili-
ated to that Society;

"care home"—

(a) in England and Wales, has the meaning given in section 3 of the
Care Standards Act 2000;

(b) in Scotland, means a care home service within the meaning of
paragraph 2 of Schedule 12 to the Public Services Reform
(Scotland) Act 2010(),

and in either case includes an independent hospital;

"croft" means a croft within the meaning of section 3(1) of the
Crofters (Scotland) Act 1993;

"full-time student" has the meaning given—

(a) in the case of income support, in regulation 61(1) of the IS
Regulations;

(b) in the case of jobseeker's allowance, in regulation 1(3) of the
JSA Regulations;

(c) in the case of employment and support allowance, in regulation
131 of the ESA Regulations;

(d) in the case of state pension credit, in regulation 1(2) of the SPC
Regulations;

"independent hospital"—

(a) in England, means a hospital as defined in section 275 of the
National Health Service Act 2006 that is not a health service
hospital as defined by that section;

(b) in Wales, has the meaning given in section 2 of the Care Standards Act 2000;

(c) in Scotland means an independent healthcare service as defined
in section 10F(1)(a) and (b) of the National Health Service
(Scotland) Act 1978;

"medically approved" means certified by a medical practitioner;

"patient" means a person who is undergoing medical or other treatment as an inpatient in a hospital or similar institution;

"period of study" has the meaning given—

(a) in the case of income support and state pension credit, in
regulation 2(1) of the IS Regulations;

(b) in the case of jobseeker's allowance, in regulation 1(3) of the JSA Regulations;

(c) in the case of employment and support allowance, in regulation 2 of the ESA Regulations;

"residential accommodation" means accommodation which is a care home, Abbeyfield Home or independent hospital;

"training course" means a course of training or instruction provided wholly or partly by or on behalf of or in pursuance of arrangements made with, or approved by or on behalf of, Skills Development Scotland, Scottish Enterprise, Highlands and Islands Enterprise, a government department or the Secretary of State.

(2) In this Schedule, a reference to a claimant being liable to make owner-occupier payments is to be read as a reference to a person being treated as liable to make owner-occupier payments under Schedule 2.

PART 2

LEGACY BENEFIT CLAIMANTS AND SPC CLAIMANTS

Application of Part 2

2. This Part applies to legacy benefit claimants and SPC claimants.   1.083

Occupying accommodation: general rule

3.—(1) Subject to the following paragraphs of this Part, the accom-   1.084
modation which the claimant occupies as the claimant's home or, if the claimant is a member of a family, the claimant and the claimant's family occupy as their home, is the accommodation which is normally occupied as the home.

(2) In determining whether accommodation is the accommodation normally occupied as the home for the purposes of sub-paragraph (1), regard shall be had to any other dwelling occupied by the claimant or, if the claimant is a member of a family, by the claimant and the claimant's family, whether or not that other dwelling is in Great Britain.

Full-time study

4.—(1) Subject to sub-paragraph (2), where a claimant is a full-time   1.085
student or on a training course and is liable to make owner-occupier payments in respect of either (but not both)—

(a) the accommodation which the claimant occupies for the purpose of attending the course of study or training course; or

(b) the accommodation which the claimant occupies when not attending the course of study or training course,

the claimant shall be treated as occupying as the claimant's home the accommodation in respect of which the claimant is liable to make the owner-occupier payments.

(2) A claimant who is a full-time student shall not be treated as occupying accommodation as the claimant's home for any week of

absence from it outside the period of study, other than an absence occasioned by the need to enter hospital for treatment.

Living in other accommodation during essential repairs

1.086   **5.** Where the claimant—

(a) has been required to move into temporary accommodation by reason of essential repairs being carried out to the accommodation which the claimant occupies as the claimant's home ("the home accommodation"); and

(b) is liable to make owner-occupier payments in respect of either (but not both) the home accommodation or the temporary accommodation,

the claimant shall be treated as occupying as the claimant's home the accommodation in respect of which the claimant is liable to make those payments.

Living in other accommodation due to fear of violence, where a claimant's partner is a full-time student or where moving into new accommodation

1.087   **6.** Where a claimant is liable to make owner-occupier payments in respect of two dwellings, the claimant shall be treated as occupying both dwellings as the claimant's home—

(a) where—

(i) the claimant has left and remains absent from the accommodation which the claimant occupies as the claimant's home ("the home accommodation") through fear of violence in the home or of violence by a close relative or former partner; and

(ii) it is reasonable that owner-occupier payments should be met in respect of both the claimant's home accommodation and the claimant's present accommodation which the claimant occupies as the home;

(b) in the case of a couple or a member of a polygamous marriage, where—

(i) one partner is a full-time student or is on a training course and it is unavoidable that the members of the couple or polygamous marriage should occupy two separate dwellings; and

(ii) it is reasonable that owner-occupier payments should be met in respect of both dwellings; or

(c) where—

(i) the claimant has moved into new accommodation occupied as the claimant's home, except where paragraph 5 applies, for a period not exceeding four benefit weeks from the first day of the benefit week in which the move occurs; and

(ii) the claimant's liability to make owner-occupier payments in respect of both the new accommodation and the accommodation from which the move was made is unavoidable.

Moving in delayed for certain reasons

7.—(1) Where— 1.088

  (a) a claimant was delayed in moving into accommodation ("the new accommodation") and was liable to make owner-occupier payments in respect of that accommodation before moving in; and

  (b) the delay was reasonable and one of the conditions in sub-paragraphs (2) to (4) applies,

the claimant shall be treated as occupying the new accommodation as the claimant's home for the period of delay, not exceeding four weeks immediately prior to the date on which the claimant moved into the new accommodation.

(2) The first condition is that the delay occurred in order to adapt the accommodation to meet the needs of the claimant or a member of the claimant's family who is a disabled person.

(3) The second condition is that—

  (a) the move was delayed pending local welfare provision to meet a need arising out of the move or in connection with setting up the claimant's home in the new accommodation; and

  (b) in the case of a legacy benefit claimant only—

    (i) a member of the claimant's family is aged 5 or under;

    (ii) the claimant's applicable amount includes a pensioner premium or disability premium under Schedule 2 to the IS Regulations, Schedule 1 to the JSA Regulations or Schedule 4 to the ESA Regulations; or

    (iii) a child tax credit is paid for a member of the claimant's family who is disabled or severely disabled for the purposes of section 9(6) of the Tax Credits Act 2002;

(4) The third condition is that the claimant became liable to make owner-occupier payments in respect of the accommodation while the claimant was a patient or was in a residential home.

Temporary absence to try new accommodation of up to 13 weeks

8.—(1) This sub-paragraph applies to a claimant who enters resi- 1.089
dential accommodation—

  (a) for the purpose of ascertaining whether the accommodation suits the claimant's needs; and

  (b) with the intention of returning to the accommodation which the claimant occupies as the claimant's home ("the home accommodation") in the event that the residential accommodation proves not to suit the claimant's needs,

and while in the residential accommodation, the home accommodation is not let or sub-let to another person.

(2) A claimant to whom sub-paragraph (1) applies shall be treated as occupying the home accommodation during the period of absence, not exceeding 13 weeks in which the claimant is resident in the residential accommodation, but only where the total absence from the home accommodation does not exceed 52 consecutive weeks.

Temporary absence of up to 13 weeks

1.090   **9.** A claimant, except where paragraph 10 applies, shall be treated as occupying accommodation as the claimant's home throughout any period of absence not exceeding 13 weeks, where—

(a) the claimant intends to return to occupy the accommodation as the claimant's home;

(b) the part of the accommodation occupied by the claimant has not been let or sub-let to another person; and

(c) the period of absence is unlikely to exceed 13 weeks.

Absences for certain reasons up to 52 weeks

1.091   **10.**—(1) Where sub-paragraph (2) applies, a claimant is to be treated as occupying accommodation as the claimant's home ("the home accommodation") during any period of absence from it not exceeding 52 weeks beginning with the first day of that absence.

(2) This paragraph applies where a claimant's absence from the home accommodation is temporary and—

(a) the claimant intends to return to occupy the home accommodation;

(b) the home accommodation has not been let or sub-let;

(c) the claimant is—

(i) detained in custody on remand pending trial or, as a condition of bail, required to reside—

(aa) in a dwelling, other than the home accommodation; or

(bb) in premises approved under section 13 of the Offender Management Act 2007;

(ii) detained pending sentence upon conviction;

(iii) resident in a hospital or similar institution as a patient;

(iv) undergoing or, the claimant's partner or child, or in the case of an SPC claimant, a person who has not attained the age of 20, is undergoing medical treatment, or medically approved convalescence, in accommodation other than residential accommodation;

(v) undertaking a training course;

(vi) undertaking medically approved care of another person;

(vii) undertaking the care of a child or, in the case of an SPC claimant, a person under the age of 20 whose parent or guardian is temporarily absent from the dwelling occupied by that parent or guardian for the purpose of receiving medically approved care or medical treatment;

(viii) a person who is receiving medically approved care provided in accommodation other than a residential home;

(ix) a full-time student to whom paragraph 4(1) or 6(b) does not apply;

(x) a person, other than a person to whom paragraph 8(1) applies, who is receiving care provided in residential accommodation; or

(xi) a person to whom paragraph 6(a) does not apply and who has left the home accommodation through fear of violence in that accommodation, or by a person who was formerly his or her partner or is a close relative; and

(d) the period of the claimant's absence is unlikely to exceed 52 weeks or, in exceptional circumstances, is unlikely substantially to exceed that period.

PART 3

UC CLAIMANTS

Application of Part 3

11. This Part applies to UC claimants.   1.092

Occupying accommodation: general rule

12.—(1) Subject to the following paragraphs of this Part, the accommodation which the claimant occupies as the claimant's home is the accommodation which the claimant normally occupies the home.

(2) Where the claimant occupies more than one dwelling, in determining whether accommodation is the accommodation normally occupied as the home for the purposes of sub-paragraph (1), regard is to be had to all the circumstances including (among other things) any persons with whom the claimant occupies each dwelling.

(3) Where accommodation which a claimant occupies as the claimant's home is situated on or pertains to a croft, croft land used for the purposes of the accommodation is to be treated as included in the accommodation.

Living in other accommodation due to essential repairs

13.—(1) Where a claimant—   1.093

(a) is required to move into accommodation ("the other accommodation") on account of essential repairs being carried out to the accommodation the claimant occupies as the claimant's home ("the home accommodation");

(b) intends to return to the home accommodation; and

(c) is liable to make owner-occupier payments in respect of either the other accommodation or the home accommodation (but not both),

the claimant is to be treated as occupying as the claimant's home the accommodation in respect of which the owner-occupier payments are made.

Moving homes: adaptations to new home for disabled person

14.—(1) Sub-paragraph (2) applies where—   1.094

(a) a claimant has moved into accommodation ("the new accommodation") and, immediately before the move, was liable to make owner-occupier payments in respect of the new accommodation; and

(b) there was a delay in moving in to adapt the new accommodation in order to meet the needs of a disabled person.

(2) The claimant is to be treated as occupying both the new accommodation and the accommodation from which the move was made ("the old accommodation") if—

(a) immediately before the move, the claimant was receiving loan payments or, in the case of an existing claimant, a qualifying benefit which includes an amount for owner-occupier payments, in respect of the old accommodation; and

(b) the delay in moving into the new accommodation was reasonable.

(3) A person is disabled under this Part if the person is—

(a) a claimant or any child or qualifying young person for whom the claimant is responsible; and

(b) in receipt of—

(i) the care component of disability living allowance at the middle or highest rate;

(ii) attendance allowance; or

(iii) the daily living component of personal independence payment.

(4) No claimant may be treated as occupying both the old accommodation and the new accommodation under this paragraph for more than one month.

Living in other accommodation due to fear of violence

1.095   **15.**—(1) Sub-paragraph (2) applies where—

(a) a claimant is occupying accommodation ("the other accommodation") other than the accommodation which the claimant occupies as the claimant's home ("the home accommodation");

(b) it is unreasonable to expect the claimant to return to the home accommodation on account of the claimant's reasonable fear of violence in the home, or by a former partner, against the claimant or any child or qualifying young person for whom the claimant is responsible; and

(c) the claimant intends to return to the home accommodation.

(2) The claimant is to be treated as occupying both the home accommodation and the other accommodation as the claimant's home if—

(a) the claimant is liable to make payments in respect of both the other accommodation and the home accommodation; and

(b) it is reasonable to make loan payments in respect of both the home accommodation and the other accommodation.

(3) Where the claimant is liable to make payments in respect of one accommodation only, the claimant is to be treated as occupying that accommodation as the claimant's home but only if it is reasonable to make loan payments in respect of that accommodation.

(4) No claimant may be treated as occupying both the home accommodation and the other accommodation under this paragraph for more than 12 months.

72

Moving in delayed by adaptations to accommodation to meet needs of disabled person

16.—(1) The claimant is to be treated as having occupied accommodation before the claimant moved into it where—
  (a) the claimant has since moved in and, immediately before the move, the claimant is liable to make payments in respect of that accommodation;
  (b) there was a delay in moving in that was necessary to enable the accommodation to be adapted to meet the needs of a disabled person; and
  (c) it was reasonable to delay moving in.

(2) No claimant may be treated as occupying accommodation under this paragraph for more than one month.

1.096

Moving into accommodation following a stay in hospital or care home

17.—(1) The claimant is to be treated as having occupied accommodation before he or she moved into it where—
  (a) the claimant has since moved in and, immediately before the move, the claimant was liable to make payments in respect of that accommodation; and
  (b) the liability to make the payments arose while the claimant was a patient or accommodated in a care home (or, in the case of joint claimants, where both individuals were patients or were accommodated in a care home).

(2) No claimant may be treated as occupying the accommodation under this paragraph for more than one month.

1.097

Temporary absence exceeding 6 months

18.—(1) Subject to sub-paragraph (2), a claimant is to be treated as no longer occupying accommodation from which the claimant is temporarily absent where the absence exceeds, or is expected to exceed, 6 months.

(2) Where a claimant who falls within paragraph 14 is temporarily absent from the relevant accommodation, the claimant is to be treated as no longer occupying that accommodation where the absence exceeds, or is expected to exceed, 12 months.

1.098

DEFINITIONS

"applicable amount"—reg.2(1).
"benefit week"—*ibid.*
"care home"—para.1(1).
"child"—reg.2(1).
"close relative"—*ibid.*
"couple"—*ibid.*
"croft"—para.1(1).
"disabled person"—reg.2(1).
"dwelling"—*ibid.*
"ESA Regulations"—*ibid.*

"existing claimant"—*ibid.*
"family"—reg.2(2)(b).
"full-time student"—para.1(1).
"IS Regulations"—reg.2(1).
"joint claimants"—*ibid.*
"JSA Regulations"—*ibid.*
"legacy benefit claimant"—*ibid.*
"loan payments"—*ibid.*
"medically approved"—para.1(1).
"owner-occupier payments"—regs 2(1) and 3(2)(a).
"partner"—reg.2(1).
"patient"—para.1(1).
"period of study"—*ibid.*
"polygamous marriage"—reg.2(1).
"qualifying benefit"—*ibid.*
"qualifying young person"—*ibid.*
"relevant accommodation"—*ibid.*
"residential accommodation"—para.1(1).
"SPC claimant"—reg.2(1).
"SPC Regulations"—*ibid.*
"training course"—para.1(1).
"UC claimant"—reg.2(1).

Regulation 17

SCHEDULE 4

DIRECT PAYMENTS TO QUALIFYING LENDERS

Direct payments

1.099   **1.** Each loan payment made to a qualifying lender directly under regulation 17(1) shall be the amount calculated under paragraph 2 or 3 of this Schedule.

Determining the amount to be paid to a qualifying lender: one qualifying loan

1.100   **2.**—(1) Where one qualifying loan or alternative finance arrangement has been made to a claimant by a qualifying lender, the amount that is to be paid direct to that lender is to be calculated as follows.

Step 1

Find the amount of each loan payment calculated under regulation 10.

Step 2

Deduct from the amount resulting from step 1 the amount referred to in paragraph (2).

(2) The amount referred to is the amount payable under a policy of insurance taken out by the claimant to insure against the risk of not being able to maintain repayments of loan interest or alternative finance payments to a qualifying lender.

Determining the amount to be paid to a qualifying lender: more than one qualifying loan

3. Where more than one qualifying loan or alternative finance arrangement has been made to a claimant by a qualifying lender, the amount that is to be paid direct to the qualifying lender is to be calculated as follows.

Step 1

Calculate an amount in accordance with Steps 1 and 2 of paragraph 2(1) in respect of each of these loans or alternative finance arrangements.

Step 2

Add those amounts together.

Qualifying lenders to apply direct payments to discharge of claimant's liability

4. Where a direct payment is made under regulation 17(1) to a qualifying lender, the lender must apply the amount of the payment determined under either paragraph 2 or 3 of this Schedule towards discharging the claimant's liability to make owner-occupier payments in respect of which the direct payment was made.

Application by qualifying lenders of any amount which exceeds liability

5.—(1) Where—
(a) a direct payment is made to a qualifying lender under regulation 17(1); and
(b) the amount paid exceeds the claimant's liability to make owner-occupier payments to the qualifying lender,
the qualifying lender must apply the amount of excess in accordance with sub-paragraph (2).

(2) Subject to sub-paragraph (3), the qualifying lender must apply the amount of excess as follows—
(a) first, towards discharging the amount of any liability of the claimant for arrears of owner-occupier payments in respect of the qualifying loan or alternative finance arrangement in question;
(b) if any amount of the excess is then remaining, towards discharging any liability of the claimant to repay—
(i) the principal sum in respect of the qualifying loan or alternative finance arrangement; or
(ii) any other sum payable by the claimant to that lender in respect of that qualifying loan or alternative finance arrangement.

(3) Where owner-occupier payments on two or more qualifying loans or alternative finance arrangements are payable to the same qualifying lender, the lender must apply the amount of the excess as follows—

1.101

1.102

1.103

1.104

1.105

   (a) first, towards discharging the amount of any liability of the claimant for arrears of owner-occupier payments in respect of the qualifying loans or alternative finance arrangements in question;

   (b) if any amount of the excess is then remaining, towards discharging any liability of the claimant to repay—

      (i) the principal sum in respect of the qualifying loans or alternative finance arrangements; or

      (ii) any other sum payable by the claimant to that lender in respect of the qualifying loans or alternative finance arrangements.

Fees payable by qualifying lenders

1.106   **6.**—(1) A fee is payable by a qualifying lender to the Secretary of State for the purpose of meeting the expenses of the Secretary of State in administering the making of direct payments to lenders.

(2) The fee is £0.39 in respect of each occasion on which a direct payment is made to the qualifying lender.

Election not to be regarded as a qualifying lender

1.107   **7.**—(1) A body or person who would otherwise be within the definition of "qualifying lender" in the Act—

   (a) may elect not to be regarded as such for the purposes of these Regulations by giving notice to the Secretary of State in writing; and

   (b) may revoke any such notice by giving a further notice in writing.

(2) In respect of any financial year, a notice under sub-paragraph (1) which is given not later than 1st February before the start of the financial year, takes effect on 1st April following the giving of the notice.

(3) Where a body or person becomes a qualifying lender in the course of a financial year—

   (a) any notice of an election by the body or person under sub-paragraph (1)(a) must be given within 6 weeks ("the initial period") beginning with the date on which the body or person becomes a qualifying lender; and

   (b) no direct payments may be made under regulation 17(1) to the body or person before the expiry of the initial period.

(4) Sub-paragraph (3)(b) does not apply in any case where—

   (a) the person or body gives the Secretary of State notice in writing that that provision should not apply; and

   (b) the notice is given before the start of the initial period or before that period expires.

(5) In relation to a notice under sub-paragraph (1)—

   (a) where the notice is given by an electronic communication, it must be given in accordance with Schedule 2 of the Universal Credit, Personal Independence Payment, Jobseeker's Allowance and Employment and Support Allowance (Claims and Payments) Regulations 2013;

(b) where the notice is sent by post, it is to be treated as having been given on the day the notice was received.

Provision of information

8.—(1) A qualifying lender must, in respect of the claimant, provide   **1.108** the Secretary of State with information as to—
  (a) the owner-occupier payments payable by the claimant to the lender;
  (b) the amount of the qualifying loan or alternative finance arrangement in respect of which owner-occupier payments are payable;
  (c) the purpose for which the qualifying loan or alternative finance arrangement was made;
  (d) the amount outstanding on the qualifying loan or alternative finance arrangement;
  (e) the amount of arrears of owner-occupier payments due in respect of the qualifying loan or alternative finance payment;
  (f) any change in the owner-occupier payments payable by the claimant to the lender; and
  (g) the redemption of the qualifying loan or alternative finance arrangement, in the circumstances specified in paragraphs (2), (3) and (6).
(2) The information referred to in paragraph (1)(a) to (e) must be provided at the request of the Secretary of State where the claimant has made a claim for a qualifying benefit, provided that the Secretary of State may only make one request under this paragraph.
(3) The information referred to in paragraph (1)(d) and (f) must be provided where the Secretary of State makes a request for that information on or after the first day in respect of which loan payments are paid, or to be paid, to the qualifying lender on behalf of the claimant ("the first day"), provided that the Secretary of State may only make a request under this paragraph once in each period of 12 months referred to in paragraph (4).
(4) The period of 12 months is the period of 12 months beginning with the first day and each subsequent period of 12 months commencing on the anniversary of that day.
(5) A request may be made under paragraph (3) for the information referred to in paragraph (1)(d) even though that information has been requested in the same 12 month period (as referred to in paragraph (4)) under paragraph (2).
(6) The information referred to in sub-paragraph (1)(g) must be provided to the Secretary of State as soon as reasonably practicable once the qualifying lender has received notice that the qualifying loan or alternative finance arrangement is to be redeemed.

Recovery of sum wrongly paid

9.—(1) In the following circumstances, a qualifying lender must at the   **1.109** request of the Secretary of State repay any amount paid to the lender under regulation 17(1) which ought not to have been paid.
(2) The circumstances are that, in respect of a claimant—

(a) the loan payments are terminated under regulation 9(2);
(b) the qualifying loan or alternative finance arrangement in respect of which owner-occupier payments are made has been redeemed; or
(c) both of the conditions in sub-paragraphs (3) and (4) are met.

t1   (3) The first condition is that the amount of each loan payment determined under regulation 10 is reduced as a result of—

(a) the standard rate determined under regulation 13 having been reduced; or
(b) the amount outstanding on the qualifying loan or alternative finance arrangement having been reduced.

(4) The second condition is that no corresponding reduction was made to the amount calculated in respect of the qualifying lender under paragraph 2 or 3 of this Schedule.

(5) A qualifying lender is not required to make a repayment in the circumstances described in sub-paragraph (2)(a) unless the Secretary of State's request is made before the end of the period of two months starting with the date on which the loan payments are terminated.

DEFINITIONS

"the Act"—reg.2(1)
"alternative finance payments"—reg.2(1).
"financial year"—*ibid.*
"loan payments"—*ibid.*
"owner-occupier payments"—regs 2(1) and 3(2)(a).
"qualifying benefit"—reg.2(1).
"qualifying lender"—*ibid.*
"qualifying loan"—*ibid.*

Regulation 18

SCHEDULE 5

CONSEQUENTIAL AMENDMENTS

[Omitted]

The Childcare Payments Act 2014 (Commencement No. 4) Regulations 2017

SI 2017/750 (C.59)

Made 13th July 2017

ARRANGEMENT OF REGULATIONS   1.110

1. Citation
2. Commencement

The Treasury, in exercise of the powers conferred on them by sections 69(2)(n) and 75(2) and (3) of the Childcare Payments Act 2014, make the following Regulations:

Citation

1. These Regulations may be cited as the Childcare Payments Act   1.111 2014 (Commencement No. 4) Regulations 2017.

Commencement

2.—(1) The day appointed for the coming into force of the provisions   1.112 of the Childcare Payments Act 2014 set out in paragraph (2) in respect of a relevant child and any sibling is 14th July 2017.

(2) The provisions referred to in paragraph (1) are—

(a) section 1;

(b) sections 3 and 4;

(c) sections 6 to 15;

(d) sections 17 to 25;

(e) section 62; and

(f) section 73(2) to (4).

(3) In this regulation—

"relevant child" means a child born on or after 1st April 2013 and before 1st September 2013;

"sibling" means any child normally living in the same household as a relevant child at the time the declaration of eligibility is made.

The Welfare Reform Act 2012 (Commencement No.17, 19, 22, 23 and 24 and Transitional and Transitory Provisions (Modification)) Order 2017

SI 2017/952

Made: September 28, 2017

The Secretary of State for Work and Pensions makes the following Order in exercise of the powers conferred by section 150(3) and (4)(a), (b)(i) and (c) of the Welfare Reform Act 2012:

ARRANGEMENT OF ARTICLES

Citation

1.114   1. This Order may be cited as the Welfare Reform Act 2012 (Commencement No.17, 19, 22, 23 and 24 and Transitional and Transitory Provisions (Modification)) Order 2017.

Interpretation

1.115   **2.**—(1) In this Order—
"claimant"—
   (a) in relation to an employment and support allowance, has the same meaning as in Part 1 of the Welfare Reform Act 2007;
   (b) in relation to a jobseeker's allowance, has the same meaning as in the Jobseekers Act 1995 (as it applies apart from the amendments made by Part 1 of Schedule 14 to the Welfare Reform Act 2012 that remove references to an income-based jobseeker's allowance);
   (c) in relation to universal credit, has the same meaning as in Part 1 of the Welfare Reform Act 2012;
"the Claims and Payments Regulations 1987" means the Social Security (Claims and Payments) Regulations 1987;
"employment and support allowance" means an employment and support allowance under Part 1 of the Welfare Reform Act 2007;
"jobseeker's allowance" means a jobseeker's allowance under the Jobseekers Act 1995;

"the No.17 Order" means the Welfare Reform Act 2012 (Commencement No.17 and Transitional and Transitory Provisions) Order 2014;

"the No.19 Order" means the Welfare Reform Act 2012 (Commencement No.19 and Transitional and Transitory Provisions and Commencement No.9 and Transitional and Transitory Provisions (Amendment)) Order 2014;

"the No.22 Order" means the Welfare Reform Act 2012 (Commencement No.22 and Transitional and Transitory Provisions) Order 2015;

"the No.23 Order" means the Welfare Reform Act 2012 (Commencement No.23 and Transitional and Transitory Provisions) Order 2015;

"the No.24 Order" means the Welfare Reform Act 2012 (Commencement No.24 and Transitional and Transitory Provisions and Commencement No.9 and Transitional and Transitory Provisions (Amendment)) Order 2015.

(2) For the purposes of this Order, the Universal Credit, Personal Independence Payment, Jobseeker's Allowance and Employment and Support Allowance (Claims and Payments) Regulations 2013 apply for the purpose of deciding—

(a) whether a claim for universal credit is made; and

(b) the date on which the claim is made.

(3) For the purposes of this Order, the Claims and Payments Regulations 1987 apply, subject to paragraphs (4) and (5), for the purposes of deciding—

(a) whether a claim for an employment and support allowance or a jobseeker's allowance is made; and

(b) the date on which the claim is made or treated as made.

(4) Subject to paragraph (6), for the purposes of this Order—

(a) a person makes a claim for an employment and support allowance or a jobseeker's allowance if that person takes any action which results in a decision on a claim being required under the Claims and Payments Regulations 1987; and

(b) it is irrelevant that the effect of any provision of those Regulations is that, for the purposes of those Regulations, the claim is made or treated as made at a date that is earlier than the date on which that action is taken.

(5) Where, by virtue of—

(a) regulation 6(1F)(b) or (c) of the Claims and Payments Regulations 1987, in the case of a claim for an employment and support allowance; or

(b) regulation 6(4ZA) to (4ZD) and (4A)(a)(i) and (b) of those Regulations, in the case of a claim for a jobseeker's allowance,

a claim for an employment and support allowance or a jobseeker's allowance is treated as made at a date that is earlier than the date on which the action referred to in paragraph (5)(a) is taken, the claim is treated as made on that earlier date.

Modification of the No.17 Order, the No.19 Order, the No.22 Order and the No.24 Order: removal of the gateway conditions

1.116   **3.** The provisions specified in the first column of the table in the Schedule have effect as though the reference in those provisions to meeting the gateway conditions were omitted, in respect of a claim for universal credit that is made, or a claim for an employment and support allowance or a jobseeker's allowance that is made or treated as made, by a claimant residing in any postcode specified in the corresponding entry in the second column, on or after the date specified in the corresponding entry in the third column.

Modifications of the No.17 Order, the No.19 Order, the No.22 Order and the No.24 Order in consequence of removal of the gateway conditions

1.117   **4.**—(1) This article applies in respect of claims in relation to which provisions of the No.17 Order, the No.19 Order, the No.22 Order and the No.24 Order are modified by article 3.

(2) Where this article applies, the following modifications also have effect—

(a) those made to the No.17 Order by article 10(2) of the Welfare Reform Act 2012 (Commencement No.29 and Commencement No.17, 19, 22, 23 and 24 and Transitional and Transitory Provisions (Modification)) Order 2017; and

(b) those made to the No.19 Order, the No.22 Order and the No.24 Order by articles 13(2), 14(2) and 15(2) respectively of the Welfare Reform Act 2012 (Commencement No.19, 22, 23 and 24 and Transitional and Transitory Provisions (Modification)) Order 2016.

Modification of the No.23 Order: claims for housing benefit, income support or a tax credit

1.118   **5.**—(1) This article applies in respect of claims in relation to which the provisions referred to in paragraph (2)(a) to (d) are modified by article 3.

(2) Where this article applies, article 7 of the No.23 Order (prevention of claims for housing benefit, income support or a tax credit) applies as though the reference in paragraph (1) of that article to article 3(1) and (2)(a) to (c) of that Order included a reference to—

(a) paragraph (1) and sub-paragraphs (c), (e) and (k) of paragraph (2) of article 3 of the No.17 Order;

(b) paragraph (1) and sub-paragraphs (a), (b), (f), (g) and (i) to (l) of paragraph (2) of article 3 of the No.19 Order;

(c) paragraph (1) and sub-paragraphs (b), (e) to (j), (l), (n) and (p) to (u) of paragraph (2) of article 3 of the No.22 Order; and

(d) paragraph (1) and sub-paragraphs (a) to (m), (o) to (u) and (w) to (bb) of paragraph (2) of article 3 of the No.24 Order.

SCHEDULE

Article 3

POSTCODE DISTRICTS AND PART-DISTRICTS WHERE GATEWAY CONDITIONS REMOVED

Provisions modified	Postcodes	Date
Articles 3(2)(f) and 4(2)(f) of the No 19 Order	M16 0.	4th October 2017
Articles 3(2)(e) and 4(2)(i) and (j) of the No.22 Order	CH4 0. CH4 9. LL11 0 to LL11 2 LL11 4 to LL11 6. LL12. LL13. LL14 1 to LL14 4. LL14 6.	4th October 2017
Articles 3(2)(g) and 4(2)(m) and (n) of the No.22 Order	SA10 6 to SA10 8. SA11 1 to SA11 4. SA11 9. SA12. SA13.	4th October 2017
Articles 3(2)(h) and 4(2)(o) and (p) of the No.22 Order	OX12 0. OX12 2. OX12 7. OX13. OX14.	4th October 2017
Articles 3(2)(n) and 4(2)(aa) and (bb) of the No.22 Order	GL5. GL6. GL10. GL11. GL12 7.	4th October 2017
Articles 3(2)(r) and 4(2)(ii) and (jj) of the No.22 Order	GL2 7.	4th October 2017
Articles 3(2)(s) and 4(2)(kk) and (ll) of the No.22 Order	OX12 8. OX12 9.	4th October 2017
Articles 3(2)(t) and 4(2)(mm) and (nn) of the No.22 Order	L11 3. LL15 9. LL16 9. LL20. LL21 1. LL21 9.	4th October 2017
Articles 3(2)(u) and 4(2)(oo) and (pp) of the No.22 Order	SA8.	4th October 2017
Articles 3(2)(c) and 4(2)(e) and (f) of the No.24 Order	EH46. G71 7 to G71 9. G72. G73. G74. G75. ML3. ML8. ML9. ML10. ML11. ML12 9.	4th October 2017
Articles 3(2)(f) and 4(2)(k) and (l) of the No.24 Order	LL21 0. SA10 9.	4th October 2017
Articles 3(2)(m) and 4(2)(y) and (z) of the No.24 Order	BN3.	4th October 2017
Articles 3(2)(s) and 4(2)(kk) and (ll) of the No.24 Order	G76 9.	4th October 2017

Provisions modified	Postcodes	Date
Articles 3(2)(x) and 4(2)(uu) and (vv) of the No.24 Order	SA11 5.	4th October 2017
Articles 3(2)(c) and 4(2)(c) of the No.17 Order	L20 0. L20 3 to L20 6. L21. L22. L23. L29. L30. L31 0. L31 2 and L31 3. L31 5 to L31 9. L37 1 to L37 4. L37 6 and L37 8. L38. PR8 1. PR8 2. PR8 6. PR8 9. PR9 0. PR9 7. PR9 9.	11th October 2017
Articles 3(2)(a) and 4(2)(a) of the No.19 Order	L31 1. L31 4. L37 0. L37 5. L37 9. PR8 3 to PR8 5. PR9 8.	11th October 2017
Articles 3(2)(b) and 4(2)(b) of the No.19 Order	L20 1. L20 2. L20 7 to L20 9.	11th October 2017
Articles 3(2)(h) and 4(2)(o) and (p) of the No.22 Order	OX10 0. OX10 1. OX10 6. OX10 8. OX10 9. OX11.	11th October 2017
Articles 3(2)(n) and 4(2)(aa) and (bb) of the No.22 Order	BN20. BN21. BN22. BN23.	11th October 2017
Articles 3(2)(p) and 4(2)(ee) and (ff) of the No.22 Order	NE8. NE9 6. NE10 0. NE10 9. NE11. NE16 3. NE16 4.	11th October 2017
Articles 3(2)(r) and 4(2)(ii) and (jj) of the No.22 Order	BH12 1 to BH12 4. BH12 9. BH13 6. BH14. BH15 2 to BH15 4. BH15 9. BH17. BH18 0. BH18 8.	11th October 2017
Articles 3(2)(a) and 4(2)(a) and (b) of the No.24 Order	NE9 5. NE16 5.	11th October 2017
Articles 3(2)(b) and 4(2)(c) and (d) of the No.24 Order	DN1. DN2. DN3. DN4. DN5. DN6 8. DN7. DN8 5. DN9 3. DN11 0. DN12 1. DN12 3. DN12 4	11th October 2017
Articles 3(2)(g) and 4(2)(m) and (n) of the No.24 Order	DH3 1. NE9 7.	11th October 2017
Articles 3(2)(h) and 4(2)(o) and (p) of the No.24 Order	DN6 0. DN6 9.	11th October 2017
Articles 3(2)(l) and 4(2)(w) and (x) of the No.24 Order	DN11 9. DN12 2. S63 6. S63 7. S64.	11th October 2017

Provisions modified	Postcodes	Date
Articles 3(2)(o) and 4(2)(cc) and (dd) of the No.24 Order	DN8 4	11th October 2017
Articles 3(2)(p) and 4(2)(cc) and (ff) of the No.24 Order	PL1 1 to PL1 3. PL1 5. PL1 9.	11th October 2017
Articles 3(2)(t) and 4(2)(mm) and (nn) of the No.24 Order	NE10 8.	11th October 2017
Articles 3(2)(aa) and 4(2)(aaa) and (bbb) of the No.24 Order	DN6 7.	18th October 2017
Articles 3(2)(f) and 4(2)(k) and (l) of the No.22 Order	IP18. IP19 8. IP19 9. NG31. NG32 2. NG33. NR34 7 to NR34 9. PE6 6. PE10 1. PE10 9	18th October 2017
Articles 3(2)(g) and 4(2)(m) and (n) of the No.22 Order	CB9 0. CB9 1. CB9 8. CB9 9. IP29 5. IP31 1. IP32. IP33.	18th October 2017
Articles 3(2)(h) and 4(2)(o) and (p) of the No.22 Order	OX1. OX2 0. OX2 6. OX2 7. OX2 9. OX3 0. OX3 3. OX3 7. OX3 8. OX4.	18th October 2017
Articles 3(2)(j) and 4(2)(s) and (t) of the No.22 Order	OX2 8. OX3 9.	18th October 2017
Articles 3(2)(r) and 4(2)(ii) and (jj) of the No.22 Order	DN9 1. DN9 2. DN15. DN16. DN17 1. DN17 2. DN17 4. DN18. DN19. DN39 6.	18th October 2017
Articles 3(2)(a) and 4(2)(a) and (b) of the No.24 Order	DH6 2. DN6 3. DN20 0. DN20 2. NR35 1. SR7 1. SR7 7. SR7 8. SR8. TS21 4. TS27 4. TS28.	18th October 2017
Articles 3(2)(b) and 4(2)(c) and (d) of the No.24 Order	CO6 5. CO10 0 to CO10 3. CO10 5. CO10 9. IP19 0. IP29 4. IP30. IP31 2 IP31 3	18th October 2017
Articles 3(2)(c) and 4(2)(e) and (f) of the No.24 Order	CB9 7. CO10 7. CO10 8. LE15.	18th October 2017
Articles 3(2)(g) and 4(2)(m) and (n) of the No.24 Order	PE6 8. PE10 0. SR7 0. SR7 9.	18th October 2017
Articles 3(2)(h) and 4(2)(o) and (p) of the No.24 Order	R34 0. NR35 2.	18th October 2017

Provisions modified	Postcodes	Date
Articles 3(2)(k) and 4(2)(u) and (v) of the No.24 Order(25)	DN17 3. DN20 8. DN20 9. DN38.	18th October 2017
Articles 3(2)(m) and 4(2)(y) and (z) of the No.24 Order	PE9.	18th October 2017
Articles 3(2)(u) and 4(2)(oo) and (pp) of the No.24 Order	CB21 4.	18th October 2017
Articles 3(2)(w) and 4(2)(ss) and (tt) of the No.24 Order	TS29.	18th October 2017
Articles 3(2)(f) and 4(2)(f) of the No.19 Order	M15. M16 6 to M16 9.	25th October 2017
Articles 3(2)(i) and 4(2)(i) of the No.19 Order	M14. M21.	25th October 2017
Articles 3(2)(j) and 4(2)(j) of the No.19 Order	M20.	25th October 2017
Articles 3(2)(b) and 4(2)(c) and (d) of the No.22 Order(28)	B49 6. B80. B97 4. B97 9. B98 0. B98 7. B98 8.	25th October 2017
Articles 3(2)(e) and 4(2)(i) and (j) of the No.22 Order	RM15 5. RM15 6. RM15 9. RM16. RM17. RM18. RM19. RM20. SS17.	25th October 2017
Articles 3(2)(n) and 4(2)(aa) and (bb) of the No.22 Order	CV7 9. CV10 8. CV11. CV12 2. CV12 8. CV12 9.	25th October 2017
Articles 3(2)(c) and 4(2)(e) and (f) of the No.24 Order	CB11. CM3 2. CM6. CM7. CM8. CM24. CM77. CO6 2. CO8. CO9.	25th October 2017
Articles 3(2)(d) and 4(2)(g) and (h) of the No.24 Order	B49 5. B96.	25th October 2017
Articles 3(2)(f) and 4(2)(k) and (l) of the No.24 Order	B47. B48. B97 5. B97 6. B98 9. CV10 0. CV10 7. CV10 9. CV12 0	25th October 2017
Articles 3(2)(l) and 4(2)(w) and (x) of the No.24 Order	CV7 8.	25th October 2017
Articles 3(2)(q) and 4(2)(gg) and (hh) of the No.24 Order	CM22 6.	25th October 2017

Provisions modified	Postcodes	Date
Articles 3(2)(s) and 4(2)(kk) and (ll) of the No.24 Order	KA1. KA2. KA3. KA4. KA5. KA16. KA17. KA18. RM14 3. RM15 4.	25th October 2017
Articles 3(2)(u) and 4(2)(oo) and (pp) of the No.24 Order	CB10.	25th October 2017
Articles 3(2)(l) and 4(2)(l) of the No.19 Order	CW6. CW7.	1st November 2017
Articles 3(2)(l) and 4(2)(w) and (x) of the No.22 Order(31)	AL1. AL2 3. AL3 4 to AL3 6. AL5 1. AL5 2. AL5 4. AL5 5.	1st November 2017
Articles 3(2)(p) and 4(2)(ee) and (ff) of the No.22 Order	NE21. NE39 2. NE39 9. NE40.	1st November 2017
Articles 3(2)(q) and 4(2)(gg) and (hh) of the No.22 Order	EN7 6. EN8 0. EN8 1.	1st November 2017
Articles 3(2)(r) and 4(2)(ii) and (jj) of the No.22 Order	BD19. HD1. HD2. HD3. HD4. HD5. HD7. HD8. HD9. WF12 9. WF13. WF14. WF15. WF16. WF17 1. WF17 5 to WF17 9.	1st November 2017
Articles 3(2)(t) and 4(2)(mm) and (nn) of the No.22 Order	EN1. EN2 0. EN2 6. EN2 7. EN2 9. EN7 5. EN8 7. EN8 8. EN9 8.	1st November 2017
Articles 3(2)(a) and 4(2)(a) and (b) of the No.24 Order	AL2 1. AL2 2. AL3 7. NE39.1.	1st November 2017
Articles 3(2)(b) and 4(2)(c) and (d) of the No.24 Order	AL4 0. AL4 9. EN2 8.	1st November 2017
Articles 3(2)(k) and 4(2)(u) and (v) of the No.24 Order	BD11 2.	1st November 2017
Articles 3(2)(q) and 4(2)(gg) and (hh) of the No.24 Order	AL4 8. EN8 9. EN9 2. EN10. WF17 0.	1st November 2017
Articles 3(2)(t) and 4(2)(mm) and (nn) of the No.24 Order	AL3 8. AL5 3. NE17 9. NE41. NE42 9.	1st November 2017
Articles 3(2)(aa) and 4(2)(aaa) and (bbb) of the No.24 Order	WF12 0. WF12 7. WF12 8.	1st November 2017

Provisions modified	Postcodes	Date
Articles 3(2)(g) and 4(2)(m) and (n) of the No.22 Order	B1. B5. B8. B15. B16 6. B16 8. B16 9. B18 5 to B18 7 B18 9. B25. B26 2. B31 1 to B31 3. B31 9. B74 4. B75 7. B76 1. B76 2.	8th November 2017
Articles 3(2)(l) and 4(2)(w) and (x) of the No.22 Order	B26 1. B26 3.	8th November 2017
Articles 3(2)(a) and 4(2)(a) and (b) of the No.24 Order	B72. B73.	8th November 2017
Articles 3(2)(f) and 4(2)(k) and (l) of the No.24 Order	B31 4. B31 5 B75 5. B75 6. B76 9.	8th November 2017
Articles 3(2)(g) and 4(2)(m) and (n) of the No.24 Order	DD1. DD2 1 to DD2 4. DD3 6 to DD3 9. DD4 6 to DD4 9 DD5 1. DD5 2.	8th November 2017
Articles 3(2)(i) and 4(2)(q) and (r) of the No.24 Order	B16 0. B18 4.	8th November 2017
Articles 3(2)(z) and 4(2)(yy) and (zz) of the No.24 Order	DD6.	8th November 2017
Articles 3(2)(bb) and 4(2)(ccc) and (ddd) of the No.24 Order	AB30. DD2 5. DD3 0. DD4 0. DD5 3. DD5 4. DD7. DD8. DD9. DD10. DD11.	8th November 2017
Articles 3(2)(e) and 4(2)(e) of the No.17 Order	CH41. CH42. CH43. CH46. CH47. CH48. CH49. CH60. CH61. CH62 0 to CH62 8.. CH63.	15th November 2017
Articles 3(2)(k) and 4(2)(k) of the No.17 Order	CH62 9.	15th November 2017
Articles 3(2)(e) and 4(2)(i) and (j) of the No.22 Order	CM11 2. CM12. CM13 1. CM13 2. CM14 4. CM14 9. CM15 8. CM15 9. SS12. SS13. SS14. SS15. SS16.	15th November 2017
Articles 3(2)(q) and 4(2)(gg) and (hh) of the No.22 Order	NP10. NP18. NP19. NP20.	15th November 2017
Articles 3(2)(b) and 4(2)(c) and (d) of the No.24 Order	CM4.	15th November 2017

Provisions modified	Postcodes	Date
Articles 3(2)(m) and 4(2)(y) and (z) of the No.24 Order	PE1. PE2 2. PE2 5. PE2 7 to PE2 . PE3. PE4. PE5. PE6 7. PE 6 9. PE7 0. PE7 8. PE8 9.	15th November 2017
Articles 3(2)(q) and 4(2)(gg) and (hh) of the No.24 Order	CM15 0. SS11.	15th November 2017
Articles 3(2)(s) and 4(2)(kk) and (ll) of the No.24 Order	CM13 3. CM14 5.	15th November 2017
Articles 3(2)(u) and 4(2)(oo) and (pp) of the No.24 Order	PE2 6. PE7 3. PE8 6.	15th November 2017
Articles 3(2)(w) and 4(2)(ss) and (tt) of the No.24 Order	PE7 1. PR7 2.	15th November 2017
Articles 3(2)(i) and 4(2)(q) and (r) of the No.22 Order	KA11. KA12 KA13 6. KA13 9. KA14. KA15. KA20. KA21 KA22 KA23. KA24. KA25. KA27. KA28. KA29. KA30. PA17.	22nd November 2017
Articles 3(2)(j) and 4(2)(s) and (t) of the No.22 Order	GL14. GL15 5. GL17. OX15. OX16. OX25. OX26. OX27 8.	22nd November 2017
Articles 3(2)(r) and 4(2)(ii) and (jj) of the No.22 Order	BH1. BH2. BH4. BH5. BH6.	22nd November 2017
Articles 3(2)(i) and 4(2)(q) and (r) of the No.24 Order	OX27 0. OX27 9.	22nd November 2017
Articles 3(2)(j) and 4(2)(s) and (t) of the No.24 Order	NN13 5. OX27 7.	22nd November 2017
Articles 3(2)(l) and 4(2)(w) and (x) of the No.24 Order	BH3.	22nd November 2017
Articles 3(2)(p) and 4(2)(ee) and (ff) of the No.24 Order	PL1 4. PL5 1 to PL5 3.	22nd November 2017
Articles 3(2)(s) and 4(2)(kk) and (ll) of the No.24 Order	KA13 7.	22nd November 2017
Articles 3(2)(b) and 4(2)(b) of the No.19 Order	M4. M40.	29th November 2017
Articles 3(2)(j) and 4(2)(j) of the No.19 Order	M11. M18.	29th November 2017

Provisions modified	Postcodes	Date
Articles 3(2)(f) and 4(2)(k) and (l) of the No.22 Order	B77 2 to B77 4. B78 3. B79 7 to B79 9. DE13 7. S40 1. S40 2. S40 4. S40 9. S41 7. S41 8. S43 1. S43 2. S49 1. WS7 0 to WS7 3. WS7 9. WS13. WS14.	29th November 2017
Articles 3(2)(h) and 4(2)(o) and (p) of the No.22 Order	OX7 3. OX18 1 to OX18 3. OX18 9. OX28. OX29 0. OX29 5 to OX29 9.	29th November 2017
Articles 3(2)(j) and 4(2)(s) and (t) of the No.22 Order	GL7 1 to GL7 5. GL7 7. GL7 9. GL8 0. GL15 4. GL15 6. GL15 9. GL16. OX7 4 to OX7 7. OX7 9. OX18 4. OX20. OX29 4.	29th November 2017
Articles 3(2)(n) and 4(2)(aa) and (bb) of the No.22 Order	GL7 6. GL8 8.	29th November 2017
Articles 3(2)(f) and 4(2)(k) and (l) of the No.24 Order	B77 1. B77 5. B78.2. B79 0.	29th November 2017
Articles 3(2)(f) and 4(2)(k) and (l) of the No.24 Order	S18. S40 3. S41 0. S41 9. S42 7.	29th November 2017
Articles 3(2)(l) and 4(2)(w) and (x) of the No.24 Order	WS15 3.	29th November 2017
Articles 3(2)(m) and 4(2)(y) and (z) of the No.24 Order	BN2.	29th November 2017
Articles 3(2)(e) and 4(2)(i) and (j) of the No.22 Order	ME9. ME10. ME11. ME12. ME13 7 to ME13 9.	6th December 2017
Articles 3(2)(g) and 4(2)(m) and (n) of the No.22 Order	ME13 0.	6th December 2017
Articles 3(2)(l) and 4(2)(w) and (x) of the No.22 Order	EX23 0. EX23 8. PL34. PL35.	6th December 2017
Articles 3(2)(n) and 4(2)(aa) and (bb) of the No.22 Order	GL20 5. GL50. GL51.	6th December 2017
Articles 3(2)(s) and 4(2)(kk) and (ll) of the No.22 Order	RG14 1 to RG14 3. RG14 5 to RG14 7. RG17. RG18. RG19 3. RG19 4. RG20 6 to RG20 8.	6th December 2017

Provisions modified	Postcodes	Date
Articles 3(2)(t) and 4(2)(mm) and (nn) of the No.22 Order	PL13. PL14. PL15 10. PL15 7. PL15 8. PL17.	6th December 2017
Articles 3(2)(a) and 4(2)(a) and (b) of the No.24 Order	RG1 1. RG1 2. RG1 4 to RG1 8. RG2 0. RG2 7. RG4 5. RG4 7 to RG4 9. RG30 1. RG30 6. RG30 9.	6th December 2017
Articles 3(2)(b) and 4(2)(c) and (d) of the No.24 Order	AL7. AL8. AL9 5. AL9 7. AL10. EN6. RG1 3. RG2 6. RG2 8. RG2 9. RG4 6. RG5. RG6. RG10 9.	6th December 2017
Articles 3(2)(d) and 4(2)(g) and (h) of the No.24 Order	GL20 7. GL20 8.	6th December 2017
Articles 3(2)(e) and 4(2)(i) and (j) of the No.24 Order(37)	DT1. DT2. DT3. DT4. DT5. DT6. DT8.	6th December 2017
Articles 3(2)(f) and 4(2)(k) and (l) of the No.24 Order	GL20 6.	6th December 2017
Articles 3(2)(h) and 4(2)(o) and (p) of the No.24 Order	DT7 EX22 6. EX22 9. EX23 9. PL15 9.	6th December 2017
Articles 3(2)(j) and 4(2)(s) and (t) of the No.24 Order	WD17 WD18. WD24. WD25 7.	6th December 2017
Articles 3(2)(o) and 4(2)(cc) and (dd) of the No.24 Order	CR4 2 to CR4 4. SW20.	6th December 2017
Articles 3(2)(p) and 4(2)(ee) and (ff) of the No.24 Order	PL16.	6th December 2017
Articles 3(2)(q) and 4(2)(gg) and (hh) of the No.24 Order	AL6. AL9 6.	6th December 2017
Articles 3(2)(r) and 4(2)(ii) and (jj) of the No.24 Order(38)	CR4 1. RG7 1. SE11 4 to SE11 6. SW8 1. SW8 2. SW8 4. SW8 5. SW8 9 SW9 0. SW9 1. SW9 6. SW9 9. SW12. SW16.	6th December 2017
Articles 3(2)(y) and 4(2)(ww) and (xx) of the No.24 Order(39)	RG7 2 to RG7 4. RG7 8. RG14 9. RG19 8. RG20 0. RG20 4. RG20 5. RG20 9.	6th December 2017

Provisions modified	Postcodes	Date
Articles 3(2)(z) and 4(2)(yy) and (zz) of the No.24 Order	FK10 4. KY1. KY2. KY3. KY4 8. KY 4 9. KY5 8. KY5 9. KY6 1. KY6 2. KY7. KY8. KY9. KY10 KY11. KY12. KY15. KY16.	6th December 2017
Articles 3(2)(bb) and 4(2)(ccc) and (ddd) of the No.24 Order	KY4 0. KY5 0. KY6 3. KY13 3. KY13 8. KY13 9.	6th December 2017
Articles 3(2)(a) and 4(2)(a) of the No.19 Order	L39. L40 0. L40 1. L40 4 to L40 9. WN8.	13th December 2017
Articles 3(2)(k) and 4(2)(k) of the No.19 Order	L40 2. L40 3. PR4 6.	13th December 2017
Articles 3(2)(l) and 4(2)(l) of the No.19 Order	CH64. CH65. CH66. CW8. CW9.	13th December 2017
Articles 3(2)(b) and 4(2)(c) and (d) of the No.22 Order	DN10 5. DN11 DN22. S80 1. S80 2. S80 9. S81 0. S81 7. S81 9.	13th December 2017
Articles 3(2)(g) and 4(2)(m) and (n) of the No.22 Order	B11. B14 6. B14 7. B19 2. B19 3. B20. B23. B28 0. B28 1. B28 8. B30. B32 1 to B32 3. B42 2. B42 9. B44.	13th December 2017
Articles 3(2)(l) and 4(2)(w) and (x) of the No.22 Order	B14 4. B28 9.	13th December 2017
Articles 3(2)(r) and 4(2)(ii) and (jj) of the No.22 Order	DN31. DN32. DN33. DN34. DN35. DN36 4. DN37 7. DN37 9. DN40. DN41 7.	13th December 2017
Articles 3(2)(u) and 4(2)(oo) and (pp) of the No.22 Order	SA1. SA2. SA3. SA4 3 to SA4 6. SA4 8. SA4 9. SA5. SA6. SA7.	13th December 2017
Articles 3(2)(a) and 4(2)(a) and (b) of the No.24 Order	DH8 0. DH8 1. DH8 5 to DH8 8. DH9. DL4 1. DL12. DL12 9. DL13. DL14. DL15. NE16 6.	13th December 2017

Provisions modified	Postcodes	Date
Articles 3(2)(b) and 4(2)(c) and (d) of the No.24 Order	DL10 6.	13th December 2017
Articles 3(2)(f) and 4(2)(k) and (l) of the No.24 Order	B14 5. B32 4. SA4 0.	13th December 2017
Articles 3(2)(g) and 4(2)(m) and (n) of the No.24 Order	DN36 5.	13th December 2017
Articles 3(2)(i) and 4(2)(q) and (r) of the No.24 Order	B42 1.	13th December 2017
Articles 3(2)(j) and 4(2)(s) and (t) of the No.24 Order	S43 4. S80 4.	13th December 2017
Articles 3(2)(k) and 4(2)(u) and (v) of the No.24 Order	DN37 0. Dn37 8. DN41 8.	13th December 2017
Articles 3(2)(l) and 4(2)(w) and (x) of the No.24 Order	S80 3. S81 8.	13th December 2017
Articles 3(2)(r) and 4(2)(ii) and (jj) of the No.24 Order	WV1. WV2. WV3. WV4. WV7. WV8. WV9. WV10 9. WV14.	13th December 2017
Articles 3(2)(t) and 4(2)(mm) and (nn) of the No.24 Order	DH8 9. NE17 7.	13th December 2017
Articles 3(2)(r) and 4(2)(ii) and (jj) of the No.24 Order	SE8 9. SE14.	20th December 2017
Articles 3(2)(bb) and 4(2)(ccc) and (ddd) of the No.24 Order	SE8 5.	20th December 2017
Articles 3(2)(g) and 4(2)(m) and (n) of the No.22 Order	B2. B3. B4. B9. B10. B33. B34. B45 5.	10th January 2018
Articles 3(2)(f) and 4(2)(k) and (l) of the No.24 Order	B38. B45 0. B45 8.	10th January 2018
Articles 3(2)(h) and 4(2)(o) and (p) of the No.22 Order	OX9 0. OX9 2. OX9.7 OX10 7. OX44. OX49. SN7.	17th January 2018
Articles 3(2)(j) and 4(2)(s) and (t) of the No.22 Order	OX5 1. OX5 3. OX5 9. OX33 1.	17th January 2018
Articles 3(2)(n) and 4(2)(aa) and (bb) of the No.22 Order	BN24. BN26. BN27. GL52. GL53. GL54. GL55. GL56. TN21.	17th January 2018

Provisions modified	Postcodes	Date
Articles 3(2)(r) and 4(2)(ii) and (jj) of the No.22 Order	BH7. BH8. BH9. BH10. BH11. BH12 5. BH13 7. BH15 1. BH16. BH18 9. BH19. BH20. BH21 1 to BH21 5. BH21 7 to BH21 9. BH22. BH23 1 to BH23 4. BH23 6. BH23 9. DT10 1. DT11.	17th January 2018
Articles 3(2)(a) and 4(2)(a) and (b) of the No.24 Order	RG1 9. RG7 5. RG7 6. RG8. RG9 1. RG9 4. RG9 5. RG9 9. RG30 2 to RG30 4. RG31.	17th January 2018
Articles 3(2)(b) and 4(2)(c) and (d) of the No.24 Order	RG9 2.	17th January 2018
Articles 3(2)(e) and 4(2)(i) and (j) of the No.24 Order	DT10 2.	17th January 2018
Articles 3(2)(i) and 4(2)(q) and (r) of the No.24 Order	OX5 2. OX9 3. OX39 RG9 3. RG9 6.	17th January 2018
Articles 3(2)(l) and 4(2)(w) and (x) of the No.24 Order	BH23 5. BH23 7. SP5 5.	17th January 2018
Articles 3(2)(m) and 4(2)(y) and (z) of the No.24 Order	BN1. BN41.	17th January 2018
Articles 3(2)(p) and 4(2)(ee) and (ff) of the No.24 Order	PL2. PL3. PL4. PL5 4. PL5 9. PL6. PL7. PL8. PL9. PL10. PL11. PL12. PL18. PL19. PL20. PL21.	17th January 2018
Articles 3(2)(e) and 4(2)(e) of the No.17 Order	CH44. CH45.	24th January 2018
Articles 3(2)(g) and 4(2)(g) of the No.19 Order	L4 5. L9.	24th January 2018
Articles 3(2)(i) and 4(2)(i) of the No.19 Order	M12. M13. M19 0.	24th January 2018
Articles 3(2)(j) and 4(2)(j) of the No.19 Order	M19 1 to M19 3.	24th January 2018
Articles 3(2)(t) and 4(2)(mm) and (nn) of the No.22 Order	EN3.	24th January 2018

Provisions modified	Postcodes	Date
Articles 3(2)(j) and 4(2)(s) and (t) of the No.24 Order	WD3. WD4. WD5. WD19. WD23. WD25 0. WD25 8. WD25 9.	24th January 2018
Articles 3(2)(r) and 4(2)(ii) and (jj) of the No.24 Order	SE19 1. SE19 9. SE27. SW2 3. SW2 4. SW17 8. SW17 9.	24th January 2018

The Childcare Payments Act 2014 (Commencement No.5) Regulations 2017

SI 2017/1116

Made: November 16, 2017

The Treasury, in exercise of the powers conferred on them by sections 69(2) and 75(2) and (3) of the Childcare Payments Act 2014, makes the following Regulations:

Citation

1.120   **1.** These Regulations may be cited as the Childcare Payments Act 2014 (Commencement No. 5) Regulations 2017.

Commencement

1.121   **2.**—(1) The day appointed for the coming into force of the provisions of the Childcare Payments Act 2014 set out in paragraph (2) in respect of a relevant child and any sibling is 24th November 2017.

(2) The provisions referred to in paragraph (1) are—

(a) section 1;

(b) sections 3 and 4;

(c) sections 6 to 15;

(d) sections 17 to 25;

(e) section 62; and

(f) section 73(2) to (4).

(3) In this regulation—

"relevant child" means a child born on or after 24th November 2011 and before 1st April 2013;

"sibling" means any child normally living in the same household as a relevant child at the time the declaration of eligibility is made.

PART II

UPDATING MATERIAL
VOLUME I

NON MEANS TESTED BENEFITS AND EMPLOYMENT AND SUPPORT ALLOWANCE

Commentary by

Ian Hooker

Richard Poynter

Robin White

Nick Wikeley

John Mesher

Edward Mitchell

p.44, *amendment to the Social Security Contribution and Benefits Act 1992 s.35(3A) (State maternity allowance for employed or self-employed earner)*

Subsection (3A) was added by s.120 of the Children and Families Act 2.001
2014 (see footnote 8 to this section). The regulations made in further-ance of it are the Maternity Allowance (Curtailment) Regulations (SI 2014/3054). The text of these regulations is produced in Vol.IV of this work.

p.60, *amendment to the Social Security Contribution and Benefits Act 1992 s.44 (Category A retirement pension)*

In subs.(4), delete "£119.30" and replace with "£122.30" and also 2.002
delete "£101.10" and replace with "£102.10".

p.62, *amendments to the Social Security Contribution and Benefits Act 1992 s.44 (Category A retirement pension)*

Delete the first item in the list of amendments (SI 2016/230) and 2.003
replace with the Social Security Benefits Up-rating Order 2017 (SI 2017/260) art.4 (April 10 2017).

p.148, *annotation to the Social Security Contributions and Benefits Act 1992 s.72(2) (The care component: qualifying period)*

The sentence that reads "As the condition is prospective it must be 2.004
judged on the basis of the information and the prognosis that was available at the time of claim" should be deleted and the following passage substituted:
On an appeal the claimant's disability must be judged on the basis of his condition at the time of claim and up to the time of the DM decision. Information that only becomes available after that time is still admissible before a tribunal provided that it relates to the claimant's condition within that period: see *R(DLA) 2/01*. Where, however the question relates to the claimant's prospective condition it is evidence as to what might then have been expected to happen, rather than what has in fact happened by the time of the tribunal determination. The case referred to (*KN v SSWP (DLA)* [2008] UKUT 2 (AAC)) to illustrate this point is incorrectly cited. The reference should be to *CDLA/2878/2000*.

p.170, *annotation to the Social Security Contributions and Benefits Act 1992 s.80 (Beneficiary's dependent children)*

In the second paragraph of the commentary substitute "£230" for 2.004.1
both "£225" and "£220"; see Social Security Benefits Up-rating Order 2015 (SI 2015/457) art.7(a) (April 1, 2015) and Social Security Benefits Up-rating Order 2017 (SI 2017/260) art.8 (April 10, 2017).

p.323, *correction to the Pensions Act 1995 Sch.4 (Equalisation of and increase in pensionable age for men and women)*

2.004.2   In para.1.657, immediately after rule (4) in Sch.4, Part I, para.1, and immediately before the heading 'Part II" insert the full text of Tables 1–4 and accompanying rules as printed in error within the text of s.128(3) (i.e. paras 1.658–1.660 to the end of rule (10), which accompanies Table 4). The Tables and rules should therefore read as correctly laid out in the 2016/17 edition of Vol.1 at pp.338–340.

p.330, *annotation to the Gender Recognition Act 2004 s.13 (Social security benefits and pensions)*

2.005   *SSWP v HY and LO (RP)* [2017] UKUT 303 (AAC) concerned a claim by two male-to-female persons that precluding their being able to receive retirement pensions in respect of periods before they acquired gender recognition certificates constituted discrimination in breach of art.4 of Directive 79/7/EEC. The first claimant underwent gender reassignment surgery in 1986, but did not obtain a gender recognition certificate until February 2015. This had been prompted by refusal to award a retirement pension from July 2014 when she reached pensionable age for a woman. The second claimant underwent gender reassignment surgery in 1988. She obtained a gender recognition certificate in February 2014 by which time she was already aged 65. She claimed a retirement pension from May 2008 when she had reached the age of 60. Judge Rowland reviews both the relevant legislative and case law history. He concludes that the circumstances of the two claimants were distinguishable from those which had arisen in the *Richards* and *Timbrell* cases. Those cases had been concerned with entitlements in respect of periods in the absence of a national scheme for recognition of a changed gender identity. In the instant cases, there had been delay in obtaining a gender recognition certificate after the scheme in the Gender Recognition Act 2004 had come into force. On the facts, both claimants could have sought gender recognition certificates in a timely manner to enable claims to be successful from the relevant pensionable ages for a woman. The claimants argued that there was nonetheless unfavourable treatment when they compared themselves to persons who had been registered as women from birth. Judge Rowland concluded that the Directive did not require the United Kingdom to establish a scheme which permitted the retrospective award of gender recognition certificates, and the United Kingdom had chosen to make them prospective only. There was accordingly no discrimination which fell foul of the prohibition in art.4 of Directive 79/7/EEC. Any difference in treatment could be objectively justified.

p.439, *annotation to the Mesothelioma Act 2014 s.3 (Eligible dependants)*

2.006   Note that in addition, and with effect from July 31, 2017, s.77 of the Digital Economy Act 2017 enables HMRC to share the name and address of an employer and associated reference numbers with the Employer Liability Tracing Office (ELTO) for the purpose of assisting with such claims. ELTO is a non-profit making company that maintains a database of insurance policies to enable employees to trace former or current employers and their insurers in order to obtain compensation for workplace injuries. It is anticipated that access to this information will help to improve the quality of the ELTO databases.

p.664, *amendment to the Social Security (Attendance Allowance) Regulations 1991 (SI 1991/2740) reg.2 (Conditions as to residence and presence in Great Britain)*

With effect from November 16, 2017, reg.6(2) of the Social Security (Miscellaneous Amendment No.4) Regulations (SI 2017/1015) amended reg.2(1) by substituting "2A, 2B and 2C" for the words and figures "2A and 2B".

2.007

p.667, *amendment to the Social Security (Attendance Allowance) Regulations 1991 (SI 1991/2740) by insertion of new reg.2C*

With effect from November 16, 2017, reg.6(3) of the Social Security (Miscellaneous Amendments No.4) Regulations 2017 (SI 2017/1015) inserted after reg.2B the following new regulation;

2.008

"Refugees
2C.—(1) Regulation 2(1)(a)(iii) shall not apply where the person has—
   (a) been granted refugee status or humanitarian protection under the immigration rules; or
   (b) leave to enter or remain in the United Kingdom as the dependant of a person granted refugee status or humanitarian protection under the immigration rules.
   (2) For the purposes of this regulation "immigration rules" means the rules laid before Parliament under section 3(2) of the Immigration Act 1971."

p.670, *amendment to the Social Security (Attendance Allowance) Regulations 1991 (SI 1991/2740) reg.7 (Persons in care homes)*

With effect from November 3, 2017, reg.7 is amended by art.3 of the Social Services and Well-being (Wales) Act 2014 and the Regulation and Inspection of Social Care (Wales) Act 2016 (Consequential Amendments) Order 2017 (SI 2017/901) as follows: in para.(2)(a) omit the word "or" at the end of para.(vii) and after that paragraph insert—

2.009

"(viii) Part 4 of the Social Services and Well-being (Wales) Act 2014 (meeting needs), or"

p.679, *amendment to the Social Security (Disability Living Allowance) Regulations 1991 (SI 1991/2890) reg.2 (Conditions as to residence and presence in Great Britain)*

2.010   With effect from November 16, 2017, reg.2(1) is amended by reg.6(2) of the Social Security (Miscellaneous Amendments No.4) Regulations 2017 (SI 2017/1015) by substituting "2A, 2B and 2C" for the words and figures "2A and 2B".

p.682, *annotation to the Social Security (Disability Living Allowance) Regulations 1991 (SI 1991/2890) reg.2 (Conditions as to residence and presence in Great Britain)*

2.011   In *FM v SSWP (DLA)* [2017] UKUT 380 (AAC) Judge Jacobs has held that the past presence test when applied in the case of a child is not discriminatory so as to be a breach of the claimant's rights under the European Convention on Human Rights and the Human Rights Act 1998. The judge doubted that the claimant's residence before coming to this country could be regarded as a status, but that in any case the difference in treatment between a child who had been resident in this country, and the claimant, was justified. He held also that no breach had been shown of the public sector equality duty under the Equality Act 2010 and that the action of the Department was in accordance with the United Nations Convention on the Rights of the Child 1989.

p.683, *amendment to the Social Security (Disability Living Allowance) Regulations 1991 (SI 1991/2890) by insertion of new reg.2C (Refugees)*

2.012   With effect from November 16, 2017, these regulations were amended by reg.7(3) of the Social Security (Miscellaneous Amendments No.4) Regulations 2017 (SI 2017/1015) by inserting after reg.2B the following new regulation:

"**Refugees**
2C.—(1) Regulation 2(1)(a)(iii) shall not apply where the person has—
   (a) been granted refugee status or humanitarian protection under the immigration rules; or
   (b) leave to enter or remain in the United Kingdom as the dependant of a person granted refugee status or humanitarian protection under the immigration rules.
(2) For the purposes of this regulation "immigration rules" means the rules laid before Parliament under section 3(2) of the Immigration Act 1971."

p.693, *amendment to the Social Security (Disability Living Allowance) Regulations 1991 (SI 1991/2890) reg.9 (Persons in care homes)*

2.013   With effect from November 3, 2017, reg.9 was amended by art.4 of the Social Services and Well-being (Wales) Act 2014 and the Regulation and Inspection of Social Care (Wales) Act 2016 (Consequential Amendments) Order 2017 (SI 2017/901) as follows: in para.(2) omit the word "or" at the end of para.(vii) and after that para. insert—

"(viii) Part 4 of the Social Services and Well-being (Wales) Act 2014 (meeting needs), or"

In addition, in the opening words of para.(4) omit the word "who" and at the beginning of each of paras.(4)(a) and (4)(b) insert the word "who". After para.(4)(b) insert the following:

"(ba) to whom section 37, 38 or 42 of the Social Services and Well-being (Wales) Act 2014 applies; or"

Finally, in para.(5) for the words "(a) and (b)" substitute "(a) (b) and (ba)".

p.717, *annotation to the Social Security (Disability Living Allowance) Regulations 1991 (SI 1991/2890) reg.12(1A) (Mobility component for the severely visually impaired)*

The validity of this regulation has been considered again in *JA-K v SSWP (DLA)* [2017] UKUT 420 (AAC). In this case the issue arose not from the method of determining what amounted to severe visual impairment, but from the fact that under s.75 of the Contributions and Benefits Act it could not be awarded to a claimant who was over the age of 65 years at the time the claim was made. The claimant was undoubtedly visually impaired to the requisite extent, but by the time the regulations were made that enabled the higher rate mobility allowance to become available by this route, in 2011, the claimant was already aged 71. She argued that to deny the benefit to her when it was available to a claimant aged less than 65, was a clear case of age discrimination. Judge Wright considered first whether the regulation might be considered to be invalid as being in breach of the public sector equality duty under the Equality Act 2010. He concluded that it could not be because the regulation was made in June 2010, but the Equality Act only came into force in April 2011. The same applied, he thought, to the decisions taken by the SSWP in not superseding the claimant's award of the mobility component to include the higher rate. As well, he pointed out that the discrimination, if there were any, resulted from s.75 of the Contributions and Benefits Act, not from reg.12(1A), and the UT was not competent to make any declaration in respect of an Act of Parliament. More importantly, however, Judge Wright considered the issue of whether the UT is competent to make a decision as to the validity of regulations in relation to the Equality Act 2010. This is a matter on which UT judges have given differing views though in some cases the matter was not put in dispute before them. Judge Wright's view was that, in consequence of s.113 of that Act, the UT was not competent to make a determination of invalidity except in the exercise of its jurisdiction in judicial review; to do that would require the claimant to commence proceedings in the High Court from where the matter might be referred to the UT. The judge would also have held that the SSWP did have due regard to the equality duty

2.014

when making the regulation. The judge considered, too, an argument based on the Human Rights Act 1998. He rejected that argument also in following *NT v SSWP (DLA)* [2009] UKUT 37 (AAC) (also reported as *R(DLA)* 1/09)—see discussion in note following s.75 of the C&BA 1992.

p.728, *annotation to the Social Security (Disability Living Allowance) Regulations 1991 (SI 1991/2890) reg.12 (Entitlement to the mobility component)*

2.015 The operation of paras.(5) and (6) of this regulation and therefore also of s.73(3) of the Act has been considered again by Judge Gray in *EC (by SC) v SSWP (DLA)* [2017] UKUT 391 (AAC). The judge held that the FTT had erred in their application of para.(6)(b) because they said that the claimant should be shown to require restraint "for the majority of the time". Judge Gray said that this was not in keeping with the interpretation of Judge Wikeley in *SSWP v MG (DLA)* [2012] UKUT 429 (AAC), where he had held that "regularly" should be interpreted more generally to mean on a significant number of occasions. The judge also observed that the FTT appeared to have treated the evidence of a medical consultant as relevant to the matter of impairment of intelligence and the evidence of the claimant's teacher as relevant to social functioning. She refers to other cases (cited in the notes to this regulation) as showing that all of the evidence was relevant to both these criteria. Judge Gray found that, on the written evidence that was before her, she was able to decide the case in the claimant's favour.

p.749, *amendment to the Social Security (Invalid Care Allowance) Regulations 1976 (SI 1976/409) reg.9 (Conditions relating to residence and presence in Great Britain)*

2.016 With effect from November 16, 2017, reg.2(2) of the Social Security (Miscellaneous Amendments No.4) Regulations 2017 (SI 2017/1015) amended reg.9(1) by substituting "9A,9B and 9C" for the numbers and words "9A and 9B".

p.752, *amendment to the Social Security (Invalid Care Allowance) Regulations 1976 (SI 1976/409) by insertion of new reg.9C (Refugees)*

2.017 With effect from November 16, 2017, reg.2(3) of the Social Security (Miscellaneous Amendments No.4) Regulations (SI 2017/1015) amended these regulations by inserting after reg. 9B the following new regulation:

"Refugees
9C.—(1) Regulation 9(1)(c) shall not apply where the person has—
  (a) been granted refugee status or humanitarian protection under the immigration rules; or
  (b) leave to enter or remain in the United Kingdom as the dependant of a person granted refugee status or humanitarian protection under the immigration rules.

(2) For the purposes of this regulation "immigration rules" means the rules laid before Parliament under section 3(2) of the Immigration Act 1971."

p.762, *annotation to the Social Security (Personal Independence Payment) Regulations 2013 (SI 2013/377) reg.3 (Personal Independence Payment Assessment: daily living activities and mobility activities)*

The circumstances in which it might be relevant for an FTT to call for medical evidence that could be available from an earlier award of DLA or of ESA has been considered in a number of cases—see *AP v SSWP (PIP)* [2016] UKUT 416 (AAC), *MA v SSWP (PIP)* [2017] UKUT 351 (AAC) and *GD v SSWP (PIP)* [2017] UKUT 415 (AAC). For a discussion of these cases see the notes following reg.8 of these regulations.   2.018

The need for a decision of supersession has been further considered in a series of cases *DS v SSWP (PIP)* [2016] UKUT 538 (AAC), *KB v SSWP (PIP)* [2016] UKUT 537 (AAC), *PM v SSWP (PIP)* [2017] UKUT 37 (AAC) and *TH v SSWP (PIP)* [2017] UKUT 231 (AAC) in the last of which Judge Wikeley confirms his acceptance of the approach that had been adopted by Judge Mesher above in this note.

On the question of whether an adjournment should be considered where the claimant is appealing against only one component of a combined award see also the more considered approach adopted by Judge Markus QC in *GA v SSWP (PIP)* [2017] UKUT 416 (AAC), although there the appeal was allowed because the FTT did not seem to have appreciated that they were making a supersession and had not given the ground upon which the supersession was made.

p.763, *annotation to the Social Security (Personal Independence Payment) Regulations 2013 (SI 2013/377) reg.4 (assessment of ability to carry out activities)*

In *RF v SSWP* [2017] EWHC 3375 Mr Justice Mostyn held that para. 2(4) of the amending regulations (SI 2017/194) was in breach of Art.14 of the ECHR and that it was *ultra vires* the regulation making power in Part 4 of the Welfare Reform Act 2012 under which it purported to have been made. The DWP has indicated that it does not intend to appeal against the decision. For the effect of this decision see the note to p.795 below. It is understood that the DWP intends to withdraw its appeal to the Court of Appeal against the decision in *MH v SSWP*.   2.018.1

p.766, *annotation to the Social Security (Personal Independence Payment) Regulations 2013 (SI 2013/377) reg.4 (Assessment of ability to carry out activities)*

A solution to this conundrum is suggested by the decision of Judge Ovey in *AB v SSWP (PIP)* [2017] UKUT 217 (AAC). This was a case in which the claimant's evidence suggested that he suffered distress when he tried to engage socially with others (Activity 9). Judge Ovey suggests   2.019

that the requirements of reg.4(2A) should apply only to those Descriptors which test what the claimant can do, and are not applicable to those descriptors that describe what the claimant cannot do. In her view the structure of PIP Activities ranges from a Descriptor at one end that specifies a claimant who can accomplish the activity described without any need for assistance at all, to another at the other extreme where the claimant cannot accomplish that activity at all. By way of illustration she refers to Activity 6—dressing and undressing; that ranges from "can dress and undress unaided" to "cannot dress or undress at all". It makes sense to test, in accordance with reg.4(2A), whether a claimant can dress (with or without aid) to a satisfactory extent, safely and in a reasonable time, but it does not, she says, make sense to ask whether someone who cannot dress at all does so satisfactorily, safely and timeously.

The inference is that reg.4(2A) was not intended to apply to the "cannot-do" descriptors. Reg. 4(2A) was a late addition to the regulations (as can be seen from the numbering) and in this, as well as other respects, the regulations as a whole, and the Descriptors in particular, have evolved somewhat piecemeal. For those Activities that are worded in the appropriate way this may provide a solution. Some Activities are worded in terms of the claimant's needs (e.g. Activity 3—Managing therapy etc) where the same problem may not arise, but for those in which the cannot-do at all Descriptor is used and is then conditioned by a further phrase, as in the case of Activity 4—washing and bathing, where the descriptor is "cannot wash at all and needs another to wash their entire body", there remains the difficulty of having to ignore the final element.

p.769, *annotation to the Social Security (Personal Independence Payment) Regulations 2013 (SI 2013/377) reg.7 (Scoring: further provision)*

2.020   The decision in *RJ v SSWP (PIP)* [2017] UKUT 105 (AAC); [2017] AACR 32 has been applied by Judge Mesher in *SSWP v NH (PIP)* [2017] UKUT 258 (AAC). There the claimant wore continence pads every day, though a leakage into them occurred, on average, only two days in the week. The judge held that such precautionary use was reasonably necessary every day and therefore the appropriate descriptor was satisfied on more than 50 percent of the days each week.

p.772, *annotation to the Social Security (Personal Independence Payment) Regulations 2013 (SI 2013/377) reg.8 (Information or evidence required for determining limited or severely limited ability to carry out activities)*

2.021   The question of whether medical reports and evidence that supported a previous award of DLA should be available to a tribunal when the claimant has appealed following transition from DLA to PIP has been considered in several cases. In *GD v SSWP (PIP)* [2017] UKUT 415 (AAC) it emerged that in all transition cases when the claimant is first interviewed by an officer of the DWP on the PIP claim, the claimant will always be asked if they wish evidence that was used for the DLA award to be considered in relation to their claim for PIP. This question does not appear on the PIP claim form. The SSWP also confirmed that where that information has been asked for by the claimant and used in making a decision it should subsequently appear as part of that claimant's file and be available on an appeal. Judge Markus QC returned the case for a rehearing, but in the light of this information and the fact that although the criteria for DLA and for PIP are different it was, in this case, likely that the information that had supported the award of DLA would have been relevant in assessing the report of the HCP, the judge directed that the SSWP provide that evidence to the new FTT if it were available. (She had also been provided with information from the DWP as to how long such evidence was retained in certain circumstances; that information appears in the judgment).

The information that claimants who are to be transitioned are asked this question will probably come as a surprise to a number of judges who have decided similar cases in the past. In *AP v SSWP (PIP)* [2016] UKUT 416 (AAC) Judge Hemingway decided just such a case. There, the representative of the SSWP had accepted that there was a duty to provide a copy of all documents in the DM's possession that were relevant to the claim, but argued that because the criteria for DLA and for PIP were different and because any medical evidence or other report would necessarily relate to a different time, that such evidence would rarely be required. Judge Hemingway decided this case on the basis that the FTT had erred in law in failing to give sufficient weight to medical evidence with which they had been provided, but he gave as his opinion, as well, that in a case like this, where the claimant had alleged that there was copious evidence relating to the DLA award, that the SSWP should provide at least a list of that evidence, and that the FTT should consider asking for that evidence to be produced where, as here, there was a marked disparity in the decision that had been reached on the award of DLA and that for PIP. He suggests that it might be so too, where there was reason to think that the HCP report might be unreliable; given the frequency with which that is said to be the case by PIP claimants this might turn out to be quite frequent. Judge Hemingway noted that a different conclusion had been reached in *DC v SSWP (PIP)* [2016] UKUT 117 (AAC) but there the DLA evidence related to the claimant's condition eight years before, as well as to the differing criteria.

The same point is made by Judge Gray in *MA v SSWP (PIP)* [2017] UKUT 351 (AAC). She directs that the new FTT to whom the case was remitted should be provided with both the relevant DLA award evidence and also evidence from an ESA examination.

p.773, *annotation to the Social Security (Personal Independence Payment) Regulations 2013 (SI 2013/377) reg.9(2) (Claimant may be called for a consultation to determine whether the claimant has limited or severely limited ability to carry out activities—negative determination)*

Two cases have been decided on the operation of this regulation. The regulation calls for a claimant to co-operate by attending for assessment with a HCP or by taking part in a telephone conversation to assist in determining their claim. Where a claimant fails to do so, without good

2.022

reason, para.(2) provides that a "negative determination must be made". Matters to be taken into account in determining "good reason" are defined in reg.10; they include the claimant's state of health and the nature of any disability.

In the first case, *SY v SSWP (PIP)* [2017] UKUT 363 (AAC) Judge Wikeley allowed the claimant's appeal against a decision that she had failed without good reason to attend or participate in a consultation to which she had been called in accordance with reg.9. This case reveals the problems that can arise in consequence of confusion about the roles of the DWP and of the provider of the independent assessment (in this case ATOS). The claimant, who had several mental health conditions, had made telephone calls to both the DWP and to ATOS. Before the UT the representative of the SSWP accepted that, as a result of these calls, the claimant had been told, and reasonably believed, that she was not required to attend for an assessment provided that she filed further medical evidence, which she had done. Indeed, before the UT a letter was produced that had been sent by ATOS clearly stating that she should not attend as the appointment was cancelled; this letter was not before the FTT. In the light of this, as well as other evidence, the judge was able to allow the appeal and directed that the claim be allowed to proceed for decision by the DM on the evidence that was available to him. What this case does highlight is the lack of any evidence provided to the FTT in support of the negative determination. The papers before the FTT and the UT simply recited that the claimant had failed to attend on four occasions when appointments had been made for her; no evidence was available in the form of appointment letters, other correspondence, records of telephone calls or otherwise, in support of these allegations. Judge Wikeley thought that, at the very least, such information should be provided.

The second case, a decision of Judge Mesher in *OM v SSWP (PIP)* [2017] UKUT 458 (AAC), has the added complication that the claimant had an appointee in respect of his dealings with the DWP. The construction of reg.9 does not sit comfortably with that situation. In this case too, the judge was able to allow the appeal and reinstate the claim. But here, the decision to discontinue the PIP claim had meant also the termination of the claimant's DLA claim, so that claim was also reinstated. This case again illustrates the confusion that arises from communication being between the appointee (this time with assistance also from a representative some of the time) and both DWP and the healthcare assessment provider (ATOS). The appointee had requested that the claimant be seen at a home visit; at some stage this was approved by the DWP, but was refused by ATOS on the ground of past incidents of aggression by the claimant. Judge Mesher allowed the appeal, ultimately, on the ground that the FTT had not taken a broad enough view of the factors to be considered in relation to the rejection of the element of good reason in reaching a decision of negative determination. Reg.10 "includes" the two reasons given above, but in the judge's view (applying an approach similar to that which has applied to jobseeker's allowance and formerly to unemployment benefit) regard should be had also to the suitability for that claimant of the arrangements that had been made for assessment. As well, he thought that the claimant should be entitled to include in his reasons the likelihood of that assessment producing any evidence that was not to be obtained already from his medical reports and possibly from evidence on his DLA award if that were relevant. The judge suggests also that where the FTT gave as the crux of their decision that the claimant had, in the end, made a conscious choice not to attend the appointment, they had failed to deal sufficiently, or at any rate failed to record their reasons for not doing so, with the fact that the claimant had an appointee whose very existence suggests that the DWP accepted that he was not capable of organising his own affairs when dealing with a claim. He observed also that the language they had used in this part of their decision—that the claimant had not shown that he was "incapable" of attending and that he was not "prevented" from attending, might indicate that they were applying a higher standard than the words of the regulation—having "good reason" not to attend.

Judge Mesher outlines a number of other concerns raised by this appeal without reaching final conclusions on them. These included the following:

(1) That reg.9 was validly made under s.80 of the Welfare Reform Act 2012.

(2) That in accordance with the regime disclosed in *GD v SSWP (PIP)* [2017] UKUT 415 (AAC) for a claimant to be offered the opportunity that his DLA award evidence be included for consideration, it was reasonable to infer that, in a case such as this, the claimant would be very likely to have done so even though no mention of that was made in the case file.

(3) Although reg.9 did not specify who should require the claimant to attend for assessment he inferred that this must be a decision for the DM, as too, would be the decision whether a telephone conversation might suffice. This raised a question as to whether that decision might be open to appeal to the tribunal, but Judge Mesher found it unnecessary to decide that point because it could be adequately subsumed in the issue of good reason as he had interpreted it. (In the UT, counsel for the Secretary of State had conceded that the FTT had erred in not considering whether a telephone consultation might have sufficed in this case, though whether as an appeal against the decision in choosing a face-to-face assessment, or as a factor in the good reason issue, was not clear).

(4) Assuming that the DM has correctly decided that an assessment appointment is necessary, can the decision and subsequent arrangements be left to another (i.e. the healthcare assessment provider) to be completed to fulfil the requirements of reg.9? The judge thought it could, though he thought that it should then be necessary for that body to provide evidence to support the allegation that appointments had been made etc. He thought that at least a standard letter with evidence that it had been used in this case would be necessary.

(5) The judge points out that the provision relating to appointees in the Claims and Payments Regulations (reg.57(5)) applies only to

things required to be done in respect of those regulations and not of other regulations. This raised the question of whether in relation to the PIP regulations requests addressed to the appointee could impose the duty to attend on the claimant and a consequent negative determination. He recognised that this might be the only effective way to communicate that requirement to a claimant, but the difficulty in applying the regulations remained unless an argument based on the principal of agency were used instead.

(6) The judge thought that even if the assessment arrangements could correctly be delegated to the healthcare assessment provider it was still competent for the DWP to remain involved in the arrangements. It might for example be appropriate for the DM to withdraw the case from the assessment process at this stage, but it was more difficult to determine how DWP involvement might impinge on other aspects of the arrangements—e.g. whether a home visit was appropriate.

(7) By not attending an appointment he accepted that the claimant would be "failing" to attend, but left open how that concept might be nuanced by a claimant's late arrival, or choice to leave early when the venue was running late, especially given the consequences of a negative determination. Most of these points, he felt, would be better dealt with as a part of the good reason issue.

(8) In judging good reason where there is an appointee there is a further question as to whose personal circumstances are to be taken account of—obviously those of the claimant are relevant, but what about those of the appointee? Does the claimant have good reason not to attend if his appointee is not available—must the possibility of another substitute be considered? Judge Mesher leaves these issues open.

p.774, *annotation to the Social Security (Personal Independence Payment) Regulations 2013 (SI 2013/377) reg.11 (Re-determination of ability to carry out activities)*

2.023   That this interpretation of the regulation is correct is now affirmed in a series of UT decisions— see *DS v SSWP (PIP)* [2016] UKUT 538 (AAC), *KB v SSWP (PIP)* [2016] UKUT 537 (AAC), *PM v SSWP (PIP)* [2017] UKUT 37 (AAC) and *TH v SSWP (PIP)* [2017] UKUT 231 (AAC). A full analysis of the provisions and the procedure to be followed is provided in the decision of Judge Wright in the *PM* case above.

p.780, *amendment to the Social Security (Personal Independence Payment) Regulations 2013 (SI 2013/377) by insertion of new reg.23A (Refugees)*

2.024   With effect from November 16, 2017, these regulations were amended by reg.14 of the Social Security (Miscellaneous Amendments No.4)

Regulations 2017 (SI 2017/1015) by the insertion after reg.23 of the following new regulation:

"Refugees
23A.—(1) Regulation 16(b) does not apply in relation to a claim for personal independence payment where C has—

(a) been granted refugee status or humanitarian protection under the immigration rules; or

(b) leave to enter or remain in the United Kingdom as the dependant of a person granted refugee status or humanitarian protection under the immigration rules.

(2) For the purposes of this regulation "immigration rules" means the rules laid before Parliament under section 3(2) of the Immigration Act 1971."

p.783, *amendment to the Social Security (Personal Independence Payment) Regulations 2013 (SI 2013/377) reg.28 (Care home residents)*

With effect from November 3, 2017, reg.28 is amended by art.16 of the Social Services and Well-being (Wales) Act 2014 and the Regulation and Inspection of Social Care (Wales) Act 2016 (Consequential Amendments) Order 2017 (SI 2017/901) as follows: in para.(2) omit the word "or" at the end of para.(eea) and after that paragraph insert: 2.025

"(eeb) Part 4 of the Social Services and Well-being (Wales) Act 2014 (meeting needs), or"

In para.(3)(a) omit the word "or" and after that paragraph insert:

"(aa) to whom section 37, 38 or 42 of the Social Services and Well-being (Wales) Act 2014 applies; or"

In para.(4) for the words "Paragraph (3)(a) only applies" substitute the words "Paragraphs (3)(a) and (aa) only apply".

p.785, *annotation to the Social Security (Personal Independence Payment) Regulations 2013 (SI 2013/377) reg.29 (Hospital in-patients aged 18 or over)*

An attempt to show that suspension of benefit under this regulation was unlawfully discriminatory as being in breach of the claimant's rights under Art.14 of the ECHR failed in *MH v SSWP (PIP)* [2017] UKUT 424 (AAC). The claimant was permanently resident in accommodation similar to a hospital and maintained out of public funds. Judge Lane held that his status as a hospital in-patient was not analogous to a similarly disabled person living at home and was only weakly analogous to a patient living in a care home (for whom only the daily living component would be removed under reg.28 above). But even if the latter case were sufficiently comparable, the judge found that the difference in treatment by withholding the mobility component as well was justified. 2.026

p.785, *annotation to the Social Security (Personal Independence Payment) Regulations 2013 (SI 2013/377) Sch.1 Part 3 (Mobility activities— planning and following journeys)*

2.026.1   In *RF v SSWP* [2017] EWHC 3375 Mr Justice Mostyn held that para.2(4) of the amending regulations (SI 2017/194) was in breach of Art.14 of the ECHR and that it was *ultra vires* the regulation making power in Part 4 of the Welfare Reform Act 2012 under which it purported to have been made. The DWP has indicated that it does not intend to appeal against the decision. This means that Descriptors (c), (d) and (f) must now be read as if the first six words of each were deleted. Each of these descriptors should now be read as if it begins with the word "Cannot" and effectively restores the original version of the descriptors. It is understood that the DWP intends to withdraw its appeal to the Court of Appeal against the decision in *MH v SSWP*.

p.797, *annotation to the Social Security (Personal Independence Payment) Regulations 2013 (SI 2013/377) Sch.1 (Personal Independence Payment Assessment)*

2.027   The approach to alcohol dependency in relation to benefits that was adopted in the ESA cases was that which had been developed for DLA in *R(DLA) 6/06*. That same approach has now been applied to PIP by Judge Hemingway in *SD v SSWP (PIP)* [2017] UKUT 310 (AAC). The judge affirms that alcohol dependency may be a mental condition for the purposes of this benefit and that an FTT must, therefore, assess and record the extent to which the claimant's ability to achieve the various Activities is affected by their condition. In this case, although the tribunal appeared to accept that the claimant's alcoholism was a mental condition, they failed to make any findings regarding the extent to which that affected his abilities. The judge points out that the degree to which a claimant's ability is affected will vary greatly and will require careful fact finding by the tribunal and that the extent to which they are affected may differ throughout the day, so that the time at which the claimant is required to perform any particular activity will also be relevant.

p.799, *annotation to the Social Security (Personal Independence Payment) Regulations 2013 (SI 2013/377) Sch.1 (Meaning of supervision)*

2.028   The meaning of supervision has been considered by Judge Wright in *LB v SSWP (PIP)* [2017] UKUT 436 (AAC). The claimant usually cooked a meal at school in a group of eight students who were watched over by two teachers. The FTT had found that this did not amount to "supervision", apparently because this was not a one-to-one relationship. Judge Wright held that there was no reason to limit the words in Part 1 of the Schedule in this way; those words required only the continuous presence of another person for the purpose of ensuring the claimant's safety. In his view that could be achieved by someone watching over a group of others.

p.800, *annotation to the Social Security (Personal Independence Payment) Regulations 2013 (SI 2013/377) Sch.1 (Activity 1—Preparing food)*

This activity is a measure of the claimant's personal ability and not 2.029
circumstances in which they are required to perform it. This has been
affirmed in *SC v SSWP (PIP)* [2017] UKUT 317 (AAC). There Judge
Gray had to consider the case of a claimant who, it was said, could not
prepare a meal because of the presence of her son who suffered from
ADHD and was autistic. She said that it was dangerous for her to cook
while he was in the kitchen and that he required constant attention. The
judge allowed an appeal, but returned the case to a fresh tribunal with a
direction that the test to be applied was of the claimant's physical and
mental ability to cook without regard to the presence or otherwise of her
son.

p.801, *annotation to the Social Security (Personal Independence Payment) Regulations 2013 (SI 2013/377) Sch.1 (Activity 1—Preparing food)*

Two recent cases relate to the question of cultural or other special 2.030
dietary requirements. In the first, *ZI v SSWP (PIP)* [2016] UKUT 572
(AAC); [2018] AACR 1 Judge Levenson has followed the line adopted in
the DLA decision in holding that a simple meal must be the same for all
claimants. The case concerned a claimant who ate an Asian diet that was
prepared for him by his wife. The FTT had concluded that, with the aid
of a perching-stool he would be able to cook for himself a meal that
included the items of an Asian diet if that were required, but the claimant
was given leave to appeal. It was argued that the FTT had given insufficient attention to the difficulty that he might have in cooking chapattis.
The judge held that it could not have been the intention of Parliament,
in making these regulations, that people from different cultural, religious
or ethnic backgrounds with the same level of disability, would have a
different entitlement to benefit on the basis of their community affilia-
tion.

The second, *SSWP v KJ (PIP)* [2017] UKUT 358 (AAC) was an
appeal by the Secretary of State against a decision awarding benefit to a
16 year old boy following his transition from DLA to PIP. The claimant
was diabetic. It appears that his mother prepared meals for him, but it
was argued that he would need supervision when cooking for himself to
ensure that he got quantities and ingredients correct and that, left to
himself, he would not eat the "right" sort of food. Judge Wright held
that, although the need for a special diet arose from his medical condition, there had been no evidence that showed that the claimant could not
prepare a simple meal for himself in the manner required by the descriptors and he allowed the appeal. The case does illustrate the different
criteria that apply as between DLA and PIP. A DLA claim could have
succeeded when the boy was under 16 because the issue would be how
much care and attention he required from his mother; the issue now was
simply how much could he do for himself.

In *SSWP v DT (PIP)* [2017] UKUT 272 (AAC) Judge Hemingway
has considered the extent to which a claimant's inability to read or to tell

the time might affect his ability to prepare a simple meal. The FTT had awarded this claimant, who was dyslexic, 4 points under descriptor 1(e) on the ground that he needed his wife's assistance to read recipes, instructions on packages and to set a timer or to tell the time. Without that help they had accepted that he would not be able to cook a meal to a satisfactory standard. The Secretary of State argued that none of these actions were necessary to satisfy this Activity because cooking a simple meal could be achieved "as a sensory and instinctive act"—in other words that it is unnecessary to read a recipe and that a person can tell when food is cooked by looking at it and testing it with a fork. Judge Hemingway took neither view. In his view the effect of an inability to read and tell the time may vary according to the limitations that it imposes on the particular individual; in such case the tribunal will be required to make careful and detailed findings of fact as to the effect on the claimant. In this case the FTT had made no such findings. The case was returned for rehearing.

p.808, *annotation to the Social Security (Personal Independence Payment) Regulations 2013 (SI 2013/377) Sch.1 (Activity 5—Managing toilet needs or incontinence)*

2.031   The use of grab handles and support bars to assist when using the toilet (and elsewhere in the bathroom) has been accepted in *FK v SSWP (PIP)* [2017] UKUT 375 (AAC). There, the point was made that such handles and bars are not mentioned in the list of items suggested to be aids and that a claimant is invited to consider when answering the relevant question on the PIP claim form. The judge suggests that might lead a claimant to answer "no" to that question, but he confirms that the handles are an aid or appliance when used to access the toilet. Note that it must be shown that it is necessary for the claimant to use those handles and that they are not there merely as a matter of convenience (see above in relation to Activity 4—Washing and bathing).

p.809, *annotation to the Social Security (Personal Independence Payment) Regulations 2013 (SI 2013/377) Sch.1 (Activity 5—Managing toilet needs or incontinence)*

2.032   The precautionary use of incontinence pads on a daily basis, even though they were soiled only infrequently, has been held to satisfy the 50 percent rule required by reg.7. See *SSWP v NH (PIP)* [2017] UKUT 258 (AAC).

p.810, *annotation to the Social Security (Personal Independence Payment) Regulations 2013 (SI 2013/377) Sch.1 (Activity 6—Dressing and undressing)*

2.033   The reference in paragraph two of this note to clothes that are appropriate in cultural sense was based originally on the inclusion of that element in the first version of the *PIP Assessment Guide* for DM. Those words have now been removed from the Guide. Nevertheless it remains the role of the tribunal to reach a decision on the basis of the claimant's ability to dress and undress in clothing that is appropriate for them. There seems no reason why this should not take account of what is culturally appropriate clothing. What might be doubted is whether dressing in such clothing, when the claimant is accustomed to doing so, should be any more difficult than any other mode of dress. Presumably if dressing in this way takes longer, the time taken is to be compared with time that would be taken to dress that way by a non-disabled person.

In *ML v SSWP (PIP)* [2017] UKUT 171 (AAC) Judge Hemingway has considered the case of a claimant whose medical condition caused her to hesitate and prolong the process of dressing. The FTT had accepted that her condition might extend the time that she took to dress—they said that "she was able to make a decision eventually", but they made no finding as to how long the delay might be and in particular did not refer to reg.4(4) and the definition there of what might be a reasonable time. For that reason the case was returned to a new tribunal, but in doing so the judge affirms that hesitation in choosing clothes, even on the basis of the appearance presented, could be reason to satisfy Activity 6, provided always that the claimant's difficulty in doing so could be attributed to their physical or mental condition.

p.812, *annotation to the Social Security (Personal Independence Payment) Regulations 2013 (SI 2013/377) Sch. 1 (Activity 6—Dressing and undressing)*

The reference to "culturally appropriate" clothing that was contained in the original version of the PIP Assessment Guide has been removed from later versions. (But see above notes to p.810). 2.034

p.812, *annotation to the Social Security (Personal Independence Payment) Regulations 2013 (SI 2013/377) Sch.1 (Activity 7—Communicating verbally)*

Judge Gray has referred again to the matter of lip-reading in *CC v SSWP (PIP)* [2017] UKUT 429 (AAC). The same concession was made by counsel representing the Secretary of State and although no general direction has been issued to judges in the Social Entitlement Chamber as the judge had requested, she was advised that guidance to this effect has been issued to decision makers, and that this should ensure a common treatment across all claimants. Judge Gray observes that DM guidance is not binding on tribunals, but suggests that, were a tribunal to reject that advice, they would need to explain their reasons with some particularity. 2.035

p.814, *annotation to the Social Security (Personal Independence Payment) Regulations 2013 (SI 2013/377) Sch.1 (Activity 8—Reading and understanding signs symbols and words)*

The importance of examining the claimant's ability to read all kinds of information has been emphasised by Judge Lane in *SSWP v SH (PIP)* 2.036

[2017] UKUT 301 (AAC). There the FTT had focused on her ability to read official letters, and her tendency to have difficulty when she got upset, rather than the whole range of any possible literature and signage. The judge said that they had erred too, in relying on the oral evidence given to them at the hearing, when there was other and contradictory evidence in the tribunal file.

The application of this Activity in the case of a claimant whose sight is severely restricted is examined by Judge Sutherland Williams in *DV v SSWP (PIP)* [2017] UKUT 244 (AAC); [2017] AACR 38. The judge reviewed several helpful passages drawn from earlier cases. The case was returned to fresh tribunal who would be required to make findings, in particular of the extent to which the claimant could read the body language of those with whom he was interacting, and of the extent to which prompting or support would assist him in that situation. The judge emphasised also, that the test was of the claimant's ability to interact generally one to one, or in a small group and in social situations. Inferences that the FTT had drawn from the claimant's interaction with them in the hearing room were either of limited relevance, or, if they were to be relied upon as the reason for their decision, they should have been put to the claimant as a part of the hearing.

p.815, *annotation to the Social Security (Personal Independence Payment) Regulations 2013 (SI 2013/377) Sch.1 (Activity 9—Engaging with people face to face)*

2.037   The meaning of prompting and of social support in relation to Activity 9— Engaging with other people face to face, has been considered by the Court of Session in Scotland in *SSWP v MMcK* [2017] CSIH 57. This was an appeal from the decision of Judge Agnew of Lochnaw Bt QC in that case. The court has affirmed his decision. In particular they have upheld the view that prompting and social support can be given prior to the event that is the social engagement and do not require the person giving assistance to be present at the time, so that the support could be, as Judge Agnew of Lochnaw Bt QC had suggested, counselling from a psychologist. But the court does point out that there must be some "temporal or causal link" with the event so that psychiatric help and other advice will, at some time, become just a matter of the past history of the claimant. The court also confirms that there may be an overlap between actions that are prompting and those that are social support. The critical difference, they say, is that social support can be given only by those who are trained or experienced in that role and they confirm too, that support can be given by friends and family on the basis that they are experienced in supporting that claimant—they need not be otherwise trained or experienced. But there does need to be some difference between what might be just prompting to make it into social support; the difference, they suggest, is that the help given, must be made effective or its effectiveness increased because it is given by that person. In other words the help given is effective either because of the training and experience of that person in a professional sense, or because of the

116

training and experience of that person as a result of their relationship with the claimant.

The reference to the decision of Judge Mark in *AM v SSWP (PIP)* [2015] UKUT 215 (AAC) should be to *SSWP v AM (PIP)* at that same citation.

p.816, *annotation to the Social Security (Personal Independence Payment) Regulations 2013 (SI 2013/377) Sch. 1 (Activity 9—Engaging with other people face to face)*

A decision of Judge Jacobs in *RC v SSWP (PIP)* [2017] UKUT 352 (AAC) has considered further the meaning of engaging socially and in particular what might be required to "establish relationships". The claimant suffered from a mental health condition which caused him to have thoughts of a homosexual nature whenever he came into contact with other men. He found this extremely distressing and said that he wished he could kill himself. The FTT had awarded 2 points for Descriptor 9(b) on the basis that, with prompting (though their reasons would suggest that they should have awarded 4 points under 9(c)), he could engage with other men (he had no difficulty in respect of women) to the extent of making a reciprocal exchange. Judge Jacobs held that this was not sufficient to constitute establishing a relationship. As he points out a brief conversation about the weather with a stranger, would be a reciprocal exchange, but we would not, as a matter of ordinary language, call that establishing a relationship. The judge returned the case to a new tribunal without attempting to prescribe what would be necessary to establish a relationship. He considered that it would be impossible to list the essential characteristics of a relationship in all circumstances—he doubted, for example, that he would have been able to anticipate the facts of this case if he had tried to list the situations that such a list might be required to encompass. This means that these words, as ordinary words of the English language, should be interpreted by a new tribunal (as the finders of the facts) relying upon their own experience and common sense.

One further point that arises from this case is the relationship between a claimant's ability to achieve an Activity to an acceptable standard, in accordance with reg.4(2A)(b), and the need to show, in Activity 9(d)(i), overwhelming psychological distress. In *SSWP v AM (PIP)* [2015] UKUT 215 (AAC) Judge Mark held that where the claimant had been unable to engage socially in a manner that was safe and to an acceptable standard, that it was not necessary to find, as well, that he would suffer overwhelming distress. In this case Judge Jacobs does not refer to the earlier case and his disposition of the case suggests that he did expect the new tribunal to make a finding about the level of distress that the claimant might suffer. Yet, he also suggests that neither prompting nor support might be sufficient to enable the claimant to engage socially to a satisfactory standard in accordance with reg.4(2A). It therefore seems open to a new tribunal, following the *AM* case, to find in the claimant's favour without needing to find overwhelming distress. The trouble with this conclusion is that the Descriptor 9(d)(i) is satisfied only when such

2.038

a finding has been made. This creates the same conundrum that emerges from cases such as *GP v SSWP (PIP)* [2016] UKUT 444 (AAC) where the FTT was forced to conclude that the claimant could not wash himself at all (because he took more than twice as long as a normal person would to do so) when the descriptor to be satisfied read "cannot wash and bathe at all and needs another person to wash their entire body". While that might have been physically possible (though unlikely) in that case, it is difficult to see how Descriptor 9(d)(i) can be said to be satisfied at all unless the overwhelming distress is shown.

But an alternative and perhaps more viable approach to this conundrum is suggested by Judge Ovey in *AB v SSWP (PIP)* [2017] UKUT 217 (AAC). This was another case where the claimant's evidence suggested that he suffered distress when he tried to engage socially with others. Judge Ovey suggests that the requirements of reg.4(2A) should apply only to those descriptors which test what the claimant *can* do, and are not applicable to those descriptors that describe what the claimant *cannot* do. In her view the structure of PIP Activities ranges from a descriptor at one end that specifies a claimant who can accomplish the activity described without any need for assistance at all, to another at the other extreme where the claimant cannot accomplish that activity at all. By way of illustration she refers to Activity 6—dressing and undressing; that ranges from "can dress and undress unaided" to "cannot dress or undress at all". It makes sense applying reg.4(2A) to test whether a claimant can dress (with or without aid) to a satisfactory extent, safely and in a reasonable time, but it does not, she says, make sense to ask whether someone who cannot dress at all does so satisfactorily, safely and timeously.

The inference is that reg.4(2A) was not intended to apply to the "cannot-do" descriptors. Regulation 4(2A) was a late addition to the regulations (as can be seen from the numbering) and in this, as well as other respects, the regulations as a whole, and the descriptors in particular, have evolved somewhat piecemeal. The advantage of this approach in relation to Activity 9 is that the tribunal can sensibly decide if the claimant can engage with others with or without prompting or support, to a satisfactory extent and do so safely, but, if it is shown that he cannot do that, then the sole question is whether, when he tries to engage, he suffers either overwhelming psychological distress or becomes a danger to himself or others.

In *CC v SSWP (PIP)* [2017] UKUT 429 (AAC) Judge Gray has reiterated her concern about the treatment of lip-reading.

p.819, *annotation to the Social Security (Personal Independence Payment) Regulations 2013 (SI 2013/377) Mobility Component—(Activity 1— Planning and following journeys)*

2.038.1   In *RF V SSWP* [2017] EWHC 3375 Mr Justice Mostyn held that para.2(4) of the amending regulations (SI 2017/194) was in breach of Art.14 of the ECHR and that it was *ultra vires* the regulation making power in Part 4 of the Welfare Reform Act 2012 under which it purported to have been made. The DWP has indicated that it does not intend to appeal against the decision. For the effect of this decision see the note to p.795 above. It is understood that the DWP intends to withdraw its appeal to the Court of Appeal against the decision in *MH v SSWP.*

p.840, *annotation to the Social Security (Personal Independence Payment) (Transitional Provisions) Regulations 2013 (SI 2013/387) reg.23 (Assessment of claim: transfer claimants to be taken to meet part of required period condition)*

This regulation provides that in the case of a transfer claimant (defined in reg.2 of these regulations as a person who is transferring from an award of DLA to one of PIP) the 3 month past period condition required by reg.12 of the PIP regulations should be deemed to have been satisfied. The complication that arose in *EB v SSWP (PIP)* [2017] UKUT 311 (AAC) was that one of the possible disabling conditions that the claimant suffered from at the time his PIP claim came to be determined may have not existed then for 3 months (it arose from prostate surgery and the FTT had not determined the exact date of the surgery) and neither did it form any part of the basis on which the claimant had been awarded DLA—(that much was clear because his DLA award had been only for the mobility component). The claimant argued that on the literal interpretation of reg.23 he should be deemed to have satisfied the past period condition, but Judge Farbey QC held that a proper interpretation of this regulation confined its meaning to those conditions that existed at the time of the DLA award and on which that award was based. The judge does this on the basis that transitional legislation is intended to facilitate transfer from one regime to another, but not to authorise innovation. (See the HL in *Britnell v Secretary of State for Social Security* [1991] 1 W.L.R. 198). But an appeal was allowed on the basis that the FTT should have gone on to consider the claim under reg.33 of the Claims and Payments Regulations which allows for an advance award for conditions arising in the 3 months period after the DM decision. As the claimant had been scored 6 points in respect of other daily living Activities this meant that he might have succeeded on a claim for the daily living component under PIP when regard was had to Activity 5—Managing toilet needs or incontinence. The case was returned for rehearing.

p.870, *amendment to the Social Security (Graduated Retirement Benefit) (No.2) Regulations 1978 (SI 1978/393) Sch 1*

In s.36(1) of the National Insurance Act 1965 as continued in force by Sch.1, delete "11.53" and replace with "13.43".

p.873, *amendments to the Social Security (Graduated Retirement Benefit) (No.2) Regulations 1978 (SI 1978/393) Sch 1*

Replace text accompanying n.12 with 'The Social Security Benefits Up-rating Order 2017 (SI 2017/260) art.12(1) (April 10, 2017)'.

2.039

2.039.1

2.039.2

p.892, *amendment to the Social Security (Maximum Additional Pension) Regulations 2010 (SI 2010/426) reg.3A (Prescribed maximum additional pension for survivors who become entitled on or after 6th April 2016)*

2.040   In subs.(2) delete "£165.60" and replace with "² £167.26". Add to list of amendments the following footnote:

2. Social Security Benefits Up-rating Order 2017 (SI 2017/260) art.14 (April 10, 2017).

p.897, *amendment to the Social Security (Widow's Benefit and Retirement Pensions) Regulations 1979 (SI 1979/642) reg.1 (Citation, commencement and interpretation)*

2.041   With effect from December 6, 2017, reg.3(2) of the Social Security (Miscellaneous Amendments No.4) Regulations 2017 (SI 2017/1015) amended this regulation by inserting after the definition of "unemploy-ability supplement" the following new definition:

"widowed mother's allowance" means an allowance referred to in section 37 of the Social Security Contributions and Benefits Act 1992 (widowed mother's allowance: deaths before 9 April 2001)".

p.907, *amendment to the Social Security (Widow's Benefit and Retirement Pensions) Regulations 1979 (SI 1979/642) reg.7 (Category B retirement pension for certain widows by virtue of husband's contributions)*

2.042   With effect from December 6, 2017, reg.3(3)(a) of the Social Security (Miscellaneous Amendments No.4) Regulations (SI 2017/1015) amended this regulation by substituting in para.(e) the words "pension-able age" for the words and figures "the age of 65". With effect from the same date, reg.3(3)(b) inserted after sub-para.(f) the following new sub-paragraph:

"(g) her having ceased to be entitled to a widowed mother's allowance at a time when she had reached the age of 65 but was under pension-able age,"

p.912, *amendment to the Social Security (Widow's Benefits and Retirement Pensions) Regulations 1979 (SI 1979/642) reg.11 (Category C retirement pension for widows of men over pensionable age on 5th July, 1948)*

2.043   In subs.(3), delete "⁴ £71.50" and replace with "⁴ £73.10". In the list of amendments delete existing text for footnote 4 and replace with the following:

4. Social Security Benefits Up-rating Order 2017 (SI 2017/260) art.13 (April 10, 2017).

p.940, *amendment to the State Pension Regulations 2015 (SI 2015/173) reg.1A (Full rate of state pension)*

Delete "£155.65" and replace with "² £159.55". In the list of amend-   2.044
ments, insert the following new footnote:

2. Social Security Benefits Up-rating Order 2017 (SI 2017/260) art.6
(April 10, 2017).

p.960, *amendment to the State Pension Regulations 2015 (SI 2015/173) reg.35 (Credits for persons providing care for a child aged under the age of 12)*

With effect from November 16, 2017, reg.17(2) of the Social Security   2.045
(Miscellaneous Amendments) Regulations 2017 (SI 2017/1015) substituted new paras.(3) and (4) as follows:

"(3) The person ('A') referred to in paragraph (1) is not entitled to be
credited with a Class 3 contribution unless
   (a) child benefit was awarded to another person ('B') in respect
       of—
         (i) the child, or each child, for whom A provided care, and
        (ii) the week in which A provided that care,
   (b) B's earnings factors, other than those derived from a Class 3
       contribution credit awarded under regulation 34, exceed the
       qualifying earnings factor for the year in which the relevant
       week falls, and
   (c) A makes an application to the Secretary of State to be so
       credited in accordance with paragraph (5) and regulation 39.
(4) Where the requirements relating to the provision of care by A in
paragraph (3)(a)(i) can be satisfied by more than one person in respect
of a week in which B was awarded child benefit—
   (a) those persons shall elect, with the agreement of B, which of
       them is to be credited with a Class 3 contribution credit (and
       then only the elected person is to be so credited), or
   (b) the Secretary of State is to exercise his discretion to determine
       which of those persons is to be credited with that contribution,
       in default of the agreement referred to in sub-paragraph (a)."

With effect from November 16, 2017, reg.17(3) of the same amending
regulations substituted "(3)(c)" for "(4)(c)" in para.(5) and in sub-paras
(a) and (c) inserted ", or each child," after "the child".

p.986, *amendment to the Employment and Support Allowance Regulations 2008 (SI 2008/794) reg.2(1) (Interpretation: definition of "approved blood scheme")*

With effect from October 23, 2017, reg.8(1) and (2)(a) of the Social   2.046
Security (Infected Blood and Thalidomide) Regulations 2017 (SI
2017/870) amended reg.2(1) by adding the following definition after the
definition of "aircraft worker":

""approved blood scheme" means a scheme established or approved by the Secretary of State, or trust established with funds provided by the Secretary of State, for the purpose of providing compensation in respect of a person having been infected from contaminated blood products;"

p.991, *amendment to the Employment and Support Allowance Regulations 2008 (SI 2008/794) reg.2(1) (Interpretation: definition of "the London Emergencies Trust")*

2.047 With effect from June 19, 2017, reg.8(2)(a) of the Social Security (Emergency Funds) (Amendment) Regulations 2017 (SI 2017/689) inserted in reg.2(1) after the definition of "the London Bombings Relief Charitable Fund" the following new definition:

""the London Emergencies Trust" means the company of that name (number 09928465) incorporated on 23rd December 2015 and the registered charity of that name (number 1172307) established on 28th March 2017;".

p.991, *amendment to the Employment and Support Allowance Regulations 2008 (SI 2008/794) reg.2(1) (Interpretation: definition of "main phase employment and support allowance")*

2.048 With effect from June 23, 2017, reg.7(1) and (2) of the Employment and Support Allowance (Miscellaneous Amendments and Transitional and Savings Provision) Regulations 2017 (SI 2017/581) amended the definition of "main phase employment and support allowance" in reg.2(1) to read as follows:

""main phase employment and support allowance" means an employment and support allowance where the calculation of the amount payable in respect of the claimant includes a component under section 2(1)(b) or 4(2)(b) of the Act [or where the claimant is a member of the work-related activity group];"

The transitional and saving provision in reg.10 of SI 2017/581 has the effect that this amendment only applies to claimants who are not protected by the transitional protections in the Employment and Support Allowance and Universal Credit (Miscellaneous Amendments and Transitional and Savings Provisions) Regulations 2017 (SI 2017/204): see paras 9.613-9.623 of Vol.I, and paras 3.564-3.574 of Vol.V, of the main work.

p.992, *amendment to the Employment and Support Allowance Regulations 2008 (SI 2008/794) reg.2(1) (Interpretation: definition of "member of the work-related activity group")*

2.049 With effect from June 23, 2017, reg.7(1) and (2) of the Employment and Support Allowance (Miscellaneous Amendments and Transitional and Savings Provision) Regulations 2017 (SI 2017/581) inserted the following new definition of "member of the work-related activity group" after the definition of "member of Her Majesty's forces" in reg.2(1):

""member of the work-related activity group" means a claimant who has or is treated as having limited capability for work under Part 5 of these Regulations other than by virtue of regulation 30 of these Regulations;"

The transitional and saving provision in reg.10 of SI 2017/581 has the effect that this amendment only applies to claimants who are not protected by the transitional protections in the Employment and Support Allowance and Universal Credit (Miscellaneous Amendments and Transitional and Savings Provisions) Regulations 2017 (SI 2017/204): see paras 9.613-9.623 of Vol.I, and paras 3.564-3.574 of Vol.V, of the main work.

p.994, *amendment to the Employment and Support Allowance Regulations 2008 (SI 2008/794) reg.2(1) (Interpretation: definition of "qualifying person")*

With effect from June 19, 2017, reg.8(1) and (2)(b) of the Social Security (Emergency Funds) (Amendment) Regulations 2017 (SI 2017/689) amended the definition of "qualifying person" in reg.2(1) to read as follows:

2.050

""qualifying person" means a person in respect of whom payment has been made from the Fund, the Eileen Trust, MFET Limited, the Skipton Fund, the Caxton Foundation, the Scottish Infected Blood Support Scheme [, the London Emergencies Trust, the We Love Manchester Emergency Fund] or the London Bombings Relief Charitable Fund"

With effect from October 23, 2017, reg.8(1) and (2)(b) of the Social Security (Infected Blood and Thalidomide) Regulations 2017 (SI 2017/870) further amended that definition to read as follows:

""qualifying person" means a person in respect of whom payment has been made from the Fund, the Eileen Trust, MFET Limited, the Skipton Fund, the Caxton Foundation, the Scottish Infected Blood Support Scheme [, an approved blood scheme], the London Emergencies Trust, the We Love Manchester Emergency Fund or the London Bombings Relief Charitable Fund."

p.995, *amendment to the Employment and Support Allowance Regulations 2008 (SI 2008/794) reg.2(1) (Interpretation: definition of "traineeship")*

With effect from November 6, 2017, reg.3(2) of the Social Security (Qualifying Young Persons Participating in Relevant Training Schemes) (Amendment) Regulations 2017 (SI 2017/987) inserted after the definition of "terminally ill" in reg.2(1) the following new definition:

2.051

""traineeship" means a course which—
   (a) is funded (in whole or in part) by, or under arrangements made by, the—

      (i) Secretary of State under section 14 of the Education Act 2002, or

      (ii) Chief Executive of Education and Skills Funding;

(b) lasts for no more than 6 months;

(c) includes training to help prepare the participant for work and a work experience placement, and

(d) is open to persons who on the first day of the course have reached the age of 16 but not the age of 25;".

p.996, *amendment to the Employment and Support Allowance Regulations 2008 (SI 2008/794) reg.2(1) (Interpretation: definition of "the We Love Manchester Emergency Fund")*

2.052   With effect from June 19, 2017, reg.8(2)(c) of the Social Security (Emergency Funds) (Amendment) Regulations 2017 (SI 2017/689) inserted in reg.2(1) after the definition of "water charges" the following new definition:

"the We Love Manchester Emergency Fund" means the registered charity of that name (number 1173260) established on 30th May 2017;".

p.1005, *amendment to the Employment and Support Allowance Regulations 2008 (SI 2008/794) reg.7(1B) (Circumstances where the condition that the assessment phase has ended before entitlement to the support component arises does not apply)*

2.053   With effect from June 23, 2017, reg.7(3)(a) of the Employment and Support Allowance (Miscellaneous Amendments and Transitional and Savings Provision) Regulations 2017 (SI 2017/581) inserted in sub-para.(a)(i) after "2(2) or 4(4) of the Act" the phrase "or the claimant was a member of the work-related activity group".

p.1006, *amendment to the Employment and Support Allowance Regulations 2008 (SI 2008/794) reg.7(1B) (Circumstances where the condition that the assessment phase has ended before entitlement to the support component arises does not apply)*

2.054   With effect from June 23, 2017, reg.7(3)(b) of the Employment and Support Allowance (Miscellaneous Amendments and Transitional and Savings Provision) Regulations 2017 (SI 2017/581) inserted in sub-para.(d)(i) after "2(2) or 4(4) of the Act" the phrase "or the claimant was a member of the work-related activity group".

p.1018, *amendment to the Employment and Support Allowance Regulations 2008 (SI 2008/794) reg.14 (Meaning of education)*

2.055   With effect from November 6, 2017, reg.3(3) of the Social Security (Qualifying Young Persons Participating in Relevant Training Schemes)

(Amendment) Regulations 2017 (SI 2017/987) inserted after para.(2A) in reg.14 the following new paragraph:

"(2B) Paragraph (2) does not apply to a traineeship."

p.1019, *amendment to the Employment and Support Allowance Regulations 2008 (SI 2008/794) reg.15 (Claimants to be treated as receiving education)*

With effect from November 6, 2017, reg.3(4) of the Social Security (Qualifying Young Persons Participating in Relevant Training Schemes) (Amendment) Regulations 2017 (SI 2017/987) amended reg.15 so that (a) the existing reg.15 becomes para.(1) of that regulation; (b) the words "and paragraph (2)" are inserted after the words "regulation 18" in the new para.(1); and (c) after para.(1) a new paragraph is inserted as follows:

2.056

"(2) A qualifying young person is not to be treated as receiving education if they are participating in a traineeship."

pp.1060-1062, *annotation to the Employment and Support Allowance Regulations 2008 (SI 2008/794) reg.29(2) (Exceptional circumstances)*

In *DB v Secretary of State for Work and Pensions (ESA)* [2017] UKUT 251 (AAC) Judge Bano gave the following guidance on the application of regulation 29:

2.057

"9. It is clear from the judgment of the Court of Appeal in *Charlton* that the question of whether regulation 29 applies to a claimant is fact-specific and that a tribunal's findings in relation to the Regulation must therefore be based specifically on a claimant's individual circumstances. That is not to say that the reasons for a tribunal's decision on whether regulation 29 applies to a claimant need necessarily be long or elaborate, and in many cases the tribunal's findings in relation to matters such as the nature and extent of a claimant's disablement will also provide a basis for their conclusions in relation to regulation 29. However, in carrying out the risk assessment required by the Regulation, it is in my view necessary that it should be reasonably apparent from the reasons, read as a whole, that the individual circumstances of the particular claimant have been fully and properly taken into account when deciding whether the Regulation applies."

p.1088, *amendment to the Employment and Support Allowance Regulations 2008 (SI 2008/794) reg.40(2)(d) (A claimant who works to be treated as not entitled to an employment and support allowance)*

With effect from November 7, 2017, reg.7(2) of the Social Security and Child Support (Care Payments and Tenant Incentive Scheme) (Amendment) Regulations 2017 (SI 2017/995) substituted "28, 29 or 29A" for "28 or 29" in reg.40(2)(d).

2.058

p.1088, *amendment to the Employment and Support Allowance Regulations 2008 (SI 2008/794) reg.40(2) (A claimant who works to be treated as not entitled to an employment and support allowance)*

2.059   With effect from November 7, 2017, reg.13(2) of the Social Security and Child Support (Care Payments and Tenant Incentive Scheme) (Amendment) Regulations 2017 (SI 2017/995) inserted after sub-para.(d) of para.(2) the following new sub-paragraph:

"(da) duties undertaken in caring for another person who is provided with continuing care by a local authority by virtue of arrangements made under section 26A of the Children (Scotland) Act 1995 and is in receipt of a payment made under that section of that Act;".

p.1097, *amendments to the Employment and Support Allowance Regulations 2008 (SI 2008/794) reg.45 (Exempt work)*

2.060   With effect from April 3, 2017, reg.3 of the Employment and Support Allowance (Exempt Work & Hardship Amounts) (Amendment) Regulations 2017 (SI 2017/205) amended reg.45 by omitting the words from ", and which—" to the end in para.(4), by omitting para.(4A) and by omitting the definitions of "relevant benefit" and "specified work" in para.(10).

p.1113, *amendments to the Employment and Support Allowance Regulations 2008 (SI 2008/794) reg.64D (The amount of a hardship payment)*

2.061   With effect from April 3, 2017, reg.5 of the Employment and Support Allowance (Exempt Work & Hardship Amounts) (Amendment) Regulations 2017 (SI 2017/205) substituted a new para.(1) as follows:

"(1) A hardship payment is either—
　(a) 80% of the prescribed amount for a single claimant as set out in paragraph (1)(a) of Part 1 of Schedule 4(2) where—
　　(i) the claimant has an award of employment and support allowance which does not include entitlement to a work-related activity component under section 4(2)(b) of the Welfare Reform Act 2007 as in force immediately before 3rd April 2017; and
　　(ii) the claimant or any other member of their family is either pregnant or seriously ill; or
　(b) 60% of the prescribed amount for a single claimant as set out in paragraph (1)(a) of Part 1 of Schedule 4 in any other case.".

p.1145, *amendments to the Employment and Support Allowance Regulations 2008 (SI 2008/794) reg.97(2)(b) (Earnings of self-employed earners)*

2.062   With effect from November 7, 2017, reg.7(3) of the Social Security and Child Support (Care Payments and Tenant Incentive Scheme)

(Amendment) Regulations 2017 (SI 2017/995) made the following amendments. The words "28, 29 or 29A" were substituted for the words "22 or 29". The words ", payments" were substituted for the words "and payments". The words "and any payments made to a claimant under section 73(1)(b) of the Children and Young People (Scotland) Act 2014 (kinship care assistance)" were added after the words "claimant's care". Payments under s.73 have been available in Scotland since April 2016 to people who have applied or are at least considering applying for a kinship care order for a child who is at risk of going into care or was previously looked after by a local authority.

With effect from the same date, reg.13(3) inserted the following provisions. After sub-para.(b) was inserted:

"(ba) any payment made in accordance with section 26A of the Children (Scotland) Act 1995 (duty to provide continuing care)—
    (i) to a claimant; or
    (ii) where paragraph (3) applies, to another person ("A") which A passes on to the claimant;".

After the end of para.(2) was inserted:

"(3) This paragraph applies only where A—
    (a) was formerly in the claimant' s care;
    (b) is aged 16 or over; and
    (c) continues to live with the claimant.".

p.1155, *amendment to the Employment and Support Allowance Regulations 2008 (SI 2008/794) reg.106(6) (Notional income— deprivation and income available on application)*

With effect from November 16, 2017, reg.13 of the Social Security (Miscellaneous Amendments No.4) Regulations 2017 (SI 2017/1015) substituted the words "rate of the annuity which may have been purchased with the fund" for the words "maximum amount of income which may be withdrawn from the fund". The Claims and Payments Regulations have been amended from the same date to require pension fund holders to provide information as to that rate on request.

2.063

p.1157, *amendments to the Employment and Support Allowance Regulations 2008 (SI 2008/794) reg.107(5)(a) (Notional income—income due to be paid or income paid to or in respect of a third party)*

With effect from June 19, 2017, reg.8(3)(a) of the Social Security (Emergency Funds) (Amendment) Regulations 2017 (SI 2017/689) inserted the words ", the London Emergencies Trust, the We Love Manchester Emergency Fund" after the words "the Scottish Infected Blood Support Scheme". Definitions of that Trust and Fund have been inserted in reg.2(1)—see the entries for pp.991 and 996 of Vol.I in this Supplement.

With effect from October 23, 2017, reg.8(3)(a) of the Social Security (Infected Blood and Thalidomide) Regulations 2017 (SI 2017/870)

2.064

inserted the words ", an approved blood scheme" after the words "the Scottish Infected Blood Support Scheme" (and therefore before the previous amendment). A definition of "approved blood scheme" has been inserted in reg.2(1)—see the entries for pp.991 and 996 in this Supplement.

p.1163, *amendments to the Employment and Support Allowance Regulations 2008 (SI 2008/794) reg.112(8) (Income treated as capital)*

2.065   With effect from June 19, 2017, reg.8(3)(b) of the Social Security (Emergency Funds) (Amendment) Regulations 2017 (SI 2017/689) inserted the words ", the London Emergencies Trust, the We Love Manchester Emergency Fund" after the words "the Scottish Infected Blood Support Scheme". Definitions of that Trust and Fund have been inserted in reg.2(1)—see the entry for p.986 of Vol.I in this Supplement.

With effect from October 23, 2017, reg.8(3)(b) of the Social Security (Infected Blood and Thalidomide) Regulations 2017 (SI 2017/870) inserted the words ", an approved blood scheme" after the words "the Scottish Infected Blood Support Scheme" (and therefore before the previous amendment). A definition of "approved blood scheme" has been inserted in reg.2(1)—see the entry for p.986 of Vol.I in this Supplement.

p.1166, *amendments to the Employment and Support Allowance Regulations 2008 (SI 2008/794) reg.115(5)(a) (Notional capital)*

2.066   With effect from June 19, 2017, reg.8(3)(c) of the Social Security (Emergency Funds) (Amendment) Regulations 2017 (SI 2017/689) inserted the words ", the London Emergencies Trust, the We Love Manchester Emergency Fund" after the words "the Scottish Infected Blood Support Scheme". Definitions of that Trust and Fund have been inserted in reg.2(1)—see the entries for pp.991 and 996 in this Supplement.

With effect from October 23, 2017, reg.8(3)(c) of the Social Security (Infected Blood and Thalidomide) Regulations 2017 (SI 2017/870) inserted the words ", an approved blood scheme" after the words "the Scottish Infected Blood Support Scheme" (and therefore before the previous amendment). A definition of "approved blood scheme" has been inserted in reg.2(1)—see the entry for p.986 of Vol.I in this Supplement.

p.1185, *amendment to the Employment and Support Allowance Regulations 2008 (SI 2008/794) reg.132(2)(j) (Calculation of grant income)*

2.067   With effect from November 3, 2017, art.13(2) of the Social Services and Well-being (Wales) Act 2014 and the Regulation and Inspection of Social Care (Wales) Act 2016 (Consequential Amendments) Order 2017

(SI 2017/901) inserted the words " or under Part 6 of the Social Services and Well-being (Wales) Act 2014" after the word "1989".

pp.1209-1211, *amendment to the Employment and Support Allowance Regulations 2008 (SI 2008/794) reg.156 (Circumstances in which a person is to be treated as being or not being a member of the household)*

With effect from November 3, 2017, art.27(1) and (2) of the Social Services and Well-being (Wales) Act 2014 and the Regulation and Inspection of Social Care (Wales) Act 2016 (Consequential Amendments) Order 2017 (SI 2017/901) amended sub-para.(5)(a) to read as follows:

    2.068

"(a)   placed with the claimant or the claimant's partner by a local authority under [section 22C(2)] of the Children Act 1989 or by a voluntary organisation under section 59(1)(a) of that Act;"

Art.13(3)(a) of the Social Services and Well-being (Wales) Act 2014 and the Regulation and Inspection of Social Care (Wales) Act 2016 (Consequential Amendments) Order 2017 (SI 2017/901) inserted a new sub-para.(5)(aa) after sub-para.(5)(a) as follows:

"(aa) placed with the claimant or his partner by a local authority under section 81(2) of the Social Services and Well-being (Wales) Act 2014; or"

while art.13(3)(b) amended the definition of "accommodation" in sub-para.(9) to read as follows:

""accommodation" means accommodation provided by a local authority in a home owned or managed by that local authority—
(a)   under sections 21 to 24 of the National Assistance Act 1948 (provision of accommodation);
(aa) under Part 1 of the Care Act 2014 (care and support);
(b)   in Scotland, under section 13B or 59 of the Social Work (Scotland) Act 1968 (provision of residential or other establishment); [. . .]
[(ba) in Wales, under section 35 or 36 of the Social Services and Well-being (Wales) Act 2014; or]
(c)   under section 25 of the Mental Health (Care and Treatment) (Scotland) Act 2003 (care and support services etc.), where the accommodation is provided for a person whose stay in that accommodation has become other than temporary;"

p.1221, *amendment to the Employment and Support Allowance Regulations 2008 (SI 2008/794) reg.165(3) (Entitlement for less than a week—amount of an employment and support allowance payable)*

With effect from April 6, 2017, art.31(2) of the Pensions Act 2014 (Consequential, Supplementary and Incidental Amendments) Order 2017 substituted "bereavement support payment under section 30 of the Pensions Act 2014" for "bereavement allowance" in the definition of "Y" in reg.165(3).

    2.069

p.1223, *amendment to the Employment and Support Allowance Regulations 2008 (SI 2008/794) reg.167(d) (Modification in the calculation of income)*

2.070   With effect from April 6, 2017, art.31(3) of the Pensions Act 2014 (Consequential, Supplementary and Incidental Amendments) Order 2017 substituted "bereavement support payment under section 30 of the Pensions Act 2014" for "bereavement allowance" in reg.167(d).

p.1250, *annotation to the Employment and Support Allowance Regulations 2008 (SI 2008/794) Sch.2 (Activity 1—Mobilising unaided)*

2.071   On the potential significance of an award of PIP to an ESA appeal concerned with mobilising unaided, see *AG v SSWP (ESA)* [2017] UKUT 413 (AAC), where Judge Hemingway ruled as follows on the comparability (if any) of a PIP award and an ESA award (at para.9):

> "The statutory tests are not the same. One is concerned with standing and moving and the other with mobilising which includes the possible use, where appropriate, of a manual wheelchair. Anyway a tribunal, whatever award has been made in respect of a different benefit, will be entitled to make its own decision with respect to entitlement to the benefit with which it is concerned on the appeal before it. It should not simply ignore the possible relevance of an award of a different benefit but that relevance is likely to be in relation to the possibility of there being further relevant evidence which might not be before the tribunal on the appeal and the appropriateness or otherwise of adjourning to get it."

p.1253, *annotation to the Employment and Support Allowance Regulations 2008 (SI 2008/794) Sch.2 (Activity 1—Mobilising unaided)*

2.072   A tribunal's fact-finding (and the relevance to that process of a claimant's own estimate as to how far s/he can walk) was in issue in *MM v Secretary of State for Work and Pensions (ESA)* [2017] UKUT 236 (AAC). Judge Hemingway held that it is perfectly permissible for a tribunal to attach weight to the claimant's own estimate as to how long in terms of time (usually expressed in minutes) he/she is able to walk for. It is also permissible for a tribunal to extrapolate as to what such an estimate, if reliable, might translate into in terms of distance. However, there is no rule to say that where a time estimate is offered it has to be accepted unless there is something specific to contradict it or to suggest it is unreliable. Further, it may be appropriate for a tribunal to consider whether such an estimate is, or is not, likely to be reliable and to probe this in questioning with a claimant. There may be reason to think that time estimates as to journeys which are undertaken regularly might be more reliable than other estimates. Finally, "the tribunal was not required to make a precise finding as to exactly how many metres the claimant could mobilise for. Absolutely precise findings as to something like that will often, realistically, be simply impossible. All it was required to do was make a finding as to which category the claimant fell into as to the range of distances contained within the relevant set of descriptors" (at paragraph 13).

Fact-finding was also an issue in *GZ v SSWP* [2017] UKUT 447 (AAC). There the tribunal, dismissing the claimant's appeal found that she qualified for 6 points for mobilising, making the following finding: "We find that she cannot unaided by another person mobilise more than 200 metres on level ground without stopping in order to avoid significant discomfort or exhaustion, or repeatedly mobilise 200 metres within a reasonable timescale because of significant discomfort or exhaustion." Judge Mesher explained why such a finding, without defining which limb of descriptor 1(d) applied, was inadequate:

"6. That [error of law] is in the form of the tribunal's finding of fact in the middle of paragraph 17 of the statement of reasons which adopted the terms of descriptor 1(d) without saying which of the two alternatives within the descriptor was satisfied. That in my judgment is not good enough as a finding of fact, because of the relationship of descriptor 1(d) with descriptors 1(a) and (c). If the tribunal considered that the claimant fell only within descriptor 1(d)(ii), because she could mobilise for more than 200 metres without stopping but could not achieve 200 metres repeatedly within a reasonable timescale, that would necessarily entail that she did not satisfy 1(c)(i) (because she could mobilise more than 100 metres) and would perhaps make it unlikely that she could satisfy descriptor 1(c)(ii) on the basis of not being able to mobilise 100 metres repeatedly. However, if the tribunal considered that the claimant fell within descriptor 1(d)(i), because she could not mobilise more than 200 metres without stopping, that would not as a matter of logical necessity exclude satisfaction of descriptor 1(c). Thus it might be necessary for a tribunal to explain why it chose descriptor 1(d)(i) rather than 1(c)(i). But more pertinently for the present case, if a claimant can only mobilise without stopping for some distance between 100 metres and 200 metres, that does not exclude the possibility that the claimant, while able to mobilise more than 100 metres without stopping, cannot achieve 100 metres repeatedly within a reasonable timescale and so satisfies descriptor 1(c)(ii). The same could potentially be said in relation to descriptor 1(a)(ii) and 50 metres. As a result, while it may not be necessary to the award of 6 points under descriptor 1(d) to specify which alternative is satisfied, in terms of the required underlying findings of fact on the whole activity of mobilising it is necessary in any statement of reasons to be more specific. It seems to me that there are two ways out where descriptor 1(d) is satisfied. The tribunal can identify the distance that it finds that the claimant can mobilise without stopping in order to avoid significant discomfort or exhaustion without considering the issue of repetition. There can then be a firm factual basis, allied to whatever explanation is appropriate, for not applying descriptor 1(c) or 1(a) and in particular for not applying descriptor 1(c)(ii). Alternatively, if the tribunal is unable to be so specific, it may be sufficient for it to explain that, while not sure precisely how far the claimant can mobilise beyond 100 metres without stopping, it has expressly considered descriptor 1(c)(ii) and is satisfied (and why) that the claimant can repeatedly mobilise 100 metres within a reasonable timescale. The question of what sort of range of estimates would be acceptable would very much depend on the circumstances of particular cases. What in my judgment is plainly not sufficient is to make a finding of fact simply in the terms used in the present case and then to say nothing at all in the statement of reasons about descriptor 1(c)."

p.1260, *annotation to the Employment and Support Allowance Regulations 2008 (SI 2008/794) Sch.2 (Activity 8—Navigation and maintaining safety)*

2.073   The meaning of "due to sensory impairment" was touched on in *Secretary of State for Work and Pensions v AI (rule 17) (ESA)* [2017] UKUT 346 (AAC). Strictly the decision is not a binding authority as it is a decision consenting to the Secretary of State (SSWP) withdrawing his appeal to the Upper Tribunal on the meaning of "sensory impairment" under descriptor 8(b) in Sch. 2. The claimant had serious balance problems caused by Meniere's disease. The SSWP appealed to the Upper Tribunal on the ground that "sensory impairment" meant a direct impairment of one the five physical senses of sight, hearing, smell, taste and touch. The SSWP subsequently sought the Upper Tribunal's consent to withdraw the appeal, having obtained further expert evidence on the nature of Meniere's disease. However, this specialist evidence may be useful in other cases.

p.1267, *annotation to the Employment and Support Allowance Regulations 2008 (SI 2008/794) Sch.2 (Activity 9—Absence or loss of control whilst conscious leading to extensive evacuation of the bowel and/or bladder, other than enuresis (bed-wetting), despite the wearing or use of any aids or adaptations which are normally, or could reasonably be, worn or used)*

2.074   In *NL v SSWP (ESA)* [2017] UKUT 397 (AAC), allowing the claimant's appeal, Judge Rowland considered it possible that the tribunal had:

"placed too much weight on the distinction between urgency and incontinence. The word 'continence', which at one time featured in the Schedules, no longer does so: the question is simply whether the claimant loses control, or is at risk of doing so, to the extent that he requires, or would require, cleaning and a change of clothing. Moreover, the words 'evacuation' of the bowel and 'voiding' of the bladder in descriptor 9(a)(i) need to be read in the light of descriptor 9(a)(ii) and I agree with the Secretary of State that the revised WCA Handbook (5 July 2016) accurately describes their effect—

'The descriptors relate to a substantial leakage of urine or faeces— such that there would be a requirement for the person to have a wash and change their clothing' (para.6)."

Judge Rowland added that "Descriptor 9(b) is satisfied when the claimant has only rare occasions of such a substantial leakage but is, for the majority of the time, at risk of having one unless able to reach a toilet quickly" (para.7).

p.1267, *annotation to the Employment and Support Allowance Regulations 2008 (SI 2008/794) Sch.2 (Activity 11—Learning tasks)*

See by analogy the guidance from Judge Rowley on this activity in the 2.075 context of Sch.3 in *Secretary of State for Work and Pensions v AT (ESA)* [2017] UKUT 338 (AAC). Note also her observation that "the words 'due to cognitive impairment or mental disorder' do not appear in the descriptors for that activity, presumably because the activity falls under Part 2 of Schedule 2 which is headed 'mental, cognitive and intellectual function assessment.' In my judgment, nothing turns on the difference" (at para.9).

p.1283, *new annotation to the Employment and Support Allowance Regulations 2008 (SI 2008/794) Sch.3 (Activity 9—Learning tasks)*

Activity 9: "learning tasks"; Descriptor: "Cannot learn how to complete a 2.076 *simple task, such as setting an alarm clock, due to cognitive impairment or mental disorder*
See the following guidance from Judge Rowley on this activity in *Secretary of State for Work and Pensions v AT (ESA)* [2017] UKUT 338 (AAC):

"cannot learn"
3. The activity is concerned with a claimant's ability to "learn" a new task, i.e. their ability to absorb, understand and retain information. As the WCA Handbook recognises, different people learn in different ways. They may prefer to watch a visual demonstration, have verbal instruction or read instructions. An inability to learn using one method would not generally lead to an overall inability to learn a new task if another way could be employed.

"how to complete a simple task"
4. "Simple task" is not defined. It would be inappropriate for me to offer any further definition, save perhaps to note the obvious—a simple task is one which is easy and straightforward. It is unlikely to involve more than one or two steps.

"such as setting an alarm clock"
5. The words "such as" are important. They confirm that the illustration given—of setting an alarm clock—is merely an example. Other instances may need to be considered by decision makers and tribunals. Further examples are listed in the WCA Handbook:

"Brushing teeth. This would involve remembering to put toothpaste onto a brush and brushing all areas of teeth.
Washing. This would involve the ability to use soap/shower gel and wash their body.
Brushing hair.

Turning on the television/using basic functions on the TV remote control.
Getting a glass of water."

Judge Rowley also stressed the further fundamental requirement that the inability to learn a simple task be "due to cognitive impairment or mental disorder", as reinforced by the requirements of reg.34(6)(b).

pp.1287–1289, *amendment to the Employment and Support Allowance Regulations 2008 (SI 2008/794) Sch.4 (Amounts)*

2.077 With effect from June 23, 2017, reg.7(1) and (2) of the Employment and Support Allowance (Miscellaneous Amendments and Transitional and Savings Provision) Regulations 2017 (SI 2017/581) amended paras (1)-(3) of the table in para.1 of Sch.4 to read as follows:

(1) Person or Couple	(2) Amount
(1) Single claimant— (a) who satisfies the conditions set out in section 2(2) or 4(4) of the Act [or who is a member of the work-related activity group]; (b) aged not less than 25; (c) aged less than 25.	(1) (a) £73.10; (b) £73.10; (c) £57.90;
(2) Lone parent or a person who has no partner and who is responsible for and a member of the same household as a young person— (a) who satisfies the conditions set out in section 4(4) of the Act [or who is a member of the work-related activity group and satisfies the conditions set out in Part 2 of Schedule 1 to the Act]; (b) aged not less than 18; (c) aged less than 18.(2)	(2) (a) £73.10; (b) £73.10; (c) £57.90;
(3) Couple— (a) where both members are aged not less than 18; (b) where one member is aged not less than 18 and the other member is a person under 18 who— (i) if that other member had not been a member of a couple, would satisfy the requirements for entitlement to income support other than the requirement to make a claim for it; or	(3) (a) £114.85; (b) £114.85;

(1) Person or Couple	(2) Amount
(ii) if that other member had not been a member] of a couple, would satisfy the requirements for entitlement to an income-related allowance; or (iii) satisfies the requirements of section 3(1)(f)(iii) of the Jobseekers Act (prescribed circumstances for persons aged 16 but less than 18); or (iv) is the subject of a direction under section 16 of that Act (persons under 18: severe hardship);	
(c) where the claimant satisfies the conditions set out in section 4(4) of the Act [or the claimant is a member of the work-related activity group and satisfies the conditions set out in Part 2 of Schedule 1 to the Act] and both members are aged less than 18 and—	(c) £114.85;
(i) at least one of them is treated as responsible for a child; or (ii) had they not been members of a couple, each would have qualified for an income-related allowance; or (iii) had they not been members of a couple the claimant's partner would satisfy the requirements for entitlement to income support other than the requirement to make a claim for it; or (iv) the claimant's partner satisfies the requirements of section 3(1)(f)(iii) of the Jobseekers Act (prescribed circumstances for persons aged 16 but less than 18); or (v) there is in force in respect of the claimant's partner a direction under section 16 of that Act (persons under 18: severe hardship);	

(1) Person or Couple	(2) Amount
(d) where both members are aged less than 18 and— (i) at least one of them is treated as responsible for a child; or (ii) had they not been members of a couple, each would have qualified for an income-related allowance; or (iii) had they not been members of a couple the claimant's partner satisfies the requirements for entitlement to income support other than a requirement to make a claim for it; or (iv) the claimant's partner satisfies the requirements of section 3(1)(f)(iii) of the Jobseekers Act (prescribed circumstances for persons aged 16 but less than 18); or (v) there is in force in respect of the claimant's partner a direction under section 16 of that Act (persons under 18: severe hardship);	(d) £87.50;
(e) where the claimant is aged not less than 25 and the claimant's partner is a person under 18 who— (i) would not qualify for an income-related allowance if the person were not a member of a couple; (ii) would not qualify for income support if the person were not a member of a couple; (iii) does not satisfy the requirements of section 3(1)(f)(iii) of the Jobseekers Act (prescribed circumstances for persons aged 16 but less than 18); and (iv) is not the subject of a direction under section 16 of that Act (persons under 18: severe hardship);	(e) £73.10;

(1) Person or Couple	(2) Amount

(f) where the claimant satisfies the conditions set out in section 4(4) of the Act [or the claimant is a member of the work-related activity group and satisfies the conditions set out in Part 2 of Schedule 1 to the Act] and the claimant's partner is a person under 18 who—
  (i) would not qualify for an income-related allowance if the person were not a member of a couple;
  (ii) (would not qualify for income support if the person were not a member of a couple,
  (iii) does not satisfy the requirements of section 3(1)(f)(iii) of the Jobseekers Act (prescribed circumstances for persons aged 16 but less than 18); and
  (iv) is not the subject of a direction under section 16 of that Act (persons under 18: severe hardship);
	(f) £73.10;

(g) where the claimant satisfies the conditions set out in section 4(4) [or the claimant is a member of the work-related activity group and satisfies the conditions set out in Part 2 of Schedule 1 to the Act] of the Act and both members are aged less than 18 and paragraph (c) does not apply;	(g) £73.10;

(h) where the claimant is aged not less than 18 but less than 25 and the claimant's partner is a person under 18 who—
  (i) would not qualify for an income-related allowance if the person were not a member of a couple;
  (ii) would not qualify for income support if the person were not a member of a couple;
	(h) £75.90;

(1) Person or Couple	(2) Amount

(iii) does not satisfy the requirements of section 3(1)(f)(iii) of the Jobseekers Act (prescribed circumstances for persons aged 16 but less than 18); and
    (iv) is not the subject of a direction under section 16 of that Act (persons under 18: severe hardship);
  (i) where both members are aged less than 18 and paragraph (d) does not apply.
	(i) £57.90.

The transitional and saving provision in reg.10 of SI 2017/581 has the effect that this amendment only applies to claimants who are not protected by the transitional protections in the Employment and Support Allowance and Universal Credit (Miscellaneous Amendments and Transitional and Savings Provisions) Regulations 2017 (SI 2017/204): see paras 9.613-9.623 of Vol.I, and paras 3.564-3.574 of Vol.V, of the main work.

p.1315, *amendment to the Employment and Support Allowance Regulations 2008 (SI 2008/794) Sch.6 para.19(8)(b) (Housing costs)*

2.078   With effect from June 19, 2017, reg.2(1) and (3)(d) of the Social Security (Emergency Funds) (Amendment) Regulations 2017 (SI 2017/689) amended Sch.6 by inserting the words ", the London Emergencies Trust, the We Love Manchester Emergency Fund" after the words "the Scottish Infected Blood Support Scheme" in para. 19(8)(b).

With effect from October 23, 2017, reg.8(1), (3)(d) and (4) of the Social Security (Infected Blood and Thalidomide) Regulations 2017 (SI 2017/870) further amended Sch.6 by inserting the words ", an approved blood scheme" after the words "the Scottish Infected Blood Support Scheme" in para.19(8)(b) and inserting a new para.19(8)(d) as follows:

"(d) any payment made under or by a trust, established for the purpose of giving relief and assistance to disabled persons whose disabilities were caused by the fact that during their mother's pregnancy she had taken a preparation containing the drug known as Thalidomide, and which is approved by the Secretary of State."

p.1327, *amendment to the Employment and Support Allowance Regulations 2008 (SI 2008/794) Sch.8 para.22(2) (Sums to be disregarded in the calculation of income other than earnings)*

With effect from June 19, 2017, reg.8(3)(e) of the Social Security (Emergency Funds) (Amendment) Regulations 2017 (SI 2017/689) inserted the words ", the London Emergencies Trust, the We Love Manchester Emergency Fund" after the words "the Scottish Infected Blood Support Scheme". Definitions of that Trust and Fund have been inserted in reg.2(1)—see the entries for pp.991 and 996 of Vol.I in this Supplement.   **2.079**

With effect from October 23, 2017, reg.8(3)(e) of the Social Security (Infected Blood and Thalidomide) Regulations 2017 (SI 2017/870) inserted the words ", an approved blood scheme" after the words "the Scottish Infected Blood Support Scheme" (and therefore before the previous amendment). A definition of "approved blood scheme" has been inserted in reg.2(1)—see the entry for p.986 of Vol.I in this Supplement.

p.1328, *amendments to the Employment and Support Allowance Regulations 2008 (SI 2008/794) Sch.8 (Sums to be disregarded in the calculation of income other than earnings)*

With effect from November 3, 2017, art.13(4)(a) of the Social Services and Well-being (Wales) Act 2014 and the Regulation and Inspection of Social Care (Wales) Act 2016 (Consequential Amendments) Order 2017 (SI 2017/901) amended para.28(a) by inserting a new head (ia) after head (i):   **2.080**

"(ia) section 81(2) of the Social Services and Well-being (Wales) Act 2014 (ways in which looked after children are to be accommodated and maintained),"

From the same date, art.13(4)(b) of that Order inserted the words "or under section 35 or 36 of the Social Services and Well-being (Wales) Act 2014 (duty and powers to meet care and support needs of an adult)" at the end of para.29(g).

From the same date, art.13(4)(c) of that Order amended para.30(1) by omitting the word "or" at the end of head (b), substituting the words "young persons); or" for the words "young persons)." at the end of head (c) and inserting a new head (d):

"(d) the following sections of the Social Services and Well-being (Wales) Act 2014—
   (aa) section 37 or 38, but excluding any direct payment made in accordance with regulations made under section 51 of that Act, or
   (bb) section 109, 110, 114 or 115."

From the same date, art.27(3) of that Order substituted head (i) of para.28(a) with the following:

"(i) section 22C(2) of the Children Act 1989 (ways in which looked after children are to be accommodated and maintained),"

With effect from November 7, 2017, reg.7(4) of the Social Security and Child Support (Care Payments and Tenant Incentive Scheme) (Amendment) Regulations 2017 (SI 2017/995) inserted the following provision after para.29:

"**29A.**—Any payment made to a claimant under section 73(1)(b) of the Children and Young People (Scotland) Act 2014 (kinship care assistance)."

Payments under s.73 have been available in Scotland since April 2016 to people who have applied or are at least considering applying for a kinship care order for a child who is at risk of going into care or was previously looked after by a local authority.

p.1329, *amendments to the Employment and Support Allowance Regulations 2008 (SI 2008/794) Sch.8 paras.32 and 34 (Sums to be disregarded in the calculation of income other than earnings)*

2.081   With effect from November 3, 2017, art.13(4)(d) of the Social Services and Well-being (Wales) Act 2014 and the Regulation and Inspection of Social Care (Wales) Act 2016 (Consequential Amendments) Order 2017 (SI 2017/901) amended para.32(1)(e) by inserting the words "or Part 4 of the Social Services and Well-being (Wales) Act 2014 (meeting needs) other than direct payments made in accordance with regulations made under section 50 or 52 of that Act" at the end.

From the same date, art.13(4)(e) of that Order amended para. 34(2)(b) by inserting the words "or under section 35 or 36 of the Social Services and Well-being (Wales) Act 2014 (duty and powers to meet care and support needs of an adult)" at the end.

pp.1330–1331, *amendment to the Employment and Support Allowance Regulations 2008 (SI 2008/794) Sch.8 para.41 (Sums to be disregarded in the calculation of income other than earnings)*

2.082   With effect from June 19, 2017, reg.8(3)(e) of the Social Security (Emergency Funds) (Amendment) Regulations 2017 (SI 2017/689) inserted the words ", the London Emergencies Trust, the We Love Manchester Emergency Fund" after the words "the Scottish Infected Blood Support Scheme" in para.41(1) and (7). Definitions of that Trust and Fund have been inserted in reg.2(1)—see the entries for pp.991 and 996 of Vol.I in this Supplement.

With effect from October 23, 2017, reg.8(3)(e) of the Social Security (Infected Blood and Thalidomide) Regulations 2017 (SI 2017/870) inserted the words ", an approved blood scheme" after the words "the Scottish Infected Blood Support Scheme" in para.41(1) and (7) (and therefore before the previous amendment). A definition of "approved blood scheme" has been inserted in reg.2(1)—see the entry for p.986 of Vol.I in this Supplement.

p.1332, *amendments to the Employment and Support Allowance Regulations 2008 (SI 2008/794) Sch.8 (Sums to be disregarded in the calculation of income other than earnings)*

With effect from November 3, 2017, art.13(4)(f) of the Social Services   2.083
and Well-being (Wales) Act 2014 and the Regulation and Inspection of Social Care (Wales) Act 2016 (Consequential Amendments) Order 2017 (SI 2017/901) amended para.53 by inserting the words ", or in accordance with regulations made under section 50 or 52 of the Social Services and Well-being (Wales) Act 2014 (direct payments)" at the end.

With effect from the same date, art.13(4)(g) of that Order amended para.56 by inserting the words ", or the provision of care and support in respect of an adult under Part 4 of the Social Services and Well-being (Wales) Act 2014" after the words "2014 (care and support)".

p.1339, *amendment to the Employment and Support Allowance Regulations 2008 (SI 2008/794) Sch.9 (Capital to be disregarded)*

With effect from November 3, 2017, art.13(5)(a) of the Social Serv-   2.084
ices and Well-being (Wales) Act 2014 and the Regulation and Inspection of Social Care (Wales) Act 2016 (Consequential Amendments) Order 2017 (SI 2017/901) amended para.22(1) by omitting the word "or" at the end of head (b), substituting the words "young persons); or" for the words "young persons)." at the end of head (c) and inserting a new head (d):

"(d) the following sections of the Social Services and Well-being (Wales) Act 2014—
    (aa) section 37 or 38, but excluding any direct payment made in accordance with regulations made under section 51 of that Act, or
    (bb) section 109, 110, 114 or 115."

pp.1340-1341, *amendments to the Employment and Support Allowance Regulations 2008 (SI 2008/794) Sch.9 paras.27 and 31 (Capital to be disregarded)*

With effect from June 19, 2017, reg.8(3)(f) of the Social Security   2.085
(Emergency Funds) (Amendment) Regulations 2017 (SI 2017/689) inserted the words ", the London Emergencies Trust, the We Love Manchester Emergency Fund" after the words "the Scottish Infected Blood Support Scheme" in para.27(1) and (7), but did not do so in para.31. Definitions of that Trust and Fund have been inserted in reg.2(1)—see the entries for pp.991 and 996 of Vol.I in this Supplement.

With effect from October 23, 2017, reg.8(3)(f) of the Social Security (Infected Blood and Thalidomide) Regulations 2017 (SI 2017/870) inserted the words ", an approved blood scheme" after the words "the Scottish Infected Blood Support Scheme" in paras 27(1) and (7) and 31 (and therefore before the previous amendment in para.27(1) and (7). A definition of "approved blood scheme" has been inserted in reg.2(1)—see the entry for p.986 of Vol.I in this Supplement.

p.1342, *amendment to the Employment and Support Allowance Regulations 2008 (SI 2008/794) Sch.9 para.42 (Capital to be disregarded)*

2.086   With effect from November 3, 2017, art.13(5)(b) of the Social Services and Well-being (Wales) Act 2014 and the Regulation and Inspection of Social Care (Wales) Act 2016 (Consequential Amendments) Order 2017 (SI 2017/901) amended para.42 by inserting the words "or under Part 4 of the Social Services and Well-being (Wales) Act 2014" after the word "1958".

p.1345, *amendments to the Employment and Support Allowance Regulations 2008 (SI 2008/794) Sch.9 (Capital to be disregarded)*

2.087   With effect from October 23, 2017, reg.8(5) of the Social Security (Infected Blood and Thalidomide) Regulations 2017 (SI 2017/870) inserted the following new para.61 after para.60:

> "**61.**—Any payment made under or by a trust, established for the purpose of giving relief and assistance to disabled persons whose disabilities were caused by the fact that during their mother's pregnancy she had taken a preparation containing the drug known as Thalidomide, and which is approved by the Secretary of State."

With effect from November 3, 2017, art.13(5)(c) of the Social Services and Well-being (Wales) Act 2014 and the Regulation and Inspection of Social Care (Wales) Act 2016 (Consequential Amendments) Order 2017 (SI 2017/901) amended para.56 by inserting the words ", or in accordance with regulations made under section 50 or 52 of the Social Services and Well-being (Wales) Act 2014 (direct payments)" at the end.

With effect from November 7, 2017, reg.7(5) of the Social Security and Child Support (Care Payments and Tenant Incentive Scheme) (Amendment) Regulations 2017 (SI 2017/995) inserted the following provision after para.61:

> "**61.**—Any payment made to a claimant under section 73(1)(b) of the Children and Young People (Scotland) Act 2014 (kinship care assistance)."

The amending regulation numbers this new paragraph as 61, it apparently having been overlooked that para.61 has already been inserted with effect from October 23, 2017. The obvious mistake can no doubt be corrected so as to use the number 62. Payments under s.73 have been available in Scotland since April 2016 to people who have applied or are at least considering applying for a kinship care order for a child who is at risk of going into care or was previously looked after by a local authority.

142

p.1412, *amendment of the Employment and Support Allowance and Universal Credit (Miscellaneous Amendments and Transitional and Savings Provisions) Regulations 2017 (SI 2017/204) Sch.2 (Transitional and savings provisions), para.1 (Transitional and savings provisions: General: definition of "a claim")*

With effect from June 23, 2017, reg.9(a) of the Employment and **2.088** Support Allowance (Miscellaneous Amendments and Transitional and Savings Provision) Regulations 2017 (SI 2017/581) amended the definition of "a claim" in para.1(2) to read as follows:

"["claim"] means [. . .] a claim for an employment and support allowance [made] in accordance with regulations 4ZC, 4G, 4H and 4I of the Social Security (Claims and Payments) Regulations 1987 or regulations 13 to 17 of the Universal Credit, Personal Independence Payment, Jobseeker's Allowance and Employment and Support Allowance (Claims and Payments) Regulations 2013;"

p.1414, *amendment of the Employment and Support Allowance and Universal Credit (Miscellaneous Amendments and Transitional and Savings Provisions) Regulations 2017(SI 2017/204) Sch.2 (Transitional and savings provisions) para.4 (Claimants on Incapacity Benefits who have or will become notified persons)*

With effect from June 23, 2017, reg.9(b) of the Employment and **2.089** Support Allowance (Miscellaneous Amendments and Transitional and Savings Provision) Regulations 2017 (SI 2017/581) amended para.4 by inserting the words "has been," after the words "where the claimant".

pp.1501-08, *annotation to the Social Security (Industrial Injuries) (Prescribed Diseases) Regulations 1985 (SI 1985/967) Sch.1 PD A10 (Occupational deafness)*

See further IIAC's Position Paper no.38, *Noise, occupational deafness* **2.090** *and Industrial Injuries Disablement Benefit* (September 2017).

p.1523, *annotation to the Social Security (Industrial Injuries) (Prescribed Diseases) Regulations 1985 (SI 1985/967) Sch.1 PD B15 (Anaphylaxis)*

IIAC has recommended an amendment to the terms of the prescrip- **2.091** tion for PD B15 (anaphylaxis) to cover any occupation involving "regular contact with products made with natural rubber latex" (see IIAC, *Extending the terms of prescription for latex anaphylaxis*, Cm 9498 (September 2017), p.11). The recommendation has yet to be given effect by amending regulations.

p.1530, *annotation to the Social Security (Industrial Injuries) (Prescribed Diseases) Regulations 1985 (SI 1985/967) Sch.1 PD D6 (Nasal carcinoma)*

IIAC has recommended an extension to the terms of the prescription **2.092** for PD D6 (nasal carcinoma) to include a new paragraph (d), namely "exposure to wood dust in the course of the machine processing of wood" (see IIAC, *Nasal carcinoma and occupational exposure to wood dust,* Cm 9499 (September 2017), p.39). The recommendation has yet to be given effect by amending regulations.

p.1530, *annotation to the Social Security (Industrial Injuries) (Prescribed Diseases) Regulations 1985 (SI 1985/967) Sch.1 PD D8a (Primary carcinoma of the lung: asbestos)*

2.093   For a further example of the fine lines that may have to be drawn in applying the terms of PD D8a, see *PC v SSWP (II)* [2017] UKUT 409 (AAC), in which Judge Jacobs held that an engineer installing fire alarm systems, whose work involved some cutting, drilling and disturbance of asbestos lagging, was not working in a prescribed occupation: "The work of cutting and drilling does not come within the prescription, as it is not lagging work. It is work related to the preparation for installing the cables. It was not lagging or preparatory to lagging" (at para.10). In so finding, Judge Jacobs followed *SSWP v ER (II)* [2012] UKUT 204 (AAC) and *SSWP v EK (II) (deceased)* [2016] UKUT 458 (AAC).

p.1590, *annotation to the Diffuse Mesothelioma Payment Scheme Regulations 2014 (SI 2014/916)*

2.094   Delete the heading 'General Note' in the second place where it occurs on p.1590. Note also that in addition, and with effect from July 31, 2017, s.77 of the Digital Economy Act 2017 enables HMRC to share the name and address of an employer and associated reference numbers with the Employer Liability Tracing Office (ELTO) for the purpose of assisting with such claims. ELTO is a non-profit making company that maintains a database of insurance policies to enable employees to trace former or current employers and their insurers in order to obtain compensation for workplace injuries. It is anticipated that access to this information will help to improve the quality of the ELTO databases.

p.1684, *amendment to the Employment and Support Allowance Regulations 2013 (SI 2013/379) reg.37(7) (A claimant who works to be treated as not entitled to an employment and support allowance)*

2.095   With effect from November 7, 2017, reg.15(2) of the Social Security and Child Support (Care Payments and Tenant Incentive Scheme) (Amendment) Regulations 2017 (SI 2017/995) inserted in sub-para.(a) in para.(ii) the words "or 26A" after "26" and the phrase "and duty to provide continuing care" after "local authority" in the second place where it occurs.

With effect from November 7, 2017, reg.9(2) of the same amending regulations inserted after para.(a) in reg.37(7) the following new sub-paragraph:

"(aa)   any payment made to the claimant under section 73(1)(b) of the Children and Young People (Scotland) Act 2014 (kinship care assistance);".

144

p.1704, *amendment to the Employment and Support Allowance Regulations 2013 (SI 2013/379) reg.62 (Prescribed amounts)*

With effect from June 23, 2017, reg.8 of the Employment and Support   **2.096**
Allowance (Miscellaneous Amendments and Transitional and Savings
Provision) Regulations 2017 (SI 2017/581) amended reg.62(1)(a) and
(b) by inserting after "the Act" in both sub-paragraphs the phrase "or the
claimant is a member of the work-related activity group and satisfies the
conditions set out in Part 1 to Schedule 1 to the Act".

PART III

UPDATING MATERIAL
VOLUME II

INCOME SUPPORT, JOBSEEKER'S ALLOWANCE, STATE PENSION CREDIT AND THE SOCIAL FUND

Commentary by

John Mesher

Richard Poynter

Nick Wikeley

pp.74-79, *annotation to the old style Jobseekers Act 1995 s.9 (The jobseeker's agreement)*

See *PG v SSWP (JSA)* [2017] UKUT 388 (AAC), discussed in the entry for p.81.

3.001

p.81, *annotation to the old style Jobseekers Act 1995 s.10 (Variation of jobseeker's agreement)*

PG v SSWP (JSA) [2017] UKUT 388 (AAC) was concerned with an employment officer's proposal to vary a jobseeker's agreement to include the provision "Search Universal Jobmatch via Gov.UK to identify and apply for jobs you can do—5 times per week minimum". Judge Wright overturned the First-tier Tribunal's upholding of the removal of entitlement to old style JSA for the claimant's failure to comply with a direction to enter into the varied agreement. That was on the basis that the tribunal had failed to decide whether the provision required the claimant to apply for jobs through Universal Jobmatch as well as search for jobs on that site. The claimant had not objected to searching for jobs on the site, because he would not need to register for an account to do so, but objected to applying for jobs because that would require such a step and he was concerned that the site was not secure and was open to fraud. It was apparently accepted on behalf of the DWP that it would not have been reasonable to require a claimant with such an objection to comply with an agreement that involved registration for an account on Universal Jobmatch (s.10(5)(b)). The judge suspected from the other provisions in the proposed agreement that, although the quoted provision did not expressly require registration with Universal Jobmatch, by inference it did require it for the claimant to apply for jobs that could only be applied for through that site, but sent that issue of fact back to a new tribunal. There was also a suggestion (paras 15 and 23) that it might be unreasonable to require a claimant to comply with an agreement whose terms are too uncertain. In relation to the test of reasonableness for the claimant, the judge suggested, in response to the tribunal's statement that there was no objection in principle to requiring a claimant to engage in actively seeking work as a full time task, that it might take very cogent reasoning to justify a person having to take very well in excess of the three steps per week that are the starting point under reg.18(1) on actively seeking employment. The principles involved in this case will apply also to s.9.

3.002

p.186, *annotation to the State Pension Credit Act 2002 s.15 (Income and capital)*

However, neither s.15 nor reg.15 seem to include as assessable income for state pension credit purposes regular payments of income from a benevolent institution (e.g. the Royal British Legion) or from a family member: see *AMS v SSWP (PC) (final decision)* [2017] UKUT 381 (AAC) at para.13.

3.003

p.226, *amendment to the Income Support (General) Regulations 1987 reg.2(1) (Interpretation: definition of "approved blood scheme")*

3.004 With effect from October 23, 2017, reg.2(1) and (2)(a) of the Social Security (Infected Blood and Thalidomide) Regulations 2017 (SI 2017/870) amended reg.2(1) by adding the following definition after the definition of "adoption leave":

""approved blood scheme" means a scheme established or approved by the Secretary of State, or trust established with funds provided by the Secretary of State, for the purpose of providing compensation in respect of a person having been infected from contaminated blood products;"

p.229, *amendment to the Income Support (General) Regulations 1987 reg.2(1) (Interpretation: definition of "the London Emergencies Trust")*

3.005 With effect from June 19, 2017, reg.2(1) and (2)(a) of the Social Security (Emergency Funds) (Amendment) Regulations 2017 (SI 2017/689) amended reg.2(1) by adding the following definition after the definition of "the London Bombings Relief Charitable Fund":

""the London Emergencies Trust" means the company of that name (number 09928465) incorporated on 23rd December 2015 and the registered charity of that name (number 1172307) established on 28th March 2017;"

p.232, *amendment to the Income Support (General) Regulations 1987 reg.2(1) (Interpretation: definition of "qualifying person")*

3.006 With effect from June 19, 2017, reg.2(1) and (2)(b) of the Social Security (Emergency Funds) (Amendment) Regulations 2017 (SI 2017/689) amended the definition of "qualifying person" in reg.2(1) to read as follows:

""qualifying person" means a person in respect of whom payment has been made from the Fund, the Eileen Trust, MFET Limited, the Skipton Fund, the Caxton Foundation, the Scottish Infected Blood Support Scheme [, the London Emergencies Trust, the We Love Manchester Emergency Fund] or the London Bombings Relief Charitable Fund"

With effect from October 23, 2017, reg.2(1) and (2)(b) of the Social Security (Infected Blood and Thalidomide) Regulations 2017 (SI 2017/870) further amended that definition to read as follows:

""qualifying person" means a person in respect of whom payment has been made from the Fund, the Eileen Trust, MFET Limited, the Skipton Fund, the Caxton Foundation, the Scottish Infected Blood Support Scheme [, an approved blood scheme], the London Emergencies Trust, the We Love Manchester Emergency Fund or the London Bombings Relief Charitable Fund"

p.234, *amendment to the Income Support (General) Regulations 1987 reg.2(1) (Interpretation: definition of "the We Love Manchester Emergency Fund")*

With effect from June 19, 2017, reg.2(1) and (2)(c) of the Social Security (Emergency Funds) (Amendment) Regulations 2017 (SI 2017/689) amended reg.2(1) by adding the following definition after the definition of "water charges":   3.007

""the We Love Manchester Emergency Fund" means the registered charity of that name (number 1173260) established on 30th May 2017;"

p.288, *amendment to the Income Support (General) Regulations 1987 reg.6 (Persons not treated as engaged in remunerative work)*

With effect from November 7, 2017, reg.10(1) and (2) of the Social Security and Child Support (Care Payments and Tenant Incentive Scheme) (Amendment) Regulations 2017 (SI 2017/995) amended reg.6(1) by inserting the following sub-paragraph after sub-para.(k):   3.008

"(ka) he is engaged in caring for a person who is provided with continuing care by a local authority by virtue of arrangements made under section 26A of the Children (Scotland) Act 1995 (duty to provide continuing care) and is in receipt of a payment made under that section of that Act;"

p.296, *amendment to Income Support (General) Regulations 1987 reg.13 (Circumstances in which persons in relevant education are to be entitled to income support)*

With effect from November 3, 2017, art.2(1) and (2) of the Social Services and Well-being (Wales) Act 2014 and the Regulation and Inspection of Social Care (Wales) Act 2016 (Consequential Amendments) Order 2017 (SI 2017/901) amended reg.13(2)(dd) to read as follows: 3.009

"(dd) has ceased to live in accommodation provided for him by a local authority under Part III of the Children Act 1989 (local authority support for children and families) or Part II of the Children (Scotland) Act 1995 (promotion of children's welfare by local authorities and by children's hearings etc.) [or Part 4 (meeting needs) or Part 6 (looked after and accommodated children) of the Social Services and Well-being (Wales) Act 2014], or by virtue of any order or warrant made under the Children's Hearings (Scotland) Act 2011, and is of necessity living away from his parents and any person acting in place of his parents;"

pp.306-307, *amendment to the Income Support (General) Regulations 1987 reg.16 (Circumstances in which a person is to be treated as being or not being a member of the household: definition of "accommodation")*

3.010   With effect from November 3, 2017, art.20(1) and (2) of the Social Services and Well-being (Wales) Act 2014 and the Regulation and Inspection of Social Care (Wales) Act 2016 (Consequential Amendments) Order 2017 (SI 2017/901) amended sub-para.(4)(a) to read as follows:

> "(a)   placed with the claimant or his partner by a local authority under [section 22C(2)] of the Children Act 1989 or by a voluntary organisation under section 59(1)(a) of that Act;"

and, art.2(1) and (3) of the Social Services and Well-being (Wales) Act 2014 and the Regulation and Inspection of Social Care (Wales) Act 2016 (Consequential Amendments) Order 2017 (SI 2017/901) amended reg.16 by inserted a new sub-para.(4)(aa) after sub-para.(4)(a) as follows:

> "(aa)   placed with the claimant or his partner by a local authority under section 81(2) of the Social Services and Well-being (Wales) Act 2014; or"

and amended the definition of "accommodation" in sub-para.(8)(za) to read as follows:

> "(za)   "accommodation" means accommodation provided by a local authority in a home owned or managed by that local authority—
>> (i)   under sections 21 to 24 of the National Assistance Act 1948 (provision of accommodation),
>> (ii)   in Scotland, under section 13B or 59 of the Social Work (Scotland) Act 1968 (provision of residential or other establishment),
>> (iii) under section 25 of the Mental Health (Care and Treatment) (Scotland) Act 2003 (care and support services etc.), [...]
>> (iv)   under section 18 or 19 of the Care Act 2014 (duty and power to meet needs for care and support),[" or
>> (v)   under section 35 or 36 of the Social Services and Well-being (Wales) Act 2014 (duty and power to meet care and support needs of an adult),"
>
> where the accommodation is provided for a person whose stay in that accommodation has become other than temporary;"

pp.307-308, *amendment to Income Support (General) Regulations 1987 reg.16 (Circumstances in which a person is to be treated as being or not being a member of the household: definition of "relevant enactment")*

3.011   With effect from November 3, 2017, art.2(1) and (3) of the Social Services and Well-being (Wales) Act 2014 and the Regulation and

Inspection of Social Care (Wales) Act 2016 (Consequential Amendments) Order 2017 (SI 2017/901) amended the definition of "relevant enactment" in sub-para.(8)(a) to read as follows:

"(a) "relevant enactment" means the Army Act 1955, the Social Work (Scotland) Act 1968, the Matrimonial Causes Act 1973, the Adoption (Scotland) Act 1978, the Family Law Act 1986 [, the Children Act 1989 and the Social Services and Well-being (Wales) Act 2014];"

p.349, *annotation to the Income Support (General) Regulations 1987 (SI 1987/1967) reg.23 (Calculation of income and capital—what constitutes income of the claimant?)*

3.011.1   See *BL v SSWP (SPC)* [2018] UKUT 4 (AAC) for a case where payments of the claimant's personal pension to his ex-wife were his income because they were made at his order and he retained practical control over the money.

p.374, *annotation to the Income Support (General) Regulations 1987 (SI 1987/1967) reg.35(1) (Earnings of employed earners)*

3.012   In *MH v SSWP and Rotherham MBC (HB)* [2017] UKUT 401 (AAC) Judge Wikeley adopted and applied the analysis in *R(TC) 2/03*. The claimant received a redundancy payment of nearly £15,000 in March 2016, which was used to pay off debts and make home improvements. In May 2016 he was offered his old job back on condition that he repaid the employer the amount of the redundancy payment by monthly deductions from salary within the 2016/17 tax year. The claimant accepted those terms. On his monthly payslips his basic salary was stated as £2,719.04 before overtime with deductions including income tax and national insurance and the sum of £1,222,22 described as "BS loan". On his claim for housing benefit the local authority (and the First-tier Tribunal) decided that under the equivalent of regs 35 and 36 the gross earnings had to be taken into account and there was nothing to allow the deduction or disregard of the £1,222.22 repayment. The judge held that the proper analysis was that the claimant's contract of employment had been varied by agreement so that he was only entitled to receive a salary reduced by the amount of the repayment and that that amount was his gross earnings. In fact, the case appears stronger than that of *R(TC) 2/03* (where the claimant agreed to repay a past overpayment of salary by monthly deductions) because the initial terms on which the claimant was re-engaged incorporated the repayments of the redundancy payment. There was hardly a variation. It might also have been arguable that the principle of *Parsons v Hogg* [1985] 2 All E.R. 897, appendix to *R(FIS) 4/85* (see para.2.269 of the main volume) could have been applied, to the effect that the £1,222.22, as an expense necessarily incurred to win the salary, did not form part of the claimant's gross earnings.

p.384, *amendments to the Income Support (General) Regulations 1987 (SI 1987/1967) reg.37(2) (Earnings of self-employed earners)*

3.013   With effect from November 7, 2017, reg.2(2) of the Social Security and Child Support (Care Payments and Tenant Incentive Scheme) (Amendment) Regulations 2017 (SI 2017/995) made the following amendments to sub-para.(b). The words "26, 27 or 27A" were substituted for the words "26 or 27". The words ", payments" were substituted for the words "and payments". The words "and any payments made to a claimant under section 73(1)(b) of the Children and Young People (Scotland) Act 2014 (kinship care assistance)" were added after the words "claimant's care". Payments under s.73 have been available in Scotland since April 2016 to people who have applied or are at least considering applying for a kinship care order for a child who is at risk of going into care or was previously looked after by a local authority.

With effect from the same date, reg.10(3) inserted the following provisions. After sub-para.(b) was inserted:

"(ba) any payment made in accordance with section 26A of the Children (Scotland) Act 1995 (duty to provide continuing care)—
(i) to a claimant; or
(ii) where paragraph (3) applies, to another person ("A") which A passes on to the claimant;".

After the end of para.(2) was inserted:

"(3) This paragraph applies only where A—
(a) was formerly in the claimant' s care;
(b) is aged 16 or over; and
(c) continues to live with the claimant.".

p.407, *amendment to the Income Support (General) Regulations 1987 (SI 1987/1967) reg.42(2B) (Notional income)*

3.014   With effect from November 16, 2017, reg.4 of the Social Security (Miscellaneous Amendments No.4) Regulations 2017 (SI 2017/1015) substituted the words "rate of the annuity which may have been purchased with the fund" for the words "maximum amount of income which may be withdrawn from the fund". The Claims and Payments Regulations have been amended from the same date to require pension fund holders to provide information as to that rate on request.

p.408, *amendments to the Income Support (General) Regulations 1987 (SI 1987/1967) reg.42(4ZA)(a) (Notional income)*

3.015   With effect from June 19, 2017, reg.2(3)(a) of the Social Security (Emergency Funds) (Amendment) Regulations 2017 (SI 2017/689) inserted the words ", the London Emergencies Trust, the We Love Manchester Emergency Fund" after the words "the Scottish Infected Blood Support Scheme". Definitions of that Trust and Fund have been inserted in reg.2(1)—see the entries for pp.229 and 234 of Vol.II in this Supplement.

With effect from October 23, 2017, reg.2(3)(a) of the Social Security (Infected Blood and Thalidomide) Regulations 2017 (SI 2017/870) inserted the words ", an approved blood scheme" after the words "the Scottish Infected Blood Support Scheme" (and therefore before the previous amendment). A definition of "approved blood scheme" has been inserted in reg.2(1)—see the entry for p.226 of Vol.II in this Supplement.

p.419, *annotation to the Income Support (General) Regulations 1987 (SI 1987/1967) reg.42(4) and (4ZA) (Notional income—payments made to third parties)*

See *BL v SSWP (SPC)* [2018] UKUT 4 (AAC) for a case where 3.015.1 payments of the claimant's personal pension to his ex-wife were his income because they were made at his order and he retained practical control over the money. It was suggested that the context of reg.42(4) may not be the same as that of reg.24(1) of the State Pension Credit Regulations 2002.

p.428, *annotation to the Income Support (General) Regulations 1987 (SI 1987/1967) reg.46 (Calculation of capital—actual capital)*

See the entry for p.438 for the application of *R(SB) 2/83* in *SSWP v* 3.016 *GF (ESA)* [2017] UKUT 333 (AAC).

p.438, *annotation to the Income Support (General) Regulations 1987 (SI 1987/1967) reg.46 (Calculation of capital—deduction of liabilities)*

SSWP v GF (ESA) [2017] UKUT 333 (AAC) is an illustration of the 3.017 application of the principle of *R(SB) 2/83* that liabilities not secured on a capital asset are not to be taken into account in calculating the value of the asset. For one part of the period in issue the claimant's brother-in-law had paid a costs order of some £48,000 made against the claimant in the expectation at least that he would be repaid once the 120-day notice period for withdrawal of funds in a building society bond with a balance of £75,000 had expired. On the evidence available the judge rightly concluded that there was no implied, resulting or constructive trust and the claimant's debt did not change the beneficial ownership of the funds in the bond. However, there could in other similar cases be evidence of the discussions or arrangements before the brother-in-law made his payment that could lead to a conclusion either that the debt had been secured on the claimant's rights in the bond or that the claimant had made a declaration of trust. In *GF* itself no such argument could have helped the claimant because even if he had not been the beneficial owner of £48,000 of the balance in the bond, the value of the remainder (even subject to the 120-day notice provision) would no doubt have exceeded £16,000.

p.439, *amendments to the Income Support (General) Regulations 1987 (SI 1987/1967) reg.48(10)(c) (Income treated as capital)*

3.018   With effect from June 19, 2017, reg.2(3)(b) of the Social Security (Emergency Funds) (Amendment) Regulations 2017 (SI 2017/689) inserted the words ", the London Emergencies Trust, the We Love Manchester Emergency Fund" after the words "the Scottish Infected Blood Support Scheme". Definitions of that Trust and Fund have been inserted in reg.2(1)—see the entries for pp.229 and 234 of Vol.II in this Supplement.

With effect from October 23, 2017, reg.2(3)(b) of the Social Security (Infected Blood and Thalidomide) Regulations 2017 (SI 2017/870) inserted the words ", an approved blood scheme" after the words "the Scottish Infected Blood Support Scheme" (and therefore before the previous amendment). A definition of "approved blood scheme" has been inserted in reg.2(1)—see the entry for p.226 of Vol.II in this Supplement.

p.448, *amendments to the Income Support (General) Regulations 1987 (SI 1987/1967) reg.51(3A)(a) (Notional capital)*

3.019   With effect from June 19, 2017, reg.2(3)(c) of the Social Security (Emergency Funds) (Amendment) Regulations 2017 (SI 2017/689) inserted the words ", the London Emergencies Trust, the We Love Manchester Emergency Fund" after the words "the Scottish Infected Blood Support Scheme". Definitions of that Trust and Fund have been inserted in reg.2(1)—see the entries for pp.229 and 234 of Vol.II in this Supplement.

With effect from October 23, 2017, reg.2(3)(c) of the Social Security (Infected Blood and Thalidomide) Regulations 2017 (SI 2017/870) inserted the words ", an approved blood scheme" after the words "the Scottish Infected Blood Support Scheme" (and therefore before the previous amendment). A definition of "approved blood scheme" has been inserted in reg.2(1)—see the entry for p.226 of Vol.II in this Supplement.

p.507, *amendment to the Income Support (General) Regulations 1987 (SI 1987/1967) reg.62(2)(k) (Calculation of grant income)*

3.020   With effect from November 3, 2017, art.2(4) of the Social Services and Well-being (Wales) Act 2014 and the Regulation and Inspection of Social Care (Wales) Act 2016 (Consequential Amendments) Order 2017 (SI 2017/901) inserted the words "or Part 6 of the Social Services and Well-being (Wales) Act 2014" after the word "1989".

p.589, *amendment to the Income Support (General) Regulations 1987 Sch.3 para.18 (housing costs)*

3.021   With effect from June 19, 2017, reg.2(1) and (3)(d) of the Social Security (Emergency Funds) (Amendment) Regulations 2017 (SI

2017/689) amended Sch.3 by inserting the words ", the London Emergencies Trust, the We Love Manchester Emergency Fund" after the words "the Scottish Infected Blood Support Scheme" in para. 18(8)(b).

With effect from October 23, 2017, reg.2(1), (3)(d) and (4) of the Social Security (Infected Blood and Thalidomide) Regulations 2017 (SI 2017/870) further amended Sch.3 by inserting the words ", an approved blood scheme" after the words "the Scottish Infected Blood Support Scheme" in para.18(8)(b) and inserting a new para.18(8)(d) as follows:

"(d) any payment made under or by a trust, established for the purpose of giving relief and assistance to disabled persons whose disabilities were caused by the fact that during their mother's pregnancy she had taken a preparation containing the drug known as Thalidomide, and which is approved by the Secretary of State."

p.671, *amendments to the Income Support (General) Regulations 1987 (SI 1987/1967) Sch.9 para.21(2) (Sums to be disregarded in the calculation of income other than earnings)*

With effect from June 19, 2017, reg.2(3)(e) of the Social Security (Emergency Funds) (Amendment) Regulations 2017 (SI 2017/689) inserted the words ", the London Emergencies Trust, the We Love Manchester Emergency Fund" after the words "the Scottish Infected Blood Support Scheme". Definitions of that Trust and Fund have been inserted in reg.2(1)—see the entries for pp.229 and 234 of Vol.II in this Supplement.

With effect from October 23, 2017, reg.8(3)(e) of the Social Security (Infected Blood and Thalidomide) Regulations 2017 (SI 2017/870) inserted the words ", an approved blood scheme" after the words "the Scottish Infected Blood Support Scheme" (and therefore before the previous amendment). A definition of "approved blood scheme" has been inserted in reg.2(1)—see the entry for p.226 of Vol.II in this Supplement.

3.022

p.672, *amendments to the Income Support (General) Regulations 1987 (SI 1987/1967) Sch.9 (Sums to be disregarded in the calculation of income other than earnings)*

With effect from November 3, 2017, art.2(5)(a) of the Social Services and Well-being (Wales) Act 2014 and the Regulation and Inspection of Social Care (Wales) Act 2016 (Consequential Amendments) Order 2017 (SI 2017/901) inserted a new head (ia) after head (i) of para.26(a):

3.023

"(ia) section 81(2) of the Social Services and Well-being (Wales) Act 2014 (ways in which looked after children are to be accommodated and maintained);"

From the same date, art.2(5)(b) of that Order inserted a new sub-para.(dzb) after sub-para.(dza) of para.27:

"(dzb)the person concerned where the payment is for the provision of accommodation to meet that person's need for care and support under section 35 or 36 of the Social Services and Well-being (Wales) Act 2014 (duty and power to meet care and support needs of an adult);"

From the same date, art.2(5)(c) of that Order amended para.28(1) by omitting the word "or" at the end of head (b), substituting the words "1995, or" for the word "1995" at the end of head (c) and inserting a new head (d):

"(d) the following sections of the Social Services and Well-being (Wales) Act 2014—
(aa) section 37 or 38, but excluding any direct payment made in accordance with regulations made under section 51 of that Act; or
(bb) section 109, 110, 114 or 115."

From the same date, art.20(3) of that Order substituted head (i) of para.26(1)(a) with the following:

"(i) section 22C(2) of the Children Act 1989 (ways in which looked after children are to be accommodated and maintained),"

With effect from November 7, 2017, reg.2(3) of the Social Security and Child Support (Care Payments and Tenant Incentive Scheme) (Amendment) Regulations 2017 (SI 2017/995) inserted the following provision after para.27:

"**27A.**—Any payment made to a claimant under section 73(1)(b) of the Children and Young People (Scotland) Act 2014 (kinship care assistance)."

Payments under s.73 have been available in Scotland since April 2016 to people who have applied or are at least considering applying for a kinship care order for a child who is at risk of going into care or was previously looked after by a local authority.

p.673, *amendments to the Income Support (General) Regulations 1987 (SI 1987/1967) Sch.9 (Sums to be disregarded in the calculation of income other than earnings)*

3.024   With effect from November 3, 2017, art.2(5)(d) of the Social Services and Well-being (Wales) Act 2014 and the Regulation and Inspection of Social Care (Wales) Act 2016 (Consequential Amendments) Order 2017 (SI 2017/901) inserted the words "or Part 4 of the Social Services and Well-being (Wales) Act 2014 (meeting needs) other than any direct payment made in accordance with regulations made under section 50 or 52 of that Act" at the end of para.30(1)(e)

From the same date, art.2(5)(e) of that Order inserted the words "or under section 35 or 36 of the Social Services and Well-being (Wales) Act 2014 (duty and power to meet care and support needs of an adult)" at the end of para.30A(2)(b).

pp.674-675, *amendments to the Income Support (General) Regulations 1987 (SI 1987/1967) Sch.9 para.39 (Sums to be disregarded in the calculation of income other than earnings)*

With effect from June 19, 2017, reg.2(3)(e) of the Social Security   3.025
(Emergency Funds) (Amendment) Regulations 2017 (SI 2017/689) inserted the words ", the London Emergencies Trust, the We Love Manchester Emergency Fund" after the words "the Scottish Infected Blood Support Scheme" in para.39(1) and (7). Definitions of that Trust and Fund have been inserted in reg.2(1)—see the entries for pp.229 and 234 of Vol.II in this Supplement.

With effect from October 23, 2017, reg.2(3)(e) of the Social Security (Infected Blood and Thalidomide) Regulations 2017 (SI 2017/870) inserted the words ", an approved blood scheme" after the words "the Scottish Infected Blood Support Scheme" in para.39(1) and (7) (and therefore before the previous amendment). A definition of "approved blood scheme" has been inserted in reg.2(1)—see the entry for p.226 of Vol.II in this Supplement.

pp.676-677, *amendments to the Income Support (General) Regulations 1987 (SI 1987/1967) Sch.9 (Sums to be disregarded in the calculation of income other than earnings)*

With effect from November 3, 2017, art.2(5)(f) of the Social Services   3.026
and Well-being (Wales) Act 2014 and the Regulation and Inspection of Social Care (Wales) Act 2016 (Consequential Amendments) Order 2017 (SI 2017/901) inserted the words ", or in accordance with regulations made under section 50 or 52 of the Social Services and Well-being (Wales) Act 2014 (direct payments)" at the end of para.58.

With effect from the same date, art.2(5)(g) of that Order inserted the words ", or the provision of care and support in respect of an adult under Part 4 of the Social Services and Well-being (Wales) Act 2014 (meeting needs)" after the words "2014 (care and support)" in para.66.

pp.705-707, *amendments to the Income Support (General) Regulations 1987 (SI 1987/1967) Sch.10 (Capital to be disregarded)*

With effect from June 19, 2017, reg.2(3)(f) of the Social Security   3.027
(Emergency Funds) (Amendment) Regulations 2017 (SI 2017/689) inserted the words ", the London Emergencies Trust, the We Love Manchester Emergency Fund" after the words "the Scottish Infected Blood Support Scheme" in para.22(1) and (7), but did not do so in para.29. Definitions of that Trust and Fund have been inserted in reg.2(1)—see the entries for pp.229 and 234 of Vol.II in this Supplement.

With effect from October 23, 2017, reg.2(3)(f) of the Social Security (Infected Blood and Thalidomide) Regulations 2017 (SI 2017/870) inserted the words ", an approved blood scheme" after the words "the Scottish Infected Blood Support Scheme" in paras 22(1) and (7) and 29 (and therefore after the previous amendment in para.22(1) and (7)). A definition of "approved blood scheme" has been inserted in reg.2(1)—see the entry for p.226 of Vol.II in this Supplement.

With effect from November 3, 2017, art.2(6)(a) of the Social Services and Well-being (Wales) Act 2014 and the Regulation and Inspection of Social Care (Wales) Act 2016 (Consequential Amendments) Order 2017 (SI 2017/901) amended para.17(1) by omitting the word "or" at the end of head (b), substituting the words "1995, or" for the word "1995" at the end of head (c) and inserting a new head (d):

"(d) the following sections of the Social Services and Well-being (Wales) Act 2014—
    (aa) section 37 or 38, but excluding any direct payment made in accordance with regulations made under section 51 of that Act; or
    (bb) section 109.110, 114 or 115."

p.708, *amendment to the Income Support (General) Regulations 1987 (SI 1987/1967) Sch.10 (Capital to be disregarded)*

3.028   With effect from November 3, 2017, art.2(6)(b) of the Social Services and Well-being (Wales) Act 2014 and the Regulation and Inspection of Social Care (Wales) Act 2016 (Consequential Amendments) Order 2017 (SI 2017/901) amended para.43 by inserting the words "or under Part 4 of the Social Services and Well-being (Wales) Act 2014" after the word "1958".

p.710, *amendments to the Income Support (General) Regulations 1987 (SI 1987/1967) Sch.10 (Capital to be disregarded)*

3.029   With effect from October 23, 2017, reg.2(5) of the Social Security (Infected Blood and Thalidomide) Regulations 2017 (SI 2017/870) inserted the following new para.73 after para.72:

"73.—Any payment made under or by a trust, established for the purpose of giving relief and assistance to disabled persons whose disabilities were caused by the fact that during their mother's pregnancy she had taken a preparation containing the drug known as Thalidomide, and which is approved by the Secretary of State."

With effect from November 3, 2017, art.2(6)(c) of the Social Services and Well-being (Wales) Act 2014 and the Regulation and Inspection of Social Care (Wales) Act 2016 (Consequential Amendments) Order 2017 (SI 2017/901) amended para.67 by inserting the words ", or in accordance with regulations made under section 50 or 52 of the Social Services and Well-being (Wales) Act 2014 (direct payments)" at the end.

With effect from November 7, 2017, reg.2(4) of the Social Security and Child Support (Care Payments and Tenant Incentive Scheme) (Amendment) Regulations 2017 (SI 2017/995) inserted the following provision after para.73:

"**74.**—Any payment made to a claimant under section 73(1)(b) of the Children and Young People (Scotland) Act 2014 (kinship care assistance)."

Payments under s.73 have been available in Scotland since April 2016 to people who have applied or are at least considering applying for a kinship care order for a child who is at risk of going into care or was previously looked after by a local authority.

pp.840-841, *commentary to Immigration (European Economic Area) Regulations 2016 (SI 2016/1052) (The personal scope of the Citizenship Directive—decision of the CJEU in Lounes v Secretary of State for the Home Department)*

The decision of the Grand Chamber of the CJEU in *Lounes v Secretary*   3.030
of State for the Home Department (Case C-165/16) was given on November 14, 2017. The Court was considering circumstances in which Ms O, a Spanish national, had exercised her rights to freedom of movement to live and work in the UK and become a naturalised British citizen, while retaining her Spanish nationality. She subsequently married Mr Lounes who was an Algerian national and, under domestic immigration law, an illegal overstayer. Mr Lounes then applied for the issue of a residence card as a family member of an EEA national (i.e., under reg.18). That application was refused and he was served with notice of a decision to remove him from the UK as an overstayer. Under UK law the third country national family members of the EEA national cannot derive a right of residence as a family member because, by becoming British, the EEA National has ceased to be an "EEA National" as defined in see reg.2(1).
The Grand Chamber ruled that, although the UK was correct to say that Ms O (and Mr Lounes) ceased to be beneficiaries of the Directive when she became British, Mr Lounes derived a right of residence directly from Art 21(1) TFEU "on conditions which must not be stricter than those provided for by [the] Directive". The Court's formal ruling was in the following terms:

"[The Citizenship Directive] must be interpreted as meaning that, in a situation in which a citizen of the European Union (i) has exercised his freedom of movement by moving to and residing in a Member State other than that of which he is a national, under Article 7(1) or Article 16(1) of that directive, (ii) has then acquired the nationality of that Member State, while also retaining his nationality of origin, and (iii) several years later, has married a third-country national with whom he continues to reside in that Member State, that third-country national does not have a derived right of residence in the Member State in question on the basis of [the Citizenship Directive].
    The third-country national is however eligible for a derived right of residence under Article 21(1) TFEU, on conditions which must not be stricter than those provided for by [the Citizenship Directive] for the grant of such a right to a third-country national who is a family member of a Union citizen who has exercised his right of freedom of

movement by settling in a Member State other than the Member State of which he is a national."

p.844, *annotation to the Immigration (European Economic Area) Regulations 2016 (SI 2016/1052)—Compatibility of the right to reside test with EU law—Commentary on Mirga v Secretary of State for Work and Pensions)*

3.031   For examples of cases decided by the Upper Tribunal after the decision of the Supreme Court in *Mirga v Secretary of State for Work and Pensions* [2016] UKSC 1; [2016] AACR 26, see *MM v SWP (ESA)* [2017] UKUT 437 (AAC) and *LO v SSWP (IS)* [2017] UKUT 440 (AAC) both of which demonstrate how very exceptional a claimant's circumstances would have to be to fall into the (possible) category of exceptional cases in which an individual consideration of those circumstances might be required by the principle of proportionality.

pp.860, *annotation to the Immigration (European Economic Area) Regulations 2016 (SI 2016/1052) reg.4 ("Worker", "self-employed person", "self-sufficient person" and "student"—self-sufficient person—sufficient resources—decision of the CJEU in* Gusa v Minister for Social Protection, Ireland, Attorney General*)*

3.031.1   The decision of the CJEU in *Gusa v Minister for Social Protection, Ireland, Attorney General* (Case C-442/16) was given on December 20, 2017. The Court did not follow the advice of Advocate General Wathelet who proposed that the it should rule that: "(1) Article 16(1) of [the Citizenship Directive] must be interpreted as meaning that it confers a right of permanent residence on a Member State national who has resided in the territory of the host Member State for an uninterrupted period of five years without relying on the social assistance system of that host Member State."

p.864, *annotation to the Immigration (European Economic Area) Regulations 2016 (SI 2016/1052) reg.5 ("Worker or self-employed person who has ceased activity"—Legal or actual residence—decision of the Court of Appeal in* Secretary of State for Work and Pensions v Gubeladze*)*

3.032   The decision of the Court of Appeal in *Secretary of State for Work and Pensions v Gubeladze* [2017] EWCA Civ 1751 (i.e. the appeal against the decision of Upper Tribunal Judge Ward in *TG v SSWP (PC)* [2015] UKUT 50 (AAC)) was given on November 7, 2017. The Court held (at para.50) that the word "reside" in Article 17(1)(a) of the Citizens Directive means "legally reside" and preferred the decision of Upper Tribunal Judge Jacobs in *ID v SSWP (IS)* [2011] UKUT 401 (AAC) to that of Upper Tribunal Judge Ward. It follows that the word "reside" (and cognate words) in reg.5 also require legal residence and not just actual residence.

p.864, *annotation to the Immigration (European Economic Area) Regulations 2016 (SI 2016/1052) reg.6 ("Qualified person"—Retaining worker status—Temporarily unable to work)*

The meaning of "temporarily unable to work" was further considered   3.033
by the Upper Tribunal (Judge Jacobs) in *HK v SSWP* [2017] UKUT 421 (AAC). After quoting from para.35 in his previous decision, CIS/4304/2007 (see main text) he added:

"4 . . . . In other words, the claimant's ability to work has to be decided as a purely factual matter without regard to the particular tests applied by domestic legislation, in this case the employment and support allowance legislation. This is subject to two qualifications.
5. First, there is a difference between the test that has to be applied and the evidence that is relevant to the test. Accordingly, the way that the employment and support allowance legislation would apply to the claimant may be relevant as evidence of inability to work.
6. Second, there is a difference between the basis of the right to reside and the entitlement to benefit. If the claimant wishes to claim for a period before the date when he submitted his claim, his *entitlement* during that period will be determined by the domestic legislation."

pp.873-875, *annotation to the Immigration (European Economic Area) Regulations 2016 (SI 2016/1052) reg.6 ("Qualified person"—Retaining worker status—Involuntary unemployment—the so-called "Genuine Prospects of Work" test)*

In *OS v SSWP (JSA)* [2017] UKUT 107 (AAC), the Upper Tribunal   3.034
(Judge Ward) confirmed that where a claimant obtains employment after the date of the Secretary of State's decision refusing jobseeker's allowance, that circumstance can be taken into account as evidence that she had a genuine chance of being engaged as at the date of that decision. Section 12(8)(b) of the Social Security Act 1998, which prevents the First-tier Tribunal from considering circumstances not obtaining at the date of the decision under appeal, "does not preclude inferences being drawn from events which occurred after the decision date about circumstances obtaining when, or before, the decision was made: see, inter alia, *R(DLA) 2/01* and *3/01*".

pp.879-880, *annotation to the Immigration (European Economic Area) Regulations 2016 (SI 2016/1052) reg.6 ("Qualified person—Retaining self-employed status—Decision of the CJEU in* Gusa v Minister for Social Protection, Ireland, Attorney General)

The decision of the CJEU in *Gusa v Minister for Social Protection,*   3.034.1
Ireland, Attorney General (Case C-442/16) was given on December 20, 2017. The Court ruled that:

"Article 7(3)(b) of [the Citizenship Directive] must be interpreted as meaning that a national of a Member State retains the status of self-employed person for the purposes of Article 7(1)(a) of that directive where, after having lawfully resided in and worked as a self-employed person in another Member State for approximately four years, that national has ceased that activity, because of a duly recorded absence of work owing to reasons beyond his control, and has registered as a jobseeker with the relevant employment office of the latter Member State."

That ruling reflects the facts of the individual case. Paragraph 45 of the judgment makes it clear that it applies whenever anyone has been self-employed for over a year.

Such a person retains self-employed status and is not a jobseeker (*i.e.*, in the EU sense). S/he can therefore claim social assistance (i.e., IS. HB, IRESA, SPC and, importantly, UC).

The decisions in *SSWP v RK* [2009] UKUT 209 (AAC) and *R. (Tilianu) v Secretary of State for Work and Pensions* [2010] EWCA Civ 1397 cannot be reconciled with the decision in *Gusa* and will need to be reconsidered.

It remains to be decided whether someone who has been self-employed for less than a year has equivalent rights to a person who has been employed for less that a year.

p.898, *annotation to the Immigration (European Economic Area) Regulations 2016 (SI 2016/1052) reg.13 (Initial right of residence)*

3.035   The decision in *GE v SSWP (ESA)* [2017] UKUT 145 (AAC) is to be reported as [2017] AACR 34.

p.898, *annotation to the Immigration (European Economic Area) Regulations 2016 (SI 2016/1052) reg.14 (Extended right of residence)*

3.036   The extended right of residence conferred on a "family member who has retained the right of residence" by reg.14(3) is not a right that is excluded by reg.21AA(3)(b)(ii) of the IS Regulations (or, by parity of reasoning, by the equivalent provisions of the JSA Regulations, the SPC Regulations, the ESA Regulations and the UC Regulations): see the decision of the Inner House of the Court of Session in *Slezak v Secretary of State for Work and Pensions* [2017] CSIH 4, [2017] AACR 21 at [30].

p.907, *annotation to the Immigration (European Economic Area) Regulations 2016 (SI 2016/1052) reg.15 (Right of permanent residence— A8 and A2 nationals—reference to the CJEU in RP v SSWP)*

3.037   The reference to the CJEU made by Upper Tribunal Judge Ward in *RP v SSWP* (ESA) [2016] UKUT 422 (AAC) has now been registered by the CJEU as *Rafal Prefeta v Secretary of State for Work and Pensions* (Case C-618/16). The questions referred are as follows:

"Did Annex XII of the Treaty of Accession permit Member States to exclude Polish nationals from the benefits of Article 7(2) of the Workers Regulation and Article 7(3) of the Citizenship Directive where the

worker, though he had belatedly complied with the national requirement that his employment be registered, had not yet worked for an
uninterrupted registered twelve month period?

If the answer to the first question is "no," may a Polish national
worker in the circumstances in question 1 rely on Article 7(3) of the
Citizenship Directive which concerns retention of worker status?"

The CJEU heard the reference on January 11, 2018. At the time of
going to press, no date has been appointed for the delivery of the
Advocate General's opinion.

p.907, *annotation to the Immigration (European Economic Area)
Regulations 2016 (SI 2016/1052) reg.15 (Permanent right of residence—
The position of jobseekers and their family members under UK domestic
law)*

The decision in *GE v SSWP (ESA)* [2017] UKUT 145 (AAC) is to be 3.038
reported as [2017] AACR 34.

p.908, *annotation to the Immigration (European Economic Area)
Regulations 2016 (SI 2016/1052) reg.15 (Right of permanent residence—
A8 and A2 nationals—decision of the Court of Appeal in Secretary of State
for Work and Pensions v Gubeladze)*

The decision of the Court of Appeal in *Secretary of State for Work and* 3.039
Pensions v Gubeladze [2017] EWCA Civ 1751 (i.e. the appeal against the
decision of Upper Tribunal Judge Ward in *TG v SSWP (PC)* [2015]
UKUT 50 (AAC)) was given on November 7, 2017. The Court held (at
para.81) that there was no error of law in the Judge Ward's conclusion
that the Accession (Immigration and Worker Registration) (Amendment) Regulations 2009 (SI 2009/892) were disproportionate and therefore incompatible with EU law. It is understood that the Secretary of
State is seeking permission to appeal to the Supreme Court against this
aspect of the decision.

p.908, *annotation to the Immigration (European Economic Area)
Regulations 2016 (SI 2016/1052) reg.15 (Right of permanent residence—
A8 and A2 nationals—decision of the UT in SSWP v NZ (ESA) (Third
interim decision))*

In *SSWP v NZ (ESA) (Third interim decision)* [2017] UKUT 360 3.040
(AAC), the Upper Tribunal (Judge Ward) decided that neither the
Accession (Immigration and Worker Registration) Regulations 2004 nor
any other provision effected a valid derogation from art.17 of the Directive. As a person who would—but for the impact of the worker registration scheme—otherwise on any view have been a worker, the claimant's
inability to point to 12 months of registered work did not preclude her
from relying on art.17 if she could satisfy its remaining conditions.

p.912, *annotation to the Immigration (European Economic Area) Regulations 2016 (SI 2016/1052) reg.16 (Derivative right to reside— Parents of British children—decision of the Supreme Court in R (HC) v Secretary of State for Work and Pensions and others)*

3.041   The decision of the Supreme Court in *R (HC) v Secretary of State for Work and Pensions and others* [2017] UKSC 73 (i.e. the appeal against the decision of the Court of Appeal in *Sanneh v Secretary of State for Work and Pensions* [2015] EWCA Civ 49) was given on November 15, 2017. The Supreme Court unanimously upheld the decision in *Sanneh* with the effect that, from November 8, 2012, a right to reside as a *Zambrano* carer does not count for the purposes of any social security benefit or tax credit.

p.987, *amendment to the Jobseeker's Allowance Regulations 1996 (SI 1996/207) reg.1(3) (Interpretation: definition of "approved blood scheme")*

3.042   With effect from October 23, 2017, reg.3(1) and (2)(a) of the Social Security (Infected Blood and Thalidomide) Regulations 2017 (SI 2017/870) amended reg.2(1) by adding the following definition after the definition of "adoption leave":

""approved blood scheme" means a scheme established or approved by the Secretary of State, or trust established with funds provided by the Secretary of State, for the purpose of providing compensation in respect of a person having been infected from contaminated blood products;"

p.994, *amendment to the Jobseeker's Allowance Regulations 1996 (SI 1996/207) reg.1(3) (Interpretation: definition of "the London Emergencies Trust")*

3.043   With effect from June 19, 2017, reg.3(1) and (2)(a) of the Social Security (Emergency Funds) (Amendment) Regulations 2017 (SI 2017/689) amended reg.1(3) by adding the following definition after the definition of "the London Bombings Relief Charitable Fund":

""the London Emergencies Trust" means the company of that name (number 09928465) incorporated on 23rd December 2015 and the registered charity of that name (number 1172307) established on 28th March 2017;"

p.996, *amendment to the Jobseeker's Allowance Regulations 1996 (SI 1996/207) reg.1(3) (Interpretation: definition of "qualifying person")*

3.044   With effect from June 19, 2017, reg.3(1) and (2)(b) of the Social Security (Emergency Funds) (Amendment) Regulations 2017 (SI 2017/689) amended the definition of "qualifying person" in reg.1(3) to read as follows:

""qualifying person" means a person in respect of whom payment has been made from the Fund, the Eileen Trust, MFET Limited, the Skipton Fund, the Caxton Foundation, the Scottish Infected Blood

Support Scheme [, the London Emergencies Trust, the We Love Manchester Emergency Fund] or the London Bombings Relief Charitable Fund"

With effect from October 23, 2017, reg.2(1) and (2)(b) of the Social Security (Infected Blood and Thalidomide) Regulations 2017 (SI 2017/870) further amended that definition to read as follows:

""qualifying person" means a person in respect of whom payment has been made from the Fund, the Eileen Trust, MFET Limited, the Skipton Fund, the Caxton Foundation, the Scottish Infected Blood Support Scheme [, an approved blood scheme], the London Emergencies Trust, the We Love Manchester Emergency Fund or the London Bombings Relief Charitable Fund"

p.998, *amendment to Jobseeker's Allowance Regulations 1996 (SI 1996/207) reg.1(3) (Interpretation: definition of "traineeship")*

With effect from November 6, 2017, reg.2 of the Social Security **3.045** (Qualifying Young Persons Participating in Relevant Training Schemes) (Amendment) Regulations 2017 (SI 2017/987) amended the definition of "traineeship" in reg.1(3) to read as follows:

""traineeship" means a course which—
(a) is funded (in whole or in part) by, or under arrangements made by, the—
  (i) Secretary of State under section 14 of the Education Act 2002, or
  (ii) Chief Executive of [Education and Skills Funding];
(b) lasts no more than 6 months;
(c) includes training to help prepare the participant for work and a work experience placement; and
(d) is open to persons who on the first day of the course have attained the age of 16 but not 25:"

p.999, *amendment to Jobseeker's Allowance Regulations 1996 (SI 1996/207) reg.1(3) (Interpretation: definition of "the We Love Manchester Emergency Fund")*

With effect from June 19, 2017, reg.3(1) and (2)(c) of the Social **3.046** Security (Emergency Funds) (Amendment) Regulations 2017 (SI 2017/689) amended reg.1(3) by adding the following definition after the definition of "water charges":

""the We Love Manchester Emergency Fund" means the registered charity of that name (number 1173260) established on 30th May 2017;"

p.1046, *amendment to the Jobseeker's Allowance Regulations 1996 (SI 1996/207) reg.14A(10) (Victims of domestic violence)*

With effect from November 3, 2017, art.19 of the Social Services and **3.047** Well-being (Wales) Act 2014 and the Regulation and Inspection of

Social Care (Wales) Act 2016 (Consequential Amendments) Order 2017 (SI 2017/901) substituted para.(b) of the definition of "registered social worker" with the following:

"(b) Social Care Wales,"

p.1069, *annotation to the Jobseeker's Allowance Regulations 1996 (SI 1996/207) reg.18 (Steps to be taken by persons actively seeking employment)*

3.048   In para.25 of *PG v SSWP (JSA)* [2017] UKUT 388 (AAC) the judge suggested (in a passage not necessary to the decision), in response to a tribunal's statement that there was no objection in principle to requiring a claimant to engage in actively seeking work as a full time task, that it might take very cogent reasoning to justify a person having to take very well in excess of the three steps per week that are the starting point under reg.18(1).

p.1114, *amendment to Jobseeker's Allowance Regulations (SI 1996/207) reg.53 (Persons not treated as engaged in remunerative work)*

3.049   With effect from November 7, 2017, reg.11(1) and (2) of the Social Security and Child Support (Care Payments and Tenant Incentive Scheme) (Amendment) Regulations 2017 (SI 2017/995) amended reg.53(1) by inserting the following sub-paragraph after sub-para. (f):

"(fa) he is engaged in caring for a person who is provided with continuing care by a local authority by virtue of arrangements made under section 26A of the Children (Scotland) Act 1995 (duty to provide continuing care) and is in receipt of a payment made under that section of that Act;"

p.1131, *amendment to the Jobseeker's Allowance Regulations 1996 (SI 1996/207) reg.60 (Young persons at the end of the child benefit extension period)*

3.050   With effect from November 3, 2017, art.6(1) and (2) of the Social Services and Well-being (Wales) Act 2014 and the Regulation and Inspection of Social Care (Wales) Act 2016 (Consequential Amendments) Order 2017 (SI 2017/901) substituted the following for reg.60(1)(a):

"(a) a person who has ceased to live in accommodation provided for him by a local authority under—
    (i) Part 3 of the Children Act 1989 (local authority support children and families), or
    (ii) Part 4 (meeting needs) or 6 (looked after and accommodated children) of the Social Services and Well-being (Wales) Act 2014, and
    is of necessity living away from his parents and any person acting in place of his parents;"

pp.1164-1166, *amendment to Jobseeker's Allowance Regulations 1996 (SI 1996/207) reg.78 (Circumstances in which a person is to be treated as being or not being a member of the household: definition of "accommodation")*

With effect from November 3, 2017, art.6(1) and (3) of the Social Services and Well-being (Wales) Act 2014 and the Regulation and Inspection of Social Care (Wales) Act 2016 (Consequential Amendments) Order 2017 (SI 2017/901) amended reg.78 by inserting a new sub-para.(4)(aa) after sub-para.(4)(a) as follows:
3.051

"(aa) placed with the claimant or his partner by a local authority under section 81(2) of the Social Services and Well-being (Wales) Act 2014; or",

by amending the definition of "accommodation" in sub-para.(9)(za) to read as follows:

"(za) "accommodation" means accommodation provided by a local authority in a home owned or managed by that local authority—
   (i) under sections 21 to 24 of the National Assistance Act 1948 (provision of accommodation),
   (ia) under section 18 or 19 of the Care Act 2014 (duty and power to meet needs for care and support); or
   (ii) in Scotland, under section 13B or 59 of the Social Work (Scotland) Act 1968 (provision of residential or other establishment), or
   (iii) under section 25 of the Mental Health (Care and Treatment) (Scotland) Act 2003 (care and support services etc.), [or
   (vi) under section 35 or 36 of the Social Services and Well-being (Wales) Act 2014 (duty and power to meet care and support needs of an adult),]
where the accommodation is provided for a person whose stay in that accommodation has become other than temporary;]",

and by amending the definition of "relevant enactment" in sub-para.(9)(a) to read as follows

"(a) "relevant enactment" means the Army Act 1955, the Social Work (Scotland) Act 1968, the Matrimonial Causes Act 1973, the Adoption (Scotland) Act 1978, the Family Law Act 1986 [, the Children Act 1989 and the Social Services and Well-being (Wales) Act 2014];"

p.1201, *amendments to the Jobseeker's Allowance Regulations 1996 (SI 1996/207) reg.100(2)(b) (Earnings of self-employed earners)*

With effect from November 7, 2017, reg.3(2) of the Social Security and Child Support (Care Payments and Tenant Incentive Scheme) (Amendment) Regulations 2017 (SI 2017/995) made the following amendments. The words "27, 28 or 28A" were substituted for the words
3.052

"27 or 28". The words ", payments" were substituted for the words "and payments". The words "and any payments made to a claimant under section 73(1)(b) of the Children and Young People (Scotland) Act 2014 (kinship care assistance)" were added after the words "claimant's care".

Payments under s.73 have been available in Scotland since April 2016 to people who have applied or are at least considering applying for a kinship care order for a child who is at risk of going into care or was previously looked after by a local authority.

With effect from the same date, reg.11(3) inserted the following provisions. After sub-para.(b) was inserted:

"(ba) any payment made in accordance with section 26A of the Children (Scotland) Act 1995 (duty to provide continuing care)—
  (i) to a claimant; or
  (ii) where paragraph (3) applies, to another person ("A") which A passes on to the claimant;".

After the end of para.(2) was inserted:

"(3) This paragraph applies only where A—
  (a) was formerly in the claimant' s care;
  (b) is aged 16 or over; and
  (c) continues to live with the claimant.".

p.1215, *amendment to the Jobseeker's Allowance Regulations 1996 (SI 1996/207) reg.105(4) (Notional income)*

3.053 With effect from November 16, 2017, reg.8 of the Social Security (Miscellaneous Amendments No.4) Regulations 2017 (SI 2017/1015) substituted the words "rate of the annuity which may have been purchased with the fund" for the words "maximum amount of income which may be withdrawn from the fund". The Claims and Payments Regulations have been amended from the same date to require pension fund holders to provide information as to that rate on request.

p.1216, *amendments to the Jobseeker's Allowance Regulations 1996 (SI 1996/207) reg.105(10A)(a) (Notional income)*

3.054 With effect from June 19, 2017, reg.3(3)(a) of the Social Security (Emergency Funds) (Amendment) Regulations 2017 (SI 2017/689) inserted the words ", the London Emergencies Trust, the We Love Manchester Emergency Fund" after the words "the Scottish Infected Blood Support Scheme". Definitions of that Trust and Fund have been inserted in reg.1(3)—see the entries for pp.994 and 999 of Vol.II in this Supplement.

With effect from October 23, 2017, reg.3(3)(a) of the Social Security (Infected Blood and Thalidomide) Regulations 2017 (SI 2017/870) inserted the words ", an approved blood scheme" after the words "the Scottish Infected Blood Support Scheme" (and therefore before the previous amendment). A definition of "approved blood scheme" has been inserted in reg.1(3)—see the entry for p.987 of Vol.II in this Supplement.

pp.1224-1225, *amendments to the Jobseeker's Allowance Regulations 1996 (SI 1996/207) reg.110(10)(c) (Income treated as capital)*

With effect from June 19, 2017, reg.3(3)(b) of the Social Security   3.055
(Emergency Funds) (Amendment) Regulations 2017 (SI 2017/689) inserted the words ", the London Emergencies Trust, the We Love Manchester Emergency Fund" after the words "the Scottish Infected Blood Support Scheme". Definitions of that Trust and Fund have been inserted in reg.1(3)—see the entries for pp.994 and 999 of Vol.II in this Supplement.

With effect from October 23, 2017, reg.3(3)(b) of the Social Security (Infected Blood and Thalidomide) Regulations 2017 (SI 2017/870) inserted the words ", an approved blood scheme" after the words "the Scottish Infected Blood Support Scheme" (and therefore before the previous amendment). A definition of "approved blood scheme" has been inserted in reg.1(3)—see the entry for p.987 of Vol.II in this Supplement.

p.1228, *amendments to the Jobseeker's Allowance Regulations 1996 (SI 1996/207) reg.113(3A)(a) (Notional capital)*

With effect from June 19, 2017, reg.3(3)(c) of the Social Security   3.056
(Emergency Funds) (Amendment) Regulations 2017 (SI 2017/689) inserted the words ", the London Emergencies Trust, the We Love Manchester Emergency Fund" after the words "the Scottish Infected Blood Support Scheme". Definitions of that Trust and Fund have been inserted in reg.1(3)—see the entries for pp.994 and 999 of Vol.II in this Supplement.

With effect from October 23, 2017, reg.3(3)(c) of the Social Security (Infected Blood and Thalidomide) Regulations 2017 (SI 2017/870) inserted the words ", an approved blood scheme" after the words "the Scottish Infected Blood Support Scheme" (and therefore before the previous amendment). A definition of "approved blood scheme" has been inserted in reg.1(3)—see the entries for pp.994 and 999 of Vol.II in this Supplement.

p.1247, *amendment to the Jobseeker's Allowance Regulations 1996 (SI 1996/207) reg.131(2)(j) (Calculation of grant income)*

With effect from November 3, 2017, art.6(4) of the Social Services   3.057
and Well-being (Wales) Act 2014 and the Regulation and Inspection of Social Care (Wales) Act 2016 (Consequential Amendments) Order 2017

(SI 2017/901) inserted the words "or Part 6 of the Social Services and Well-being (Wales) Act 2014" after the word "1989".

p.1259-1261, *amendment to the Jobseeker's Allowance Regulations 1996 (SI 1996/207) reg.140 (Meaning of "person in hardship")*

3.058   With effect from October 23, 2017, reg.2(1) and (2) of the Jobseeker's Allowance (Hardship) (Amendment) Regulations 2017 (SI 2017/760) amended reg.140(1)(g) to read as follows:

> "(g) suffers, or whose partner suffers from a chronic medical condition which results in functional capacity being limited or restricted by physical [or mental] impairment and the Secretary of State is satisfied that—
> > (i) the suffering has already lasted, or is likely to last, for not less than 26 weeks; and
> > (ii) unless a jobseeker's allowance is paid to the claimant the probability is that the health of the person suffering would, within 2 weeks of the Secretary of State making his decision, decline further than that of a normally healthy adult and that person would suffer hardship;",

inserted "or" after the semicolon at the end of sub-paras (j) and "; or" before the full-stop at the end of sub-para.(k) and inserted a new sub-para.(l) after sub-para.(k) as follows:

> "(l) is a person who is homeless within the meaning of Part 7 of the Housing Act 1996, Part 2 of the Housing (Wales) Act 2014 or Part 2 of the Housing (Scotland) Act 1987, as the case may be."

With effect from November 3, 2017, art.6(1) and (5) of the Social Services and Well-being (Wales) Act 2014 and the Regulation and Inspection of Social Care (Wales) Act 2016 (Consequential Amendments) Order 2017 (SI 2017/901) amended reg.140(1)(k) to read as follows:

> "(k) is a person—
> > (i) who, pursuant to the Children Act 1989 [or the Social Services and Well-being (Wales) Act 2014], was being looked after by a local authority;
> > (ii) with whom the local authority had a duty, pursuant to [either of those Acts], to take reasonable steps to keep in touch; or
> > (iii) who, pursuant to [either of those Acts], qualified for advice and assistance from a local authority,
> > but in respect of whom (i), (ii) or, as the case may be, (iii) above had not applied for a period of three years or less as at the date on which he complies with the requirements of regulation 143; and
> > (iv) as at the date on which he complies with the requirements of regulation 143, is under the age of 21."

p.1266, *amendment to Jobseeker's Allowance Regulations 1996 (SI 1996/207) reg.141 (Circumstances in which an income-based jobseeker's allowance is payable to a person in hardship)*

With effect from October 23, 2017, reg.2(1) and (3) of the Jobseeker's Allowance (Hardship) (Amendment) Regulations 2017 (SI 2017/760) amended reg.141(2) to read as follows: **3.059**

"(2) Subject to paragraph (3) a person in hardship, other than a person to whom regulation 46(1) (waiting days) applies, shall be treated as entitled to an income-based jobseeker's allowance for the period beginning with the 8th day of the jobseeking period or, if later, from the day he first becomes a person in hardship and ending on the day before the claim is determined where the sole reason for the delay in determining the claim is that a question arises as to whether the claimant satisfies any of the conditions of entitlement specified in section 1(2)(a) to (c) provided he satisfies the conditions of entitlement specified in [paragraph (b) of subsection (2A)] of section 1."

pp.1272–1274, *amendment to the Jobseeker's Allowance Regulations 1996 (SI 1996/207) reg.146A (Meaning of "couple in hardship")*

With effect from October 23, 2017, reg.2(1) and (4) of the Jobseeker's Allowance (Hardship) (Amendment) Regulations 2017 (SI 2017/760) amended reg.146A(1)(d) to read as follows: **3.060**

"(d) either member of the couple suffers from a chronic medical condition which results in functional capacity being limited or restricted by physical [or mental] impairment and the Secretary of State is satisfied that—
  (i) the suffering has already lasted or is likely to last, for not less than 26 weeks; and
  (ii) unless a joint-claim jobseeker's allowance is paid, the probability is that the health of the person suffering would, within two weeks of the Secretary of State making his decision, decline further than that of a normally healthy adult and the member of the couple who suffers from that condition would suffer hardship;"

inserted "or" after the semicolon at the end of sub-para.(g) and ", or" before the full-stop at the end of sub-para. (h) and inserted a new sub-para.(i) after sub-para.(h) as follows:

"(i) either member of the couple is a person who is homeless within the meaning of Part 7 of the Housing Act 1996, Part 2 of the Housing (Wales) Act 2014 or Part 2 of the Housing (Scotland) Act 1987, as the case may be."

With effect from November 3, 2017, art.6(1) and (6) of the Social Services and Well-being (Wales) Act 2014 and the Regulation and Inspection of Social Care (Wales) Act 2016 (Consequential Amendments) Order 2017 (SI 2017/901) amended reg.146A(1)(h) to read as follows:

"(h) one or both members of the couple is a person—
   (i) who, pursuant to the Children Act 1989 [or the Social Services and Well-being (Wales) Act 2014], was being looked after by a local authority;
   (ii) with whom the local authority had a duty, pursuant to [either of those Acts], to take reasonable steps to keep in touch; or
   (iii) who, pursuant to [either of those Acts], qualified for advice or assistance from a local authority,
   but in respect of whom head (i), (ii) or, as the case may be, (iii) above had not applied for a period of three years or less as at the date on which the requirements of regulation 146F are complied with; and
   (iv) as at the date on which the requirements of regulation 146F are complied with, that member is, or both of those members are, under the age of 21."

p.1312, *amendment to the Jobseeker's Allowance Regulations 1996 (SI 1996/207) Sch.2 para.1(3) (Housing costs: definition of "disabled person")*

3.061   With effect from June 23, 2017, reg.3 of the Employment and Support Allowance (Miscellaneous Amendments and Transitional and Savings Provision) Regulations 2017 (SI 2017/581) amended para.1(3)(e)(i) of Sch.2 to read as follows:

"(i) is in receipt of an employment and support allowance which includes an amount under section 2(2) or 4(4) of the Welfare Reform Act (component) [or who is a member of the work-related activity group];"

The transitional and saving provision in reg.10 of SI 2017/581 has the effect that this amendment only applies to claimants who are not protected by the transitional protections in the Employment and Support Allowance and Universal Credit (Miscellaneous Amendments and Transitional and Savings Provisions) Regulations 2017 (SI 2017/204): see paras 9.613-9.623 of Vol.I, and paras 3.564-3.574 of Vol.V, of the main work.

p.1326, *amendment to the Jobseeker's Allowance Regulations 1996 (SI 1996/207) Sch.2 para.17 (housing costs)*

3.062   With effect from June 19, 2017, reg.3(1) and (3)(d) of the Social Security (Emergency Funds) (Amendment) Regulations 2017 (SI 2017/689) amended Sch.2 by inserting the words ", the London Emergencies Trust, the We Love Manchester Emergency Fund" after the words "the Scottish Infected Blood Support Scheme" in para. 17(8)(b).

With effect from October 23, 2017, reg.3(1), (3)(d) and (4) of the Social Security (Infected Blood and Thalidomide) Regulations 2017 (SI 2017/870) further amended Sch.2 by inserting the words ", an approved blood scheme" after the words "the Scottish Infected Blood Support

Scheme" in para.17(8)(b) and inserting a new para.17(8)(d) as follows:

"(d) any payment made under or by a trust, established for the purpose of giving relief and assistance to disabled persons whose disabilities were caused by the fact that during their mother's pregnancy she had taken a preparation containing the drug known as Thalidomide, and which is approved by the Secretary of State."

p.1354, *amendments to the Jobseeker's Allowance Regulations 1996 (SI 1996/207) Sch.7 para.22(2) (Sums to be disregarded in the calculation of income other than earnings)*

With effect from June 19, 2017, reg.3(3)(e) of the Social Security 3.063 (Emergency Funds) (Amendment) Regulations 2017 (SI 2017/689) inserted the words ", the London Emergencies Trust, the We Love Manchester Emergency Fund" after the words "the Scottish Infected Blood Support Scheme". Definitions of that Trust and Fund have been inserted in reg.1(3)—see the entries for pp.994 and 999 of Vol.II in this Supplement.

With effect from October 23, 2017, reg.3(3)(e) of the Social Security (Infected Blood and Thalidomide) Regulations 2017 (SI 2017/870) inserted the words ", an approved blood scheme" after the words "the Scottish Infected Blood Support Scheme" (and therefore before the previous amendment). A definition of "approved blood scheme" has been inserted in reg.1(3)—see the entry for p.987 of Vol.II in this Supplement.

p.1355, *amendments to the Jobseeker's Allowance Regulations 1996 (SI 1996/207) Sch.7 (Sums to be disregarded in the calculation of income other than earnings)*

With effect from November 3, 2017, art.6(7)(a) of the Social Services 3.064 and Well-being (Wales) Act 2014 and the Regulation and Inspection of Social Care (Wales) Act 2016 (Consequential Amendments) Order 2017 (SI 2017/901) inserted a new head (ia) after head (i) of para.27(a):

"(ia)   section 81(2) of the Social Services and Well-being (Wales) Act 2014 (ways in which looked after children are to be accommodated and maintained);"

From the same date, art.6(7)(b) of that Order inserted a new sub-para.(dzb) after sub-para.(dza) of para.27:

"(dzb)the person concerned where the payment is for the provision of accommodation to meet that person's need for care and support under section 35 or 36 of the Social Services and Well-being (Wales) Act 2014 (duty and power to meet care and support needs of an adult);"

From the same date, art.6(7)(c) of that Order amended para.29(1) by omitting the word "or" at the end of head (b), substituting the words

"1995, or" for the word "1995" at the end of head (c) and inserting a new head (d):

"(d) the following sections of the Social Services and Well-being (Wales) Act 2014—
 (aa) section 37 or 38, but excluding any direct payment made in accordance with regulations made under section 51 of that Act; or
 (bb) section 109.110, 114 or 115."

From the same date, art.21(3) of that Order substituted head (i) of para.27(a) with the following:

"(i) section 22C(2) of the Children Act 1989 (ways in which looked after children are to be accommodated and maintained),"

With effect from November 7, 2017, reg.3(3) of the Social Security and Child Support (Care Payments and Tenant Incentive Scheme) (Amendment) Regulations 2017 (SI 2017/995) inserted the following provision after para.28:

"**28A.**—Any payment made to a claimant under section 73(1)(b) of the Children and Young People (Scotland) Act 2014 (kinship care assistance)."

Payments under s.73 have been available in Scotland since April 2016 to people who have applied or are at least considering applying for a kinship care order for a child who is at risk of going into care or was previously looked after by a local authority.

p.1356, *amendments to the Jobseeker's Allowance Regulations 1996 (SI 1996/207) Sch.7 (Sums to be disregarded in the calculation of income other than earnings)*

3.064.1　　With effect from November 3, 2017, art.6(7)(d) of the Social Services and Well-being (Wales) Act 2014 and the Regulation and Inspection of Social Care (Wales) Act 2016 (Consequential Amendments) Order 2017 (SI 2017/901) inserted the words "or Part 4 of the Social Services and Well-being (Wales) Act 2014 (meeting needs) other than any direct payment made in accordance with regulations made under section 50 or 52 of that Act" at the end of para.31(1)(e).

From the same date, art.6(7)(e) of that Order inserted the words "or under section 35 or 36 of the Social Services and Well-being (Wales) Act 2014 (duty and powers to meet care and support needs of an adult)" at the end of para.32(2)(b).

pp.1357-1358, *amendments to the Jobseeker's Allowance Regulations 1996 (SI 1996/207) Sch.7 para 41 (Sums to be disregarded in the calculation of income other than earnings)*

3.065　　With effect from June 19, 2017, reg.3(3)(e) of the Social Security (Emergency Funds) (Amendment) Regulations 2017 (SI 2017/689) inserted the words ", the London Emergencies Trust, the We Love

Manchester Emergency Fund" after the words "the Scottish Infected Blood Support Scheme" in para.41(1) and (7). Definitions of that Trust and Fund have been inserted in reg.1(3)—see the entries for pp.994 and 999 of Vol.II in this Supplement.

With effect from October 23, 2017, reg.3(3)(e) of the Social Security (Infected Blood and Thalidomide) Regulations 2017 (SI 2017/870) inserted the words ", an approved blood scheme" after the words "the Scottish Infected Blood Support Scheme" in para.41(1) and (7) (and therefore before the previous amendment). A definition of "approved blood scheme" has been inserted in reg.1(3)—see the entry for p.987 of Vol.II in this Supplement.

p.1359, *amendments to the Jobseeker's Allowance Regulations 1996 (SI 1996/207) Sch 7 (Sums to be disregarded in the calculation of income other than earnings)*

With effect from November 3, 2017, art.6(7)(f) of the Social Services   3.066
and Well-being (Wales) Act 2014 and the Regulation and Inspection of Social Care (Wales) Act 2016 (Consequential Amendments) Order 2017 (SI 2017/901) inserted the words "or in accordance with regulations made under section 50 or 52 of the Social Services and Well-being (Wales) Act 2014 (direct payments)" at the end of para.56.

From the same date, art.6(7)(g) of that Order inserted the words "or the provision of care and support in respect of an adult under Part 4 of the Social Services and Well-being (Wales) Act 2014 (meeting needs)" after the word "2014" in para.64.

p.1370, *amendment to the Jobseeker's Allowance Regulations 1996 (SI 1996/207) Sch.8 para.22(1) (Capital to be disregarded)*

With effect from November 3, 2017, art.6(8)(a) of the Social Services   3.067
and Well-being (Wales) Act 2014 and the Regulation and Inspection of Social Care (Wales) Act 2016 (Consequential Amendments) Order 2017 (SI 2017/901) amended para.22(1) by omitting the word "or" at the end of head (b), substituting the words "1995, or" for the word "1995" at the end of head (c) and inserting a new head (d):

"(d) the following sections of the Social Services and Well-being (Wales) Act 2014—
    (aa) section 37 or 38, but excluding any direct payment made in accordance with regulations made under section 51 of that Act; or
    (bb) section 109.110, 114 or 115."

pp.1371-1372, *amendments to the Jobseeker's Allowance Regulations 1996 (SI 1996/207) Sch.8 (Capital to be disregarded)*

With effect from June 19, 2017, reg.3(3)(f) of the Social Security   3.068
(Emergency Funds) (Amendment) Regulations 2017 (SI 2017/689) inserted the words ", the London Emergencies Trust, the We Love Manchester Emergency Fund" after the words "the Scottish Infected

Blood Support Scheme" in para.27(1) but did not do so in para.31. Definitions of that Trust and Fund have been inserted in reg.1(3)—see the entries for pp.994 and 999 of Vol.II in this Supplement.

With effect from October 23, 2017, reg.3(3)(f) of the Social Security (Infected Blood and Thalidomide) Regulations 2017 (SI 2017/870) inserted the words ", an approved blood scheme" after the words "the Scottish Infected Blood Support Scheme" in paras 27(1) and 31 (and therefore before the previous amendment in para.27(1). A definition of "approved blood scheme" has been inserted in reg.1(3)—see the entry for p.987 of Vol.II in this Supplement.

With effect from November 3, 2017, art.6(8)(b) of the Social Services and Well-being (Wales) Act 2014 and the Regulation and Inspection of Social Care (Wales) Act 2016 (Consequential Amendments) Order 2017 (SI 2017/901) amended para.41 by inserting the words "or under Part 4 of the Social Services and Well-being (Wales) Act 2014" after the word "1958".

p.1375, *amendments to the Jobseeker's Allowance Regulations 1996 (SI 1996/207) Sch.8 (Capital to be disregarded)*

3.069   With effect from October 23, 2017, reg.3(5) of the Social Security (Infected Blood and Thalidomide) Regulations 2017 (SI 2017/870) inserted the following new para.66 after para.65:

"**66.**—Any payment made under or by a trust, established for the purpose of giving relief and assistance to disabled persons whose disabilities were caused by the fact that during their mother's pregnancy she had taken a preparation containing the drug known as Thalidomide, and which is approved by the Secretary of State."

With effect from November 3, 2017, art.6(8)(c) of the Social Services and Well-being (Wales) Act 2014 and the Regulation and Inspection of Social Care (Wales) Act 2016 (Consequential Amendments) Order 2017 (SI 2017/901) amended para.60 by inserting the words ", or in accordance with regulations made under section 50 or 52 of the Social Services and Well-being (Wales) Act 2014 (direct payments)" at the end.

With effect from November 7, 2017, reg.3(4) of the Social Security and Child Support (Care Payments and Tenant Incentive Scheme) (Amendment) Regulations 2017 (SI 2017/995) inserted the following provision after para.65:

"**66.**—Any payment made to a claimant under section 73(1)(b) of the Children and Young People (Scotland) Act 2014 (kinship care assistance)."

Payments under s.73 have been available in Scotland since April 2016 to people who have applied or are at least considering applying for a kinship care order for a child who is at risk of going into care or was previously looked after by a local authority. The amending regulations clearly number the new paragraph as 66, apparently overlooking the previous insertion of a para.66 with effect from October 23, 2017. No doubt the obvious mistake can be corrected and this paragraph regarded as numbered 67.

pp.1383–1384, *annotation to the Jobseeker's Allowance (Mandatory Work Activity Scheme) Regulations 2011 (SI 2011/688)*

See the discussion of *SSWP v DC (JSA)* [2017] UKUT 464 (AAC) in the entry for pp.1388-1390 for what is sufficient evidence of the giving of an effective notice under reg.4 and authorisation under reg.20.   3.070

pp.1388-1390, *annotation to the Jobseeker's Allowance (Employment, Skills and Enterprise Scheme) Regulations 2011 (SI 2011/917)*

SSWP v DC (JSA) [2017] UKUT 464 (AAC) concerned two sanctions imposed in August 2013 for failures, without good cause, to participate in a Scheme as required under reg.4 of the ESES Regulations in June and August 2012. By August 2013 the Regulations had been revoked, but continued to apply in relation to failures to participate that occurred while they were in force. For the same reason, the sanctions provisions in reg.8 (revoked with effect from October 22, 2012) applied in the present case, rather than s.19A of the old style Jobseekers Act 1995.   3.071

The first appeal (in relation to August 2012) raised the issue of the effect of the Secretary of State being unable to provide to the First-tier Tribunal, as directed, a copy of the appointment letter known as a Mandatory Activity Notification (MAN) sent or handed to the claimant in respect of the appointment that he failed to attend. The tribunal had allowed the claimant's appeal on the basis that the Secretary of State had failed to show that the claimant had been properly notified in accordance with the conditions in reg.4(2). In concluding that there was no error of law in that, Judge Rowland held that this was not a matter of the drawing of adverse inferences, but of the Secretary of State simply having failed to come forward with evidence on a matter on which the burden of proof was on him. Although there was evidence before the tribunal that the claimant had been given an appointment letter, that evidence did not go beyond showing the date and time of the appointment. It did not show where the claimant was to attend or what other information was provided and how it was expressed. The judge rejected the Secretary of State's submission relying on the presumption of regularity and the "inherent probabilities". Although the tribunal could, using its specialist experience, properly have concluded that the letter had contained enough information to make it effective, it was not bound to do so, given that it is not unknown for documents to be issued in an unapproved form or to use language that is not intelligible to an uninitiated recipient. The judge agreed with the tribunal that a copy of the appointment letter should have been in the tribunal bundle: a decision-maker might be able to rely on the presumption of regularity, but on an appeal (where it is not known what issues may eventually emerge) a copy of the letter should be provided.

Judge Rowland accepted that the tribunal had erred in law in deciding against the Secretary of State on the authorisation point (discussed below) without giving him an opportunity to provide relevant evidence, but that error was not material as, even if there was evidence that the provider was authorised to issue reg.4 notices, the tribunal would have been entitled to allow the claimant's appeal on the basis of the lack of necessary evidence that an effective notice had been given.

The second appeal (in relation to June 2012) raised the issue of whether the tribunal had been entitled to conclude that the Secretary of State had not shown that the Scheme provider in question had been authorised under reg.18 to give reg.4 notices when he was unable to produce a copy of a letter of authorisation. Judge Rowland held that the tribunal had gone wrong in law. Regulation 18 did not specify the form in which authorisation had to be given, so that it was a matter of fact and degree. So authority could be found to exist in evidence as to the conduct of those concerned, including what they have said and written over a period. The tribunal did not consider that possibility, raised by the provider acting as though authorised and the Secretary of State asserting that authority had been given. The judge went on to re-make the decision on the appeal. It had emerged that, by an administrative mistake, no formal letter of authority had ever been issued, but the existence of a contract between the Secretary of State and the main contractor for the sub-contractor to act in the area in question and a draft authorisation letter was sufficient to satisfy reg.18. He found that the claimant had been properly notified and had not shown good cause for his failure to participate, so that a sanction was to be imposed. On close analysis of reg.8 the sanction was to be for four weeks, rather than the 26 that had originally been imposed.

pp.1394-1395, *annotation to the Jobseeker's Allowance (Schemes for Assisting Persons to Obtain Employment) Regulations 2013 (SI 2013/276)*

3.072   See the discussion of *SSWP v DC (JSA)* [2017] UKUT 464 (AAC) in the entry for pp.1388-1390 for what is sufficient evidence of the giving of an effective notice under reg.5 and authorisation under reg.17.

pp.1396-1397, *amendments to the Jobseeker's Allowance (Schemes for Assisting Persons to Obtain Employment) Regulations 2013 (SI 2013/276) reg.3 (Schemes for Assisting Persons to Obtain Employment)*

3.073   With effect from November 20, 2017, reg.2(2)(a) of the Jobseeker's Allowance (Schemes for Assisting Persons to Obtain Employment) (Amendment) Regulations 2017 (SI 2017/1020) amended reg.3 by omitting paras (2), (3) and (8A). From the same date, reg.2(2)(b) inserted a new para.(8C) before para.(9):

"(8C) The Work and Health Programme is a scheme designed to assist a claimant who is long-term unemployed in which, for a period of up to 456 calendar days, the claimant is given such support, and required to participate in such activity, as the provider of the Work and Health Programme considers appropriate and reasonable in the claimant's circumstances to assist the claimant to obtain and sustain employment."

From the same date, reg.2(2)(c) amended para.(9) by omitting the definitions of "EHC plan", "Learning Difficulty Assessment" and "work history". Note that, in error, the insertion of "EHC plan" into para.(8B) and its definition into para.(9) was not included in the 2015/16 and subsequent editions of the main volume. But the definition was rendered irrelevant by the revocation of para.(8B) as a whole with effect from March 17, 2015, although it was not removed from para.(9) on that date.

The 2017 amendments are in the main to remove references to schemes that no longer operate. The Work and Health Programme (WHP) is newly prescribed in para.(8C). There may perhaps be some doubt whether para.(8C) provides sufficient description of the scheme to satisfy the test for validity under s.17A of the old style Jobseekers Act 1995 as laid down in *R (Reilly and Wilson) v Secretary of State for Work and Pensions* [2013] UKSC 68, [2014] 1 A.C. 453 (that a description is prescribed, not merely a label), since the nature of the support and activity in which participation can be required is left to the provider to identify in the light of a claimant's particular circumstances. On the other hand, the statements of the aim of assisting a claimant to obtain and sustain employment and of a maximum length indicating long-term assistance may point towards satisfaction of the test. Paragraph (8C) also leaves open who might count as long-term unemployed and what the "health" part of the name of the scheme might imply.

The revised Explanatory Memorandum to the amending regulations reveals (para.7.3) that the great majority of participants in the scheme will be those with disabilities (75%) or within an Early Access Disadvantaged Group (up to 10%), who can volunteer to take part. The mandatory process under s.17A is restricted to the long-term unemployed, i.e claimants who have not moved into employment within 24 months of their claim. There may be further doubt whether a description in the SAPOE Regulations that is restricted to the mandatory part of a scheme rather than of the scheme as a whole is sufficient and how far there could be reference to the Explanatory Memorandum to flesh out the statutory description in determining validity or otherwise under s.17A.

The Explanatory Memorandum says (para.4.6) that a Designation Order will be made designating employees of WHP providers as "employment officers" for the purposes of s.19(2)(c) of the old style Jobseekers Act 1995 in relation to informing a claimant of an existing or imminent employment vacancy, with the consequence of a higher-level sanction for, without a good reason, failing or refusing to apply for such a vacancy or accept an offer. See the notes to the definition of "employment officer" in s.35(1) of the old style Jobseekers Act 1995 in the main volume. No Designation Order had appeared in the "Deposited Papers" section of the Parliament website by the time of going to press.

p.1405, *annotation to the State Pension Credit Regulations 2002 (SI 2002/1792), reg.1 (Citation, commencement and interpretation)*

3.074 With effect from October 23, 2017, reg.5(2)(a) of the Social Security (Infected Blood and Thalidomide) Regulations 2017 (SI 2017/870) inserted in reg.1(2) after the definition of "the appointed day" the following new definition:

> ""approved blood scheme" means a scheme established or approved by the Secretary of State, or trust established with funds provided by the Secretary of State, for the purpose of providing compensation in respect of a person having been infected from contaminated blood products;".

p.1407, *annotation to the State Pension Credit Regulations 2002 (SI 2002/1792), reg.1 (Citation, commencement and interpretation)*

3.075 With effect from June 19, 2017, reg.4(2)(a) of the Social Security (Emergency Funds) (Amendment) Regulations 2017 (SI 2017/689) inserted in reg.1(2) after the definition of "the London Bombings Relief Charitable Fund" the following new definition:

> ""the London Emergencies Trust" means the company of that name (number 09928465) incorporated on 23rd December 2015 and the registered charity of that name (number 1172307) established on 28th March 2017;".

p.1408, *annotation to the State Pension Credit Regulations 2002 (SI 2002/1792), reg.1 (Citation, commencement and interpretation)*

3.076 With effect from June 19, 2017, reg.4(2)(b) of the Social Security (Emergency Funds) (Amendment) Regulations 2017 (SI 2017/689) inserted in the definition of "qualifying person" in reg.1(2), after "the Scottish Infected Blood Support Scheme", the words ", the London Emergencies Trust, the We Love Manchester Emergency Fund".

With effect from October 23, 2017, reg.5(2)(b) of the Social Security (Infected Blood and Thalidomide) Regulations 2017 (SI 2017/870) inserted in the definition of "qualifying person" in reg.1(2), after "the Scottish Infected Blood Support Scheme", the words "an approved blood scheme".

p.1409, *annotation to the State Pension Credit Regulations 2002 (SI 2002/1792), reg.1 (Citation, commencement and interpretation)*

3.077 With effect from June 19, 2017, reg.4(2)(c) of the Social Security (Emergency Funds) (Amendment) Regulations 2017 (SI 2017/689) inserted in reg.1(2) after the definition of "water charges" the following new definition:

> "the We Love Manchester Emergency Fund" means the registered charity of that name (number 1173260) established on 30th May 2017;".

p.1437, *amendment to the State Pension Credit Regulations 2002 (SI 2002/1792) reg.15 (Income for the purposes of the Act)*

With effect from November 16, 2017, reg.10(2) of the Social Security   3.078
(Miscellaneous Amendments) Regulations 2017 (SI 2017/1015) amended reg.15(3) by inserting the phrase ", or retirement pension income to which section 16(1)(za) to (e)(2) applies," after "prescribed under paragraph (1)" and inserting the words ", or section 16(1)(za) to (e)," after "taken into account under paragraph (1)".

With effect from November 16, 2017, reg.10(3) of the same amending regulations inserted after reg.15(4)(d) the following new sub-para-grpahs:

"(e) section 14 of the Pensions Act 2014 (pension sharing: reduction in the sharer's section 4 pension);
 (f) section 45B or 55B of the Social Security Contributions and Benefits Act 1992 (reduction of additional pension in Category A retirement pension and shared additional pension: pension sharing)".

p.1439, *annotation to the State Pension Credit Regulations 2002 (SI 2002/1792) reg.15 (Income for the purposes of the Act)*

Note that neither s.15 of the Act nor reg.15 seem to include as   3.079
assessable income for state pension credit purposes regular payments of income from a benevolent institution (e.g. the Royal British Legion) or from a family member: see *AMS v SSWP (PC) (final decision)* [2017] UKUT 381 (AAC) at para.13.

p.1448, *amendment to the State Pension Credit Regulations 2002 (SI 2002/1792) reg.17B(4) (Earnings of self-employed earners)*

With effect from November 7, 2017, reg.4(2) of the Social Security   3.080
and Child Support (Care Payments and Tenant Incentive Scheme) (Amendment) Regulations 2017 (SI 2017/995) inserted in reg.17B(4) in the text of the inserted para.(2), after sub-para.(da), the following new sub-paragraph:

"(db) any payment made to a claimant under section 73(1)(b) of the Children and Young People (Scotland) Act 2014 (kinship care assistance)."

p.1451, *amendment to the State Pension Credit Regulations 2002 (SI 2002/1792) reg.18 (Notional income)*

With effect from November 16, 2017, reg.10(2)(a) of the Social   3.081
Security (Miscellaneous Amendments) Regulations 2017 (SI 2017/1015) amended reg.15(3) by deleting "maximum amount of income which may be withdrawn from the fund" and substituting "rate of the annuity which may have been purchased with the fund and is to be determined by the Secretary of State, taking account of information

provided by the pension fund holder in accordance with regulation 7(5) of the Social Security (Claims and Payments) Regulations 1987".

p.1465, *amendment to the State Pension Credit Regulations 2002 (SI 2002/1792) Sch II para.1(2)(a)(iii)(ddd) (Housing costs)*

3.082   With effect from June 23, 2017, reg.4 of the Employment and Support Allowance (Miscellaneous Amendments and Transitional and Savings Provision) Regulations 2017 (SI 2017/581) substituted in para. 1(2)(a)(iii)(ddd) "Welfare Reform Act (component)" for "Welfare Reform Act "(component)".

p.1478, *amendment to the State Pension Credit Regulations 2002 (SI 2002/1792) Sch II para.14(8)(b) (Persons residing with the claimant)*

3.083   With effect from June 19, 2017, reg.4(3)(a) of the Social Security (Emergency Funds) (Amendment) Regulations 2017 (SI 2017/689) inserted in para.14(8)(b) of Sch.2 after "the Scottish Infected Blood Support Scheme" the words ", the London Emergencies Trust, the We Love Manchester Emergency Fund".

     With effect from October 23, 2017, reg.5(3)(a) of the Social Security (Infected Blood and Thalidomide) Regulations 2017 (SI 2017/870) inserted in para.14(8)(b) after "the Scottish Infected Blood Support Scheme" the words "an approved blood scheme".

p.1478, *amendment to the State Pension Credit Regulations 2002 (SI 2002/1792) Sch II para.14(8)(c) (Persons residing with the claimant)*

3.084   With effect from October 23, 2017, reg.5(4) of the Social Security (Infected Blood and Thalidomide) Regulations 2017 (SI 2017/870) inserted in Sch.2 after para.14(8)(c) the following new sub-paragraph:

> "(d) any payment made under or by a trust, established for the purpose of giving relief and assistance to disabled persons whose disabilities were caused by the fact that during their mother's pregnancy she had taken a preparation containing the drug known as Thalidomide, and which is approved by the Secretary of State.".

pp.1492-1493, *amendments to the State Pension Credit Regulations 2002 (SI 2002/1792) Sch.V para.15 (Income from capital)*

3.085   With effect from June 19, 2017, reg.4(3)(b) of the Social Security (Emergency Funds) (Amendment) Regulations 2017 (SI 2017/689) inserted in para.15(1) and (7) after "the Scottish Infected Blood Support Scheme" the words ", the London Emergencies Trust, the We Love Manchester Emergency Fund".

     With effect from October 23, 2017, reg.5(3)(b) of the Social Security (Infected Blood and Thalidomide) Regulations 2017 (SI 2017/870) inserted in para.15(1) and (7) after "the Scottish Infected Blood Support Scheme" the words "an approved blood scheme".

p.1496, *amendments to the State Pension Credit Regulations 2002 (SI 2002/1792) Sch.V new para.23F (Income from capital)*

With effect from October 23, 2017, reg.5(5) of the Social Security   3.086
(Infected Blood and Thalidomide) Regulations 2017 (SI 2017/870)
inserted in Sch.V after para.23E the following new paragraph:

> "**23F.** Any payment made under or by a trust, established for the
> purpose of giving relief and assistance to disabled persons whose
> disabilities were caused by the fact that during their mother's preg-
> nancy she had taken a preparation containing the drug known as
> Thalidomide, and which is approved by the Secretary of State."

p.1506, *amendment to Social Fund Cold Weather Payments (General) Regulations 1988 (SI 1988/1724) reg.1(3) (Citation, commencement and interpretation: definitions of "member of the support group" and "member of the work-related activity group")*

With effect from June 23, 2017, reg.2(1) of the Employment and   3.087
Support Allowance (Miscellaneous Amendments and Transitional and
Savings Provision) Regulations 2017 (SI 2017/581) substituted the fol-
lowing for the definition of "member of the support group":

> ""member of the support group" means a person who has or is treated
> as having limited capability for work-related activity under Part 6 of
> the Employment and Support Allowance Regulations 2008;"

and the following for the definition of "member of the work-related
activity group":

> ""member of the work-related activity group" means a person who has
> or is treated as having limited capability for work under Part 5 of the
> Employment and Support Allowance Regulations 2008 other than by
> virtue of regulation 30 of the Employment and Support Allowance
> Regulations 2008;"

The transitional and saving provision in reg.10 of SI 2017/581 has the
effect that this amendments only apply to claimants who are not protected by the transitional protections in the Employment and Support
Allowance and Universal Credit (Miscellaneous Amendments and Transitional and Savings Provisions) Regulations 2017 (SI 2017/204): see
paras 9.613-9.623 of Vol.I, and paras 3.564-3.574 of Vol.V, of the main
work.

pp.1536-1537, *amendment to the Social Fund Maternity and Funeral Expenses (General) Regulations 2005 (SI 2005/3061) reg.4A (Persons to be treated as responsible for children)*

With effect from November 3, 2017, art.10 of the Social Services and   3.088
Well-being (Wales) Act 2014 and the Regulation and Inspection of
Social Care (Wales) Act 2016 (Consequential Amendments) Order 2017
(SI 2017/901) amended reg.10(4)(a) to read as follows:

"(a) being looked after by a local authority within the meaning of section 22 of the Children Act 1989, or section 93 of the Children (Scotland) Act 1995, [or section 74 of the Social Services and Well-being (Wales) Act 2014,] unless the child usually lives with P;"

p.1546, *correction to Social Fund Maternity and Funeral Expenses (General) Regulations 2005 (SI 2005/3061) reg.7 (Funeral payments: entitlement)*

3.089   The text of reg.7(4)(a)(iv) should read:

"(iv) working tax credit where the disability element or the severe disability element of working tax credit as specified in regulation 20(1)(b) and (f) of the Working Tax Credit (Entitlement and Maximum Rate) Regulations 2002 is included in the award,"

p.1564, *amendment to the Social Fund Maternity and Funeral Expenses (General) Regulations 2005 (SI 2005/3061) reg.10 (Deductions from an award of a funeral payment)*

3.090   With effect from June 19, 2017, reg.3(1) and (3)(d) of the Social Security (Emergency Funds) (Amendment) Regulations 2017 (SI 2017/689) amended paras (2) and (3) of reg.10 by omitting the word "or" at the end of para.(2)(i), inserting the following after para.(2)(j):

"(k) the London Emergencies Trust, or
(l) the We Love Manchester Emergency Fund,"

and inserting the words ", the London Emergencies Trust, the We Love Manchester Emergency Fund" after the words "the London Bombings Relief Charitable Fund" in para.(3).

pp.1581-1584, *annotation to the new style Jobseekers Act 1995 s.6A (Claimant commitment)*

3.090.1   Two universal credit appeals before the Upper Tribunal in Scotland may possibly address the question of whether the current standard terms of claimant commitments, e.g. in the form of a provision like "I will attend and take part in appointments with my adviser when required" are sufficient in themselves to be a notification of the imposition of a work-related requirement (e.g. the work-focused interview requirement under s.15 of the WRA 2012) under s.24(4) (the equivalent of s.6H(4) of the new style Jobseekers Act 1995).

p.1593, *annotation to the new style Jobseekers Act 1995 s.6H(4) (Imposition of work-related and connected requirements: supplementary)*

3.090.2   Two universal credit appeals before the Upper Tribunal in Scotland may possibly address the question of whether the current standard terms of claimant commitments, e.g. in the form of a provision like "I will attend and take part in appointments with my adviser when required" are sufficient in themselves to be notification of the imposition of a work-related requirement (e.g. the work-focused interview requirement under s.15 of the WRA 2012) under s.24(4) (the equivalent of s.6H(4)).

p.1598, *annotation to the new style Jobseekers Act 1995 s.6J (Higher-level sanctions)*

See *S v SSWP (UC)* [2017] UKUT 477 (AAC), discussed in the entry for pp.79-80 of Vol.V in this Supplement, on the approach to "for no good reason".   3.090.3

p.1603, *annotation to the new style Jobseekers Act 1995 s.6K (Other sanctions)*

See *S v SSWP (UC)* [2017] UKUT 477 (AAC), discussed in the entry for pp.79-80 of Vol.V in this Supplement, on the approach to "for no good reason" in relation to the equivalent of s.6K(2)(a).   3.090.4

p.1687, *amendments to the Jobseeker's Allowance Regulations 2013 (SI 2013/378) reg.45(1A)(a)(ii) (Relevant education)*

With effect from November 6, 2017, reg.5 of the Social Security (Qualifying Young Persons Participating in Relevant Training Schemes) (Amendment) Regulations (SI 2017/987) substituted the words "Education and Skills Funding" for the words "Skills Funding".   3.091

p.1710, *amendments to the Jobseeker's Allowance Regulations 2013 (SI 2013/378) reg.60(2) (Earnings of self-employed earners)*

With effect from November 3, 2017, art.17(a) of the Social Services and Well-being (Wales) Act 2014 and the Regulation and Inspection of Social Care (Wales) Act 2016 (Consequential Amendments) Order 2017 (SI 2017/901) amended reg.60(2)(b) by inserting a new head (ia) after head (i):   3.092

"(ia)   under section 81(2), (3), (5) or (6)(a) or (b) of the Social Services and Well-being (Wales) Act 2014 (ways in which looked after children are to be accommodated and maintained);"

From the same date, art 17(b) of that Order amended reg.60(2)(c) by omitting the word "or" at the end of head (vi) and inserting after head (vii):

"or
(vii)   the person concerned where the payment is for the provision of accommodation to meet that person's needs for care and support under section 35 or 36 of the Social Services and Well-being (Wales) Act 2014 (duty and power to meet needs for care and support of an adult);"

The amending Order clearly numbers the new head as (vii) when it should be (viii).

With effect from November 7, 2017, reg.8(2) of the Social Security and Child Support (Care Payments and Tenant Incentive Scheme) (Amendment) Regulations 2017 (SI 2017/995) inserted the following provision after sub-para.(b):

"(ba) any payment made to the claimant under section 73(1)(b) of the Children and Young People (Scotland) Act 2014 (kinship care assistance);"

Payments under s.73 have been available in Scotland since April 2016 to people who have applied or are at least considering applying for a kinship care order for a child who is at risk of going into care or was previously looked after by a local authority.

From the same date reg.14(2) amended reg.60(2)(b)(ii) by inserting the words "or 26A" after "26" and the words "and duty to provide continuing care" after the words "local authority" the second time they appear.

PART IV

UPDATING MATERIAL
VOLUME III

ADMINISTRATION, ADJUDICATION AND
THE EUROPEAN DIMENSION

Commentary by

Mark Rowland

Robin White

p.188, *ERRATUM—Social Security (Recovery of Benefits) Act 1997 s.11 (Appeals against certificates of recoverable benefits)*

With effect from October 1, 2009, para.1(2) of Sch.11 to the Constitutional Reform Act 2005, s.148(1), amended s.11(4)(a) of the 1997
Act by substituting "Senior Courts Act 1981" for "Supreme Court Act
1981". This amendment was overlooked in the main work.

4.001A

p.214, *amendment to the Social Security Act 1998 s.2 (Use of computers)*

With effect from July 27, 2017, s.20(3) of the Welfare Reform and
Work Act 2016 amended subs.(2) by omitting "or" after paragraph (m)
and inserting after paragraph (n)—

4.001

"or
(o) sections 18 to 21 of the Welfare Reform and Work Act 2016."

p.218, *amendment to the Social Security Act 1998 s.8 (Decisions by
Secretary of State)*

With effect from July 27, 2017, s.20(4) of the Welfare Reform and
Work Act 2016 made two amendments to s.8. In subs.(3) (meaning of
"relevant benefit"), it inserted after paragraph (bb)—

4.002

"(bc) a loan under section 18 of the Welfare Reform and Work Act
2016;".

In subs.(4) (meaning of "relevant enactment"), for "or section 30 of that
Act" it substituted—

", section 30 of that Act or sections 18 to 21 of the Welfare Reform
and Work Act 2016".

The amendment made to s.39 (see below) at the same time as these
amendments puts it beyond doubt that an application for a loan under
s.18 of the 2016 Act is to be treated as a claim for benefit for the
purposes of all the adjudication provisions of the 1998 Act.

p.231, *amendment to the Social Security Act 1998 s.11 (Regulations with
respect to decisions)*

With effect from July 27, 2017, s.20(5) of the Welfare Reform and
Work Act 2016 amended the definition of "the current legislation" in
subs.(3) by substituting for "and section 30 of that Act" the words ",
section 30 of that Act and sections 18 to 21 of the Welfare Reform and
Work Act 2016".

4.003

pp.234-254, *annotation to the Social Security Act 1998 s.12 (Appeal to
First-tier Tribunal)*

Regulation 25(a) of the Social Security and Child Support (Decisions
and Appeals) Regulations 1999 prescribes an appointee as a person who
has a right of appeal to the First-tier Tribunal. In *RH v SSWP (DLA)*

4.004

[2018] UKUT 48 (AAC), it was held that that did not preclude the claimant from himself bringing an appeal and that, if the claimant lacked capacity, the First-tier Tribunal had the power to appoint a litigation friend if that was necessary in order to avoid unfairness.

There is an important distinction between the First-tier Tribunal remitting a case to the Secretary of State to make an "outcome decision", where the First-tier Tribunal has dealt with the issue arising on the appeal and the consequence is that other issues that have not previously been considered need to be determined (as in *R(IS) 2/08*, mentioned in the main work on p.238), and the First-tier Tribunal making an "outcome decision" but leaving to the Secretary of State a precise assessment or calculation necessary to implement the decision (which was held in *R(SB) 11/86* to be an acceptable procedure). In the former, the Secretary of State is left to make the "outcome decision" and any challenge to it can be brought before the First-tier Tribunal only by way of a fresh appeal (after "mandatory reconsideration"). In the latter, the First-tier Tribunal has made an "outcome decision" but it is incomplete if there is no agreement as to the assessment or calculation and so the First-tier Tribunal remains seised of the case and it was stated in *R(SB) 11/86* that "it is essential, when such a course is adopted, that the appeal tribunal should make it clear that, in the event that the issue cannot be disposed of by agreement between the parties, the matter must be restored before the appeal tribunal so that it—and it alone—may discharge its duty of finally determining the claimant's appeal thereto". Thus the parties have what lawyers call "liberty to appeal", although it may not be helpful to use that term when the parties do not have legal representation. In *MQ v SSWP (CSM)* [2017] UKUT 392 (AAC), it was held that a request to the First-tier Tribunal to resolve such a disagreement about an assessment or calculation was a form of post-hearing application that might be considered by the judge sitting alone even though the main decision had been given by a panel consisting of the judge and another member.

R(IB) 2/04, mentioned several times in the main Volume, was cited by Ryder LJ in *Singh v Secretary of State for the Home Department* [2017] EWCA Civ 362; [2017] 1 W.L.R. 4340, when referring to "the undoubted practice before the modern tribunal system came into being that appeals tribunals have some powers of decision-making sufficient to substitute a decision for the decision appealed against". In that case, the Court of Appeal rejected an argument that, where the First-tier Tribunal found a decision of the Secretary of State to be legally flawed, it was bound to allow the appeal so that the Secretary of State had to re-make the decision. The appellant's argument was based on section 83(3)(a) of the Nationality, Immigration and Asylum Act 2002, which provided that an appeal had to be allowed if the Secretary of State's decision "was not in accordance with the law". It was held that the First-tier Tribunal, and on any further appeal, the Upper Tribunal, was empowered to re-make the Secretary of State's decision, their appellate functions being an extension of the Secretary of State's decision-making function because, while they were independent, they undertook the same task. Therefore, the Secretary of State's decision was in accordance with the law unless the decision read as a whole was unlawful. An error of law by the

Secretary of State that was immaterial to the result did not require the appeal to be allowed. The reference to *R(IB) 2/04* confirms that the appellant's argument would never have got off the ground at all had the appeal to the First-tier Tribunal been under s.12 of the 1998 Act.

pp.254-256, *annotation to the Social Security Act 1998 s.13 (Redetermination etc. of appeals by tribunal)*

Section 13(3) was described in *AF v SSWP (DLA) (No.2)* [2017] UKUT 366 (AAC) as "a less than helpful provision" and reference was made to the criticism of the provision in the 2016/17 edition of this work (repeated in the first full paragraph on p.255 of the 2017/18 edition).

4.004.1

p.274, *ERRATUM—Social Security Act 1998 s.25 (Decisions involving issues that arise on appeal in other cases)*

With effect from October 1, 2009, para.1(2) of Sch.11 of the Constitutional Reform Act 2005, s.148(1), amended s.25(6)(a) of the 1998 Act by substituting "Senior Courts Act 1981" for "Supreme Court Act 1981". This amendment was overlooked in the main work.

4.004.2

p.276, *ERRATUM—Social Security Act 1998 s.26 (Appeals involving issues that arise in other cases)*

With effect from October 1, 2009, para.1(2) of Sch.11 to the Constitutional Reform Act 2005, s.148(1), amended s.26(7)(b)(i) of the 1998 Act by substituting "Senior Courts Act 1981" for "Supreme Court Act 1981". This amendment was overlooked in the main work.

4.004.3

p.282, *amendment to the Social Security Act 1998 s.28 (Correction of errors and setting aside of decisions)*

With effect from July 27, 2017, s.20(6) of the Welfare Reform and Work Act 2016 amended subs.(3) (meaning of "relevant enactment") by omitting "or" after para.(i) and inserting after para.(j)—

4.005

"or
(k) sections 18 to 21 of the Welfare Reform and Work Act 2016."

p.289, *amendment to the Social Security Act 1998 s.39 (Interpretation etc of Chapter 2 of Part 1)*

With effect from July 27, 2017, s.20(7) of the Welfare Reform and Work Act 2016 inserted after subs.(1)—

4.006

"(1A) In this Chapter—
  (a) a reference to a benefit includes a reference to a loan under section 18 of the Welfare Reform and Work Act 2016;
  (b) a reference to a claim for a benefit includes a reference to an application for a loan under section 18 of the Welfare Reform and Work Act 2016;

(c) a reference to a claimant includes a reference to an applicant for a loan under section 18 of the Welfare Reform and Work Act 2016 or, in relation to a couple jointly applying for a loan under that section, a reference to the couple or either member of the couple;

(d) a reference to an award of a benefit to a person includes a reference to a decision that a person is eligible for a loan under section 18 of the Welfare Reform and Work Act 2016;

(e) a reference to entitlement to a benefit includes a reference to eligibility for a loan under section 18 of the Welfare Reform and Work Act 2016."

p.378, *amendment to the Social Security (Claims and Payments) Regulations 1987 (SI 1987/1968) reg.7 (Evidence and information)*

4.007   With effect from November 16, 2017, reg.5(3) of the Social Security (Miscellaneous Amendments No.4) Regulations 2017 (SI 2017/1015) amended:

(1) reg.7(6)(b)(i) by substituting the words "rate of annuity which may have been purchased with the funds held under the scheme" for the words "maximum amount of income which may be withdrawn from the scheme"; and

(2) reg.7(6)(b)(ii) by substituting the words "rate of annuity which might have been purchased with the fund" for the words "maximum amount of income which might be withdrawn from the fund".

p.494, *amendment to the Social Security (Claims and Payments) Regulations 1987 (SI 1987/1968) reg.32 (Information to be given and changes to be notified)*

4.008   With effect from November 16, 2017, reg.5(4) of the Social Security (Miscellaneous Amendments No. 4) Regulations 2017 (SI 2017/1015) amended:

(1) reg.32(5)(b)(i) by substituting the words "rate of annuity which may have been purchased with the funds held under the scheme" for the words "maximum amount of income which may be withdrawn from the scheme"; and

(2) reg.32(5)(b)(ii) by substituting the words "rate of annuity which might have been purchased with the fund" for the words "maximum amount of income which might be withdrawn from the fund".

p.571, *amendment to the Universal Credit, Personal Independence Payment, Jobseeker's Allowance and Employment and Support Allowance (Claims and Payments) Regulations 2013 (SI 2013/380) reg.41 (Evidence and information required from pension fund holders)*

4.009   With effect from November 16, 2017, reg.15 of the Social Security (Miscellaneous Amendments No. 4) Regulations 2017 (SI 2017/1015) amended:

(1) reg.41(3)(b)(i) by substituting the words "rate of annuity which may have been purchased with the funds held under the scheme" for the words "maximum amount of income which may be withdrawn from the scheme"; and

(2) reg.42(3)(b)(ii) by substituting the words "rate of annuity which might have been purchased with the fund" for the words "maximum amount of income which might be withdrawn from the fund".

p.619, *amendment to the Social Security and Child Support (Decisions and Appeals) Regulations 1999 reg.3(7CD) (Revision of decisions)*

With effect from November 16, 2017, reg.9 of the Social Security (Miscellaneous Amendments No.4) Regulations 2017 (SI 2017/1015) amended reg.3(7CD) of the 1999 Regulations by inserting ", without showing good cause," before "failed to satisfy a requirement". It thus makes it clear that only a decision under regulation 6(2) of the Income Support (Work-Related Activity) and Miscellaneous Amendments Regulations 2014 to the effect that a claimant has *not* shown good cause for a failure to undertake work-related activity may be revised under reg.3(7CD). The explanatory note to the amending Regulations says that the "amendment makes clear that a decision may only be revised where the claimant has not shown good cause for a failure to undertake work-related activity", which is not quite the same thing and appears to be inaccurate. Regulation 3(7CD) confers a wide power to revise a supersession decision made in consequence of a determination under reg.6(2) of the 2014 Regulations "if it contained an error to which the claimant did not materially contribute" and the purpose of the amendment seems to be to ensure that the power may be used only to revise a decision that was adverse to a claimant. **4.010**

p.635, *annotation to the Social Security and Child Support (Decisions and Appeals) Regulations 1999 reg.3ZA (Consideration of revision before appeal)*

In *R(CJ) v Secretary of State for Work and Pensions* [2017] UKUT 324 (AAC); [2018] AACR 5, a three-judge panel of the Upper Tribunal has held that, when he has refused under reg.4 to extend time for applying for a revision of a decision, the Secretary of State "has considered an application for a revision of the decision" so that there is a right of appeal against the original decision. The Upper Tribunal left open the question whether there is a right of appeal where an application for revision is rejected on the ground that it was made more than 13 months after the original decision (see reg.4(2)(b)). The Secretary of State has not appealed and has issued guidance to decision-makers in DMG Memo 17/17, making it clear that previous guidance was wrong and that a refusal to extend time for applying for revision must be treated as a refusal to revise: **4.011**

"If a late application is made within 13 months but cannot be admitted and the decision cannot be revised for official error, a decision refusing to revise should be given and an MR notification issued. DMs must ensure that the MR notification includes appeal rights. If the claimant appeals, the FtT will be able to consider the substance of the decision that the claimant applied to have revised and not just the question of lateness."

Since the appeal is against the original decision and could not be against the decision made on the application for revision, the guidance seems to be wrong insofar as it suggests that the question of the lateness of the application for revision the only respect in which the First-tier Tribunal could consider "the question of lateness" would presumably be for the purpose of determining whether the application had been made within 13 months (if that is relevant).

pp.638-639, *annotation to the Social Security and Child Support (Decisions and Appeals) Regulations 1999 reg.4 (Late application for revision)*

4.012   Where an application for revision is submitted late but within the 13-month absolute time limit, a refusal to extend time is a refusal to revise. See the above supplementary annotation to reg.3ZA of the Social Security and Child Support (Decisions and Appeals) Regulations 1999.

p.664, *amendment to Social Security and Child support (Decisions and Appeals) Regulations 1999 reg.7(7B) (Date from which a decision superseded under section 10 takes effect)*

4.012.1   With effect from December 1, 2017, reg.4 of the Social Security (Miscellaneous Amendments No.5) Regulations 2017 (SI 2017/1187) amended reg.7(7B) of the 1999 Regulations by omitting subpara.(b).

p.735, *amendment to the Universal Credit, Personal Independence Payment, Jobseeker's Allowance and Employment and Support Allowance (Decisions and Appeals) Regulations 2013 reg.6(3)(c) (Late application for a revision)*

4.013   With effect from November 16, 2017, reg.16 of the Social Security (Miscellaneous Amendments No.4) Regulations 2017 (SI 2017/1015) amended reg.6(3)(c) of the 2013 Regulations by substituting "12" for "13", thus reducing the absolute time limit for applying for revision from 14 months to 13 months and bringing it into line with reg.4 of the Social Security and Child Support (Decisions and Appeals) Regulations 1999. The original period may have been the result of a drafting error.

Note also that, where an application for revision is submitted late but within the 13-month absolute time limit, a refusal to extend time is effectively a refusal to revise. See the supplementary annotation to reg.3ZA of the 1999 Regulations, above, although the guidance for decision-makers applying the 2013 Regulations is in ADM Memo 21/17 rather than in DMG Memo 17/17.

p.736, *annotation to the Universal Credit, Personal Independence Payment, Jobseeker's Allowance and Employment and Support Allowance (Decisions and Appeals) Regulations 2013 reg.7 (Consideration of revision before appeal)*

When an application for revision is submitted late but within the 13-month absolute time limit and the Secretary of State has refused to extend time for making the application, he "has considered an application for the revision of the decision", so that there is a right of appeal against the original decision (*R(CJ) v Secretary of State for Work and Pensions* [2017] UKUT 324 (AAC); [2018] AACR 5). See the supplementary annotation to reg.3ZA Social Security and Child Support (Decisions and Appeals) Regulations 1999, above. Guidance for decision-makers applying the 2013 Regulations is in ADM Memo 21/17, rather than in DMG Memo 17/17, but is to the same effect.

4.014

p.785, *amendment to the Social Security (Information-sharing in relation to Welfare Services etc.) Regulations 2012 (SI 2012/1483) reg.2 (Interpretation)*

With effect from November 15, 2017, reg.2(2) of the Social Security (Information-sharing in relation to Welfare Services etc.) (Amendment) Regulations 2017 (SI 2017/1016) amended reg.2 by adding the following definition after the definition of "the benefit cap":

4.015

""Careers Wales" means the company with the name Career Choices Dewis Gyrfa Ltd. which is trading as Careers Wales and which is established by the Welsh Government to provide careers services in Wales under sections 2, 8 and 10 of the Employment and Training Act 1973;"

In addition, a new reg.2A is inserted after reg.2 as follows:

"Prescription of Welsh body
2A. Careers Wales is prescribed as a Welsh body for the purpose of section 131 of the 2012 Act."

p.790, *amendment to the Social Security (Information-sharing in relation to Welfare Services etc.) Regulations 2012 (SI 2012/1483) reg.5 (Supply of relevant information by the Secretary of State)*

With effect from November 15, 2017, reg.2(3) of the Social Security (Information-sharing in relation to Welfare Services etc.) (Amendment) Regulations 2017 (SI 2017/1016) amended reg.5(1) as follows:

4.016

(1) by omitting the word "and" and the end of sub-para.(e); and
(2) by inserting the following after sub-para.(h):
    "; and

(i) where the qualifying person is Careers Wales—
  (i) identifying persons in Wales aged 18 and over but under 25 who are not in employment or receiving either education or training;
  (ii) providing advice, assistance and support to such persons;
  (iii) monitoring and evaluating the provision of such advice, assistance and support."

p.792, *amendment to the Social Security (Information-sharing in relation to Welfare Services etc.) Regulations 2012 (SI 2012/1483) reg.6 (Holding purposes)*

4.017   With effect from November 15, 2017, reg.2(4) of the Social Security (Information-sharing in relation to Welfare Services etc.) (Amendment) Regulations 2017 (SI 2017/1016) amended reg.6(1) by inserting the following after sub-para.(q):

"(r) where the qualifying person is Careers Wales—
  (i) identifying persons in Wales aged 18 and over but under 25 who are not in employment or receiving either education or training;
  (ii) providing advice, assistance and support to such persons;
  (iii) monitoring and evaluating the provision of such advice, assistance and support."

p.797, *amendment to the Social Security (Information-sharing in relation to Welfare Services etc.) Regulations 2012 (SI 2012/1483) reg.10 (Qualifying persons)*

4.018   With effect from November 15, 2017, reg.2(5) of the Social Security (Information-sharing in relation to Welfare Services etc.) (Amendment) Regulations 2017 (SI 2017/1016) amended reg.10(1) by inserting the following after sub-para.(e):

"(f) for the purposes of regulations 5(1)(i) and 6(1)(r), Careers Wales."

p.839, *amendment to the Social Security (Loss of Benefit) Regulations 2001 reg.5(1)(k) (Meaning of "person in hardship")*

4.019   With effect from November 3, 2017, art.8(1) and (2) of the Social Services and Well-being (Wales) Act 2014 and the Regulation and Inspection of Social Care (Wales) Act 2016 (Consequential Amendments) Order 2017 (SI 2017/901) amended reg.5(1)(k) of the 2001 Regulations by inserting "or the Social Services and Well-being (Wales) Act 2014" after "1989" in paragraph (i) and by substituting "either of those Acts" for "that Act" in paragraphs (ii) and (iii).

pp.843-844, *amendment to the Social Security (Loss of Benefit)*
Regulations 2001 reg.11(2)(h) (Application of Part IV and "meaning of
"couple in hardship")

With effect from November 3, 2017, art.8(1) and (3) of the Social   4.020
Services and Well-being (Wales) Act 2014 and the Regulation and
Inspection of Social Care (Wales) Act 2016 (Consequential Amend-
ments) Order 2017 (SI 2017/901) amended reg.11(2)(h) of the 2001
Regulations by inserting "or the Social Services and Well-being (Wales)
Act 2014" after "1989" in paragraph (i) and by substituting "either of
those Acts" for "that Act" in paragraphs (ii) and (iii).

p.941, *amendment to the Social Security (Recovery of Benefit)*
Regulations 1997 reg.2(2) (Exempted trusts and payments)

With effect from October 23, 2017, reg.4 of the Social Security   4.021
(Infected Blood and Thalidomide) Regulations 2017 (SI 2017/870)
amended reg.2(2) of the 1997 Regulations by adding after sub-
para.(n):

"(o) any payment made from a scheme established or approved by the
Secretary of State, or trust established with funds provided by
the Secretary of State, for the purpose of providing compensation in respect of a person having been infected from contaminated blood products;
(p) any payment made under or by a trust, established for the purpose of giving relief and assistance to disabled persons whose
disabilities were caused by the fact that during their mother's
pregnancy she had taken a preparation containing the drug
known as Thalidomide, and which is approved by the Secretary
of State.".

p.955, *amendment to the Social Security (Recovery of Benefit) (Lump*
Sum Payments) Regulations 2008 reg.7(2) (Exempted trusts and
payments)

With effect from October 23, 2017, reg.9 of the Social Security   4.022
(Infected Blood and Thalidomide) Regulations 2017 (SI 2017/870)
amended reg.7(2) of the 2008 Regulations by adding after sub-
para.(k):

"(l) any payment made from a scheme established or approved by the
Secretary of State, or trust established with funds provided by
the Secretary of State, for the purpose of providing compensation in respect of a person having been infected from contaminated blood products;
(m) any payment made under or by a trust, established for the purpose of giving relief and assistance to disabled persons whose
disabilities were caused by the fact that during their mother's
pregnancy she had taken a preparation containing the drug

known as Thalidomide, and which is approved by the Secretary of State.".

p.1078, *annotation to the Treaty of the Functioning of the European Union art.21*

4.023   See *MM v SSWP (ESA)* [2017] UKUT 437 (AAC) for a further example of the rejection of exceptional circumstances under the *Mirga* doctrine (para.3.74 refers).

LO v SSWP (IS) [2017] UKUT 440 (AAC) contains a detailed analysis of whether the *Mirga* doctrine assists a Spanish national, the mother of twins, who was separated from her unmarried partner (a British national) in circumstances where there was an order of the family courts precluding her from removing the children from the United Kingdom. Judge Ward concluded that her circumstances did not bring her within the category of exceptional circumstances set out in the *Mirga* case. Nor could she have any claim to a right to reside in the United Kingdom based on derivative rights, or founded solely on Article 8 of the European Convention on Human Rights.

p.1151, *annotation to Directive 2004/38/EC art.7 (Right of residence for more than three months)*

4.024   *AMS v SSWP (PC)* [2017] UKUT 381 (AAC) is the final decision in the consideration of the claimant's entitlement to state pension credit, and examines how the earlier analysis applies to the claimant's circumstances.

p.1168, *annotation to Directive 2004/38/EC art.12 (Retention of the right of residence by family members in the event of death or departure of the Union Citizen)*

4.025   In *Slezak v Secretary of State for Work and Pensions* [2017] CSIH 4; [2017] AACR 21, the Court of Session ruled that a person in the circumstances of the appellant had a right under EU law having regard to art.12(1) and (3), and art.14(2) of the Citizenship Directive [para. 28]. The appellant is a Polish citizen who had arrived in the United Kingdom as a 15-year-old in 2013 and had attended school here. Her father had never lived in the United Kingdom, but her mother did come to the United Kingdom in 2014 as a work seeker but subsequently returned to Poland. The appellant was estranged from both parents and claimed income support in September 2014. The Court of Session allowed her appeal, ruling that she was entitled to income support provided that she could establish habitual residence in the United Kingdom and the other conditions of entitlement to the benefit. In particular, the retained right of residence she enjoyed is not an excluded right of residence under regulation 21AA(3)(b)(ii) of the Income Support (General) Regulations 1987.

p.1175, *annotation to Directive 2004/38/EC art.17 (Exemptions for persons no longer working in the host Member State and their family members)*

The appeal in *Secretary of State for Work and Pensions v Gubeladze* has been determined: [2017] EWCA Civ 1751. The Court of Appeal ruled, reversing the Upper Tribunal, that the word 'resided' in art.17(1)(a) has the same meaning as in art.16 and so must be interpreted as meaning 'resided legally'. On the second point—the validity of the extension of the Worker Registration Scheme—the Court of Appeal upheld Judge Ward's analysis. Since the Secretary of State needed to succeed on both points, the appeal was dismissed.   4.025.1

p.1216, *annotation to Regulation (EC) No. 883/2004 art.7 (Waiving of residence clauses)*

The *Tolley* litigation, which concerned the interpretation of provisions of Regulation 1408/71, has limped to a conclusion. Following the judgment of the Court of Justice on the reference from the Supreme Court, the Secretary of State has decided not to pursue the appeal and not to seek permission to appeal on the prior authorisation point. The proceedings have been terminated by an order of the Supreme Court dated June 27, 2017 dismissing the appeal with costs. The effect is essentially to approve the reasoning of the three-judge panel at [2012] UKUT 282 (AAC). This lengthy litigation may not provide that much assistance on the interpretation of corresponding provisions of the 2004 Regulation which are worded somewhat differently. Regulation 1408/71 was replaced by Regulation 883/2004 in May 2010, although it still has effect in relation to Regulation 859/2003 which applies to third country nationals.   4.026

The decision of the Court of Justice *SSWP v Tolley* (C-430/15) is reported as [2017] AACR 40.

p.1221, *annotation to Regulation (EC) 883/2004 art.11 (General rules)*

I v Health Service Executive (C-255/13) Judgment of June 5, 2015 indicates that a person's habitual residence may change and affect the application of art.11(3)(e): see, in particular, in relation to the commentary at para.3.349 of the main volume.   4.027

Where reg.11(3) comes into play in circumstances where a person is employed in one Member State and self-employed in a different Member State, the rules in arts 14 to 16 of the implementing regulation (Regulation 987/2009) are mandatory and must be taken into account: *Radoslaw Szoja v WEBUNG, ebung s.r.o* (Case C-89/16) Judgment of July 13, 2017.

p.1235, *Regulation (EC) No. 883/2004 art.21 (Cash benefits)*

The relevant provisions of the Implementing Regulation should be Articles 27 and 28 and not as stated.   4.028

p.1275, *annotation to Regulation (EC) No 883/2004 art.68 (Priority rules in the event of overlapping)*

4.029   It should be noted that HMRC does not agree with the analysis in *JL v HMRC (CB)* [2017] UKUT 193 (AAC). Permission to appeal was sought from the Upper Tribunal but refused on the grounds that the appeal would serve no useful purpose since HMRC had conceded that the claimant should receive the benefit. In refusing permission to appeal, Judge Rowland noted that the analysis in *JL* is, strictly speaking, obiter, though he did not, in the light of his reasons for refusing permission to appeal, make any observations on the merits of the analysis in the decision against which appeal was sought. In the event of the matter proceeding no further, it should be noted that it will be open to HMRC to argue before a First-tier Tribunal that the analysis in *JL* is defective, since it is obiter dicta.

p.1355, *annotation to Regulation (EC) No 987/2009 art.6 (Provisional application of legislation and provisional granting of benefits)*

4.029.1   The decision of Judge Jacobs in *SSWP v FF* [2015] UKUT 488 (AAC)—wrongly cited on page 1357 of the Main Volume as [2015] UKUT 288 (AAC)—has been upheld in glowing terms in *Secretary of State for Work and Pensions v Fileccia* [2017] EWCA Civ 1907, reported as [2018] AACR 9.

4.030   **p.1363,** *annotation to Regulation (EC) No. 987/2009 art.14 (Details relating to Articles 12 and 13 of the basic Regulation)*

General note

4.031   Add the following General Note: The provisions of art.14(5b) and art.16 are mandatory and must be taken into account when art.13(3) of the basic regulation (Regulation 883/2004) comes into play: *Radoslaw Szoja v WEBUNG, ebung s.r.o* (Case C-89/16) Judgment of July 13, 2017.

p.1432, *annotation to Council Directive 79/7/EC art.4*

4.032   The reference by the Supreme Court to the Court of Justice in *MB v Secretary of State for Work and Pensions* has been registered at the Court of Justice as Case C-451/16 (para.3.655 refers).
    SSWP v HY and LW (RP) [2017] UKUT 303 (AAC) concerned a claim by two male-to-female persons that precluding their being able to receive retirement pensions in respect of periods before they acquired gender recognition certificates constituted discrimination in breach of art.4. The first claimant underwent gender reassignment surgery in 1986, but did not obtain a gender recognition certificate until February 2015. This had been prompted by refusal to award a retirement pension from July 2014 when she reached pensionable age for a woman. The second claimant underwent gender reassignment surgery in 1988. She

obtained a gender recognition certificate in February 2014 by which time she was already aged 65. She claimed a retirement pension from May 2008 when she had reached the age of 60. Judge Rowland reviews both the relevant legislative and case-law history. He concludes that the circumstances of the two claimants were distinguishable from those which had arisen in the *Richards* and *Timbrell* cases. Those cases had been concerned with entitlements in respect of periods in the absence of a national scheme for recognition of a changed gender identity. In the instant cases, there had been delay in obtaining a gender recognition certificate after the scheme in the Gender Recognition Act 2004 had come into force. On the facts, both claimants could have sought gender recognition certificates in a timely manner to enable claims to be successful from the relevant pensionable ages for a woman. The claimants argued that there was nonetheless unfavourable treatment when they compared themselves to persons who had been registered as women from birth. Judge Rowland concluded that the Directive did not require the United Kingdom to establish a scheme which permitted the retrospective award of gender recognition certificates, and the United Kingdom had chosen to make them prospective only. There was accordingly no discrimination which fell afoul of the prohibition in art.4. Any difference in treatment could be objectively justified.

p.1469, *annotation to Human Rights Act 1998 Sch.1 European Convention on Human Rights art.8 (right to respect for private and family life)*

The report of *Cameron Mathieson, a deceased child (by his father Craig Mathieson) v SSWP* cited at para.4.99 should be [2015] AACR 19.   4.033

pp.1519-1530, *annotation to the Tribunals, Courts and Enforcement Act 2007 s.3(1) (The First-tier Tribunal)*

R(C) v First-tier Tribunal [2016] EWHC 707 (Admin) cannot be   4.034
found on the *BAILLI* website but can be found on-line in the *Administrative Court Digest* at [2016] A.C.D. 60. In any event, in *AM (Afghanistan) v Secretary of State for the Home Department* [2017] EWCA Civ 1123, the Court of Appeal has now agreed that the First-tier Tribunal may appoint a litigation friend (see the supplementary annotation to s.25 of the Tribunals, Courts and Enforcement Act 2007, below).
SSWP v HS (JSA) [2016] UKUT 272 (AAC) has been reported at [2017] AACR 29. It was distinguished in *SSWP v DC (JSA)* [2017] UKUT 464 (AAC) where, in two separate cases concerning the same claimant, the First-tier Tribunal had directed the Secretary of State to produce evidence and, when he had failed to do so, had relied simply on the lack of evidence rather than drawing an adverse inference. The First-tier Tribunal was held at [33] to be entitled, although not bound, to require strict proof of a matter, whether or not it has expressly been put in issue by a party, rather than relying on the presumption of regularity. However, it could only rely on a simple lack of evidence if there was no other evidence at all. In one of the two cases, no copy of a letter requiring

the claimant to attend an appointment had been provided and, although there was evidence that a letter had been issued requiring the claimant to attend an appointment at a specific time on a particular date, there was no evidence as to what the letter had said as to the place where the claimant should go and so the First-tier Tribunal was entitled to find that it had not been sufficiently clear to be effective. On the other hand, in the other case, the Secretary of State had been unable to provide a letter authorising a company to issue such appointment letters but had nonetheless maintained that it was authorised to issue them. Because authorisation did not need to be in writing, the First-tier Tribunal had erred in finding that there was no evidence at all of authorisation when the company was acting as though authorised and the Secretary of State was asserting that it was authorised.

p.1554, *annotation to the Tribunals, Courts and Enforcement Act 2007 s.11(1) (Right to appeal to Upper Tribunal—challenging misdirections of law)*

4.035   Although tribunals may find subordinate legislation to be invalid on procedural grounds so that provisions of the legislation must be ignored, it has been held in *JA-K v SSWP (DLA)* [2017] UKUT 420 (AAC) that this does not extend to failures of a legislator to comply with the public sector equality duty imposed by s.149(1) of the Equality Act 2010, because s.113 of that Act has the effect of ousting the jurisdiction of tribunals in relation to contraventions of the Act except when the Upper Tribunal is exercising its judicial review jurisdiction or when express provision is made (e.g., by Sch.17 to the Act which confers jurisdiction on the First-tier Tribunal in relation to disability discrimination in schools).

In contrast, in *SSWP v Carmichael (HB)* [2017] UKUT 174 (AAC), the Upper Tribunal rejected the Secretary of State's submission that it had no power to provide a remedy when it held subordinate legislation to be incompatible with the European Convention on Human Rights. It held at [62] that "courts and tribunals ultimately have the power to determine and so order or direct that to the extent that subordinate legislation is incompatible with a person's Convention rights it should not be given effect to in determining the person's lawful entitlement, or should be otherwise applied or disapplied in a way that does not breach the person's Convention rights". The Secretary of State has been given permission to appeal and the appeal is due to be heard in the Court of Appeal in February 2018.

pp.1555–1559, *annotation to the Tribunals, Courts and Enforcement Act 2007 s.11(1) (Right to appeal to Upper Tribunal—procedural and other irregularities)*

4.035.1   The rule against bias was considered again in *Zuma's Choice Pet Products Limited v Azumi Limited* [2017] EWCA Civ 2133, where it was held that the fact that a part-time judge was a barrister in the same chambers as an advocate appearing before him did not necessarily give rise to an appearance of bias, although, in considering whether there had been an appearance of bias, it was necessary to consider all of the appellant's allegations together, rather than to consider them individually and conclude that, merely because there was nothing in them individually, there could be nothing in them in combination.

pp.1569-1572, *annotation to the Tribunals, Courts and Enforcement Act 2007 s.13(1) and (2) (Right to appeal to Court of Appeal etc.)*

Where the Upper Tribunal remits a case to the First-tier Tribunal, an appeal may be brought against the decision notwithstanding that there is no challenge to the remittal. In *Secretary of State for Work and Pensions v MMcK* [2017] CSIH 57, the Court of Session said: 4.036

> "[36] The Secretary of State does not challenge the decision by the UT judge to remit the matter back to the FTT for reconsideration. In those circumstances it might be open to question whether he was entitled to bring this appeal. In general, an appeal lies against a decision or order, not the reasons given for that decision or order. The matter was 24 canvassed briefly before us, and properly so, though we should make it clear that it was not contended on behalf of M that the appeal was incompetent. In our opinion the Secretary of State is entitled to bring this appeal. The decision of the UT was that the decision of the FTT be set aside and the case remitted to the FTT for rehearing before a differently constituted tribunal "in accordance with the directions set out below", in other words in accordance with the directions set out in the Reasons given by the UT judge. That is part of the decision and, unless this court is persuaded to the contrary, that is the basis upon which the FTT will have to reconsider the case. In those circumstances it is open to the dissatisfied party to challenge the directions given by the UT judge and to seek an order that the FTT rehear the case in accordance with directions given by this court. That is what has been done in this case. That is what was done in *Secretary of State for Work and Pensions v Brade* [2014] CSIH 29; 2014 SC 742; [2014] AACR 29 at paragraph [39]. Support for that approach, albeit under reference to English rules of procedure, is to be found in *Curtis v London Rent Assessment Committee* [1999] QB 92 at 107D-109D."

The Court of Appeal has a discretion whether to consider arguments not raised before either the First-tier Tribunal or the Upper Tribunal and, in *LC (Albania) v Secretary of State for the Home Department* [2017] EWCA Civ 351; [2017] 1 W.L.R. 4173, did so because the ground on which permission to appeal had been given raised a pure point of law that was potentially of some importance.

p.1582, *ERRATUM—Tribunals, Courts and Enforcement Act 2007 s.15 (Upper Tribunal's "judicial review" jurisdiction)*

With effect from October 1, 2009, para.1(2) of Sch.11 to the Constitutional Reform Act 2005, s.148(1), amended s.15(5)(a) of the 2007 Act by substituting "Senior Courts Act 1981" for "Supreme Court Act 1981". This amendment was overlooked in the main work. 4.036.1

p.1588, *ERRATUM—Tribunals, Courts and Enforcement Act 2007 s.19 (Transfer of judicial review applications from High Court)*

4.036.2   With effect from October 1, 2009, para.1(2) of Sch.11 to the Constitutional Reform Act 2005, s.148(1), amended s.19(3) and (4)(a) of the 2007 Act by substituting "Senior Courts Act 1981" for "Supreme Court 1981" in each place where it occurs. These amendments were overlooked in the main work.

p.1598, *annotation to the Tribunals, Courts and Enforcement Act 2007 s.25 (The First-tier Tribunal)*

4.037   *R(C) v First-tier Tribunal* [2016] EWHC 707 (Admin) cannot be found on the *BAILLI* website but can be found on-line in the *Administrative Court Digest* at [2016] A.C.D. 60. In any event, the Court of Appeal has now agreed that the First-tier Tribunal may appoint a litigation friend. In *AM (Afghanistan) v Secretary of State for the Home Department* [2017] EWCA Civ 1123, Ryder LJ, with whom Underhill and Gross LJJ agreed, said—

> "44. I have come to the conclusion that there is ample flexibility in the tribunal rules to permit a tribunal to appoint a litigation friend in the rare circumstance that the child or incapacitated adult would not be able to represent him/herself and obtain effective access to justice without such a step being taken. In the alternative, even if the tribunal rules are not broad enough to confer that power, the overriding objective in the context of natural justice requires the same conclusion to be reached. It must be remembered that this step will not be necessary in many cases because a child who is an asylum seeker in the UK will have a public authority who may exercise responsibility for him or her and who can give instructions and assistance in the provision of legal representation of the child".

In *RH v Secretary of State for Work and Pensions (DLA)* [2018] UKUT 48 (AAC), it was held that the fact that the Secretary of State had, under reg.33 of the Social Security (Claims and Payments) Regulations 1987, appointed someone to act on behalf of a claimant did not necessary preclude someone else acting in the interests of the claimant from bringing an appeal to the First-tier Tribunal in the claimant's name and applying to be appointed as a litigation friend. Nor did it prevent a claimant from bringing an appeal in his own name, if he had capacity to do so.

p.1600, *annotation to the Tribunals, Courts and Enforcement Act 2007 s.29 (Costs or expenses)*

4.038   A specially-convened two-judge panel of the Immigration and Asylum Chamber of the First-tier Tribunal, comprised of the Chamber President of the Immigration and Asylum Chamber of the Upper Tribunal sitting with the First-tier Tribunal Chamber President, has held that a wasted costs order may not be imposed on a Home Office presenting officer but may be imposed only on professional advocates, including registered immigration service providers, who may exercise a formal right of audience (*Awuah v SSHD (Wasted Costs Orders—HOPOs— Tribunal Powers)* [2017] UKFTT 555 (IAC)). This decision, while not technically binding, is plainly authoritative. The First-tier Tribunal pointed out that the language of s.29(5) of the 2007 Act is obviously drawn directly from that of s.51(7) of the Senior Courts Act 1981 and it referred to decisions of the courts made under the 1981 Act. It further held that, when Tribunal Procedure Rules (equivalent to r.11 of the Tribunal Procedure (First-tier Tribunal) (Social Entitlement Chamber) Rules 2008) allowed other people to be representatives, they did not thereby confer additional rights of audience for the purposes of s.29(5). In immigration and asylum cases, s.84 of the Immigration and Asylum Act 1999 has the effect that, apart from Government presenting officers, only people who are professional advocates exercising a formal right of audience may provide representation before the First-tier Tribunal or Upper Tribunal "in the course of a business". However, it appears to follow from the decision that, in other types of case, wasted costs orders cannot be imposed on litigants' representatives who are not relevant professional representatives, even if they are paid for their services. This is a side-effect of such paid representatives not being regulated.

pp.1617-1621, *annotation to the First-tier Tribunal and Upper Tribunal (Composition of Tribunal) Order 2008 (SI 2008/2835) art.2 (Number of members of the First-tier Tribunal)*

In *TC v SSWP (PIP)* [2017] UKUT 335 (AAC) it was pointed out   4.039
that the effect of the Senior President of Tribunals' practice statement mentioned in the main work is that, whereas any appeal against a decision that a claimant did not have good cause for failing to attend a medical examination in connection with employment and support allowance is heard by a judge alone, any appeal against a decision that a claimant did not have good cause for failing to attend a medical examination in connection with personal independence payment must be heard by a judge sitting with two members. The facts of that case, where the First-tier Tribunal had not addressed the impact that the claimant's disabilities might have had on his non-attendance, may be thought to illustrate why it might not be bad idea for there to be medically-qualified members sitting on some such cases, but others do not turn on medical issues at all. Some flexibility might be in order.

Indeed, that may be the result of a consultation about tribunal composition carried out in late 2016. It was proposed that art.2(2)(a) be revoked and also that, rather than issuing practice statements, the composition of tribunals should be determined through practice directions made under s.23 of the Tribunals, Courts and Enforcement Act 2007, so that the Lord Chancellor's approval would be required. More controversially, it was suggested that a tribunal panel in the First-tier Tribunal should consist of a single member unless otherwise determined by the Senior President of Tribunals. In view of the opposition to the idea that single judge panels would be the default position, the Government's response, published in February 2017 (available with the consultation documents at *https://consult.justice.gov.uk/digital-communications/panel-composition-in-tribunals/*), was a bit more circumspect, it being stated that single member panels "would only exist for cases for which the SPT has determined that there is no need for additional members" and the emphasis being on the need for flexibility whatever the default position for a type of case. However, as yet, there has been no new order, amending or replacing the existing one, and therefore there have been no practice directions.

Where a hearing is adjourned (as opposed to being postponed before it has started), the members of the First-tier Tribunal on the rehearing should either be entirely the same as the composition at the first hearing or else should be entirely different (*R(U) 3/88*). In the latter case, of course, the panel would have to start the hearing again from scratch, although it could take into account any record of the evidence and arguments advanced at the first hearing that had been available to the parties. However, where a hearing is concluded subject to calculations being carried out by the Secretary of State and the matter is referred back to the First-tier Tribunal because there is a dispute about the calculations—under what is sometimes called "liberty to apply"—the request to resolve the dispute can best be seen as a post-hearing application for a direction under rules 5 and 6 of the 2008 Rules mentioned in paragraph 10 of the Practice Statement and so may be dealt with by a judge alone even though the main hearing was before a panel composed of a judge and one or two other members (*MQ v SSWP (CSM)* [2017] UKUT 392 (AAC) at [34] to [37]). Whether it is necessary for the judge to be the same one as was a party to the original decision was not an issue that arose in that case and it may depend on whether the principles upon which the calculation is to be made can clearly be discerned from the decision notice and any statement of reasons that has been produced.

pp.1635–1636, *annotation to the Tribunal Procedure (First-tier Tribunal) (Social Entitlement Chamber) Rules 2008 (SI 2008/2685) r.5(3)(d) (Case management powers)*

4.040   Rule 5(3)(d), providing that the First-tier Tribunal may require a party to provide documents to another party, does not enable the First-tier Tribunal to fulfil its duty to issue its decision to the parties by asking one party to provide copies of the decision and the other information required by r.33(2) to the other parties (*Hyslop v 38/41 CHG Residents Co Limited* [2017] UKUT 398 (LC)).

pp.1645–1650, *annotation to the Tribunal Procedure (First-tier Tribunal) (Social Entitlement Chamber) Rules 2008 (SI 2008/2685) r.8 (Striking out a party's case)*

4.041   The decision of the Court of Appeal in *BPP Holdings v Commissioners for Her Majesty's Revenue and Customs*, mentioned twice in the main work as requiring directions of tribunals to be enforced with the same rigour as orders of courts, has been upheld by the Supreme Court (*BPP Holdings v Commissioners for Her Majesty's Revenue and Customs* [2017] UKSC 55; [2017] 1 W.L.R. 2945). Lord Neuberger PSC, with whom the other Justices agreed, said: "In a nutshell, the cases on time-limits and sanctions in the CPR do not apply directly, but the Tribunals should generally follow a similar approach." As to whether the order barring HMRC from further participation in the proceedings, made by the First-tier Tribunal in that case, was beyond the scope of what was reasonable, he said:

"[33] . . . , before they can interfere, appellate judges must not merely disagree with the decision: they must consider that [it] is unjustifiable. HMRC cannot in my view cross that high hurdle in this case.

[34] That is not to say that an appellate tribunal cannot interfere in a case where a debarring order has been imposed or confirmed. The decision to impose a debarring order (unlike case management decisions of a more routine nature) can often have the effect of determining the substantive case. Further, as already mentioned in para 27 above, an important function of the UT and the Court of Appeal is to ensure a degree of consistency of approach among F-tT judges. In the context of court decisions, this concern was plainly in the mind of the Court of Appeal in *Mitchell* and *Denton*. There must be a limit to the permissible harshness (or indeed the permissible generosity) of a decision relating to the imposition or confirmation (or discharge) of a debarring order. It may well be that this case is not far from that limit (a view which obviously draws support from Judge Bishopp's careful judgment in the UT). However, I do not consider that it was on the wrong side of the line, given the combination of the nature and extent of HMRC's failure to reply to BPP's request, the length of the delay in rectifying the failure and the length of the consequential delay to the proceedings, the absence of any remedy to compensate BPP for the delay, and the absence of any explanation or excuse for the failure, coupled with the existence of other failures by HMRC to comply with directions."

In conclusion, he added:

"[35] . . . it may be worth considering whether tribunals should be accorded additional sanction powers to those which they currently have. As Judge Mosedale explained, she was faced with a binary question, involving two unpalatable choices. Making the debarring order, which she described as draconian, or not making the order, which, to use the vernacular, would have meant that HMRC effectively would have got away with it. There may be force in the notion that the tribunal rules should provide for the possibility of more nuanced sanctions, such as a fine or even the imposition of some procedural advantage. Experience suggests that such ideas, while attractive in theory, can often be difficult to formulate or to apply satisfactorily in practice, so I mention the point with some diffidence."

p.1654, *annotation to the Tribunal Procedure (First-tier Tribunal) (Social Entitlement Chamber) Rules 2008 (SI 2008/2685) r.11(1) (Representatives)*

4.042 *R.(C) v First-tier Tribunal* [2016] EWHC 707 (Admin) cannot be found on the *BAILLI* website but can be found on-line in the *Administrative Court Digest* at [2016] A.C.D. 60. In any event, in *AM (Afghanistan) v Secretary of State for the Home Department* [2017] EWCA Civ 1123, the Court of Appeal has now agreed that the First-tier Tribunal may appoint a litigation friend (see the supplementary annotation to s.25 of the Tribunals, Courts and Enforcement Act 2007, above).

pp.1676-1680, *annotation to the Tribunal Procedure (First-tier Tribunal) (Social Entitlement Chamber) Rules 2008 (SI 2008/2685) r.24 (Responses and replies)*

4.042.1 The Upper Tribunal's decision in *SSWP v G (VDP)* [2015] UKUT 321 (AAC) was upheld by the Court of Appeal in *Secretary of State for Work and Pensions v G* [2017] EWCA Civ 61 and both decisions have been reported at [2017] AACR 20.

In *IS v Craven DC (HB)* [2013] UKUT 9 (AAC), the Upper Tribunal said that a response to an appeal ought to set out the relevant law, both statutory and caselaw. However, in *LH v SSWP (PIP)* [2018] UKUT 57 (AAC), the Upper Tribunal was critical of a response that did not set out the descriptors in a personal independence payment case but it did not go as far as to say it was unlawful, allowing the claimant's appeal on another ground.

pp.1683-1691, *annotation to the Tribunal Procedure (First-tier Tribunal) (Social Entitlement Chamber) Rules 2008 (SI 2008/2685) r.27 (Decision with or without a hearing)*

4.043 Guidance as to reasonable adjustments that may need to be made at a hearing where a litigant suffers from Asperger's syndrome may be derived from *Rackham v New Professionals Limited* UKEAT/0110/15/LA and *Galo v Bombardier Aerospace UK* [2016] NICA 25.

pp.1692-1695, *annotation to the Tribunal Procedure (First-tier Tribunal) (Social Entitlement Chamber) Rules 2008 (SI 2008/2685) r.30 (Public and private hearings)*

4.044 Under s.53 of the Courts Act 2003, as applied and modified by art.3 of the Tribunal Security Order 2014 (SI 2014/786), tribunal security officers may exclude members of the public from a tribunal building or part of a tribunal building if the person refuses to be searched under s.52 or to surrender an article if asked to do so under s.54 or for the purposes of enabling tribunal business to be carried on without interference or delay, maintaining order or securing the safety of any person in the tribunal building and may remove any person from a tribunal room at the request of a judge, and they may use reasonable force for those purposes. Section 53 was considered in *R. (O'Connor) v Aldershot Magistrates' Court* [2016] EWHC 2792 (Admin); [2017] 1 W.L.R. 2833. It was held that, where there is a dispute as to whether the conditions for exclusion are satisfied or there is room for such a dispute (e.g., because it is proposed in advance to exclude a particular category of person), the matter should be referred to a judge or justice of the peace who will be the final arbiter. Moreover, where it is proposed to exclude a group of people, fairness may require that one of them should be able to make representations before a final decision is made. However, wrongly excluding people from a hearing does not necessarily have the effect that the hearing is not in public, although it may have that effect and thus invalidate the proceedings.

pp.1714-1716, *annotation to the Tribunal Procedure (First-tier Tribunal) ('Social Entitlement Chamber) Rules 2008 ('SI 2008/2685) r.37 ('Setting aside a decision which disposes of proceedings)*

In *RR v SSWP (ESA)* [2017] UKUT 403 (AAC), the claimant 4.045
appealed to the First-tier Tribunal against a refusal of employment and support allowance and the First-tier Tribunal decided that she had limited capacity for work. She had argued that she had limited capacity for work-related activity and she asked for a statement of reasons. The presiding judge, realising that the First-tier Tribunal had not considered whether the claimant had limited capacity for work-related activity, indicated to a district tribunal judge that she would support an application for the decision to be set aside. The district tribunal judge set the decision aside without further ado and the case was reheard by another panel who decided that the claimant was not entitled to employment and support allowance at all. The Upper Tribunal allowed the claimant's appeals against both the setting aside and the subsequent decision on the ground that the first decision had been wrongly set aside because there had been no written application for a setting aside. The Upper Tribunal appears to have taken the view (at [14]) that the First-tier Tribunal had no power to set aside a decision on its own initiative, which arguably does not follow from r.37(3). However, that point may be fairly academic because setting aside a decision on the tribunal's own initiative without giving the parties an opportunity to say whether that was what either of them wanted would generally be unfair to a successful, or partially successful party. Moreover, in *RR*, it was unlikely that there were grounds for setting aside under r.37, unlike in *DC v SSWP (ESA)* [2015] UKUT 150 (AAC), to which the Upper Tribunal referred, where it was suggested that the First-tier Tribunal should have invited an application for setting aside because there had been clear grounds for doing so. The best approach in the situation that arose in *RR* would probably have been for the presiding judge simply to have written the statement of reasons that had been requested, drawing attention to the error of law and inviting an application for permission to appeal which, if made, could have resulted in the decision being set aside on review under s.9(4)(c) of the Tribunals, Courts and Enforcement Act 2007 (see rr.39(1) and 40). Indeed, a statement of reasons drawing attention to the

error of law was written and issued, but only after the decision had been set aside. The Upper Tribunal set aside both the setting aside decision and the second substantive decision, which left the claimant able to apply for permission to appeal against the first decision if she still wished to do so.

pp.1731-1732, *amendments to the Tribunal Procedure (Upper Tribunal) Rules 2008 (SI 2008/2698) r.1 (Citation, commencement, application and interpretation)*

4.046   With effect from July 23, 2017, rr.5 and 7 of the Tribunal Procedure (Amendment) Rules 2017 (SI 2017/723) amended r.1 of the 2008 Rules by inserting a definition of "financial sanctions case" and a new para.(d) in the definition of "interested party". A "financial sanctions case" is "an appeal to the Upper Tribunal under section 147(6) of the Policing and Crime Act 2017". Such appeals are heard by the Tax and Chancery Chamber of the Upper Tribunal and are outside the scope of this book. The amendment to the definition of "interested party" applies only to such cases and is therefore not set out here.

Also, with effect from October 1, 2009, para.1(2) of Sch.11 to the Constitutional Reform Act 2005, s.148(1), amended head (b) of the definition of "interested party" and head (c)(ii) of the definition of "respondent" by substituting "Senior Courts Act 1981" for "Supreme Court Act 1981" in both provisions. These amendments were over-looked in the main work.

p.1738, *amendment to the Tribunal Procedure (Upper Tribunal) Rules 2008 (SI 2008/2698) r.5 (Case management powers)*

4.047   With effect from July 23, 2017, rr.5 and 8 of the Tribunal Procedure (Amendment) Rules 2017 (SI 2017/723) amended r.5 of the 2008 Rules by inserting a new para.(5A) that applies only to financial sanctions cases (see, above, the supplementary annotation to r.1) and therefore is not set out here.

pp.1744-1745, *annotation to the Tribunal Procedure (Upper Tribunal) Rules 2008 (SI 2008/2698) r.8 (Striking out a party's case)*

4.048   In the main work, it is stated that a case should be struck out under r.8(2) if the Upper Tribunal lacks jurisdiction because the appeal brought to it has lapsed. *LS v HMRC (TC)* [2017] UKUT 257 (AAC); [2018] AACR 2 is cited as authority for that proposition but that case raises the question whether an appeal to the Upper Tribunal can ever lapse. It was held that, where a decision under s.16 of the Tax Credits Act 2002 against which an appeal has been brought lapses as the result of a subsequent decision made under s.18, any appeal to the First-tier Tribunal should be struck out under r.8(2) Tribunal Procedure (First-tier Tribunal) (Social Entitlement Chamber) Rules 2008 on the ground that the First-tier Tribunal no longer has jurisdiction in relation to the proceedings. However, it was also held that the Upper Tribunal had jurisdiction under s.11 of the Tribunals. Courts and Enforcement Act 2007 to set aside a decision of the First-tier Tribunal given on an appeal against a s.16 decision notwithstanding that a s.18 decision had been made, irrespective of whether the s.18 decision was made before or after the First-tier Tribunal's decision.

The Upper Tribunal's decision as to its own jurisdiction is probably not controversial in a case where the s.18 decision was made before the First-tier Tribunal's decision, since the Upper Tribunal would otherwise be unable to correct a failure by the First-tier Tribunal to strike out the appeal before it. However, it is not obvious why an appeal to the Upper Tribunal should not lapse where a subsequent decision renders the First-tier Tribunal's decision, and the question whether it erred in law, entirely academic, and why the Upper Tribunal should not then be under the same obligation to strike the case out as the First-tier Tribunal is when an appeal to it has lapsed. Striking an appeal out need not always be done summarily and need not prevent the Upper Tribunal from expressing a view on the merits of the First-tier Tribunal's decision if it considers it desirable to do so.

This point is not of a great deal of practical importance, given that the Upper Tribunal in *LS* did accept that, when a s.18 decision had been given, any decision of the Upper Tribunal on an appeal from a decision of the First-tier Tribunal under s.16 would be of only academic interest between the parties. In one of the cases before it, in which a s.18 decision had been made since the First-tier Tribunal's decision and it found the First-tier Tribunal to have erred in law, it merely set aside the First-tier Tribunal's decision and neither remitted the case nor re-made the decision. However, the Upper Tribunal's decision does require all such appeals to be determined once permission has been given (unless they are withdrawn), albeit that a fairly summary determination may be possible in many cases. This is because there is no power to strike an appeal from the First-tier Tribunal out under r.8(3)(c) for lack of prospects of success.

The decision of the Court of Appeal in *BPP Holdings v Commissioners for Her Majesty's Revenue and Customs*, mentioned twice in the main work, has been upheld by the Supreme Court (*BPP Holdings v Commissioners for Her Majesty's Revenue and Customs* [2017] UKSC 55; [2017] 1 W.L.R. 2945). See the supplementary annotation to r.8 of the Tribunal Procedure (First-tier Tribunal) (Social Entitlement Chamber) Rules 2008, above.

p.1746, *amendment to the Tribunal Procedure (Upper Tribunal) Rules 2008 (SI 2008/2698) r.10 (Orders for costs)*

With effect from July 23, 2017, rr.5 and 9 of the Tribunal Procedure (Amendment) Rules 2017 (SI 2017/723) amended r.10(3) of the 2008 Rules by inserting a new sub-para.(f) that applies only to financial sanctions cases (see, above, the supplementary annotation to r.1) and therefore is not set out here.

4.049

pp.1748-1749, *annotation to the Tribunal Procedure (Upper Tribunal) Rules 2008 (SI 2008/2698) r.10 (Orders for costs)*

4.050   In *Awuah v SSHD (Wasted Costs Orders—HOPOs—Tribunal Powers)* [2017] UKFTT 555 (IAC), it has been held that there is no power to make wasted costs orders against representatives who are not professional advocates (see, above, the supplementary annotation to s.29 of the Tribunals, Courts and Enforcement Act 2007).

The *Administrative Court Judicial Review Guide 2017* has replaced the 2016 edition and can most easily be found on-line by putting the title into a search engine. The full URL is: *https://www.gov.uk/government/uploads/system/uploads/attachment_data/file/647052/Admin_Court_JRG_2017_180917.pdf.*

The rule that a successful judicial review applicant should normally be awarded his or her costs does not apply where the claim is brought against the First-tier Tribunal and is not opposed by any party (*R. (Gudanaviciene) v First-tier Tribunal (Immigration and Asylum Chamber)* [2017] EWCA Civ 352; [2017] 1 W.L.R. 4095, applying *R. (Davies) v Birmingham Deputy Coroner* [2004] EWCA Civ 207; [2004] 1 W.L.R. 2739).

pp.1755-1756, *annotation to the Tribunal Procedure (Upper Tribunal) Rules 2008 (SI 2009/2698) r.14 (Use of documents and information)*

4.050.1   *Adams v SSWP (CSM)* [2017] UKUT 9 (AAC) has been reported at [2017] AACR 28.

pp.1766-1767, *annotation to the Tribunal Procedure (Upper Tribunal) Rules 2008 (SI 2008/2698) r.22 (Decision in relation to permission to appeal)*

4.051   There is no specific provision for adding grounds of appeal after permission has been given, in cases where the grant of permission has not been expressly limited. In these circumstances, the Upper Tribunal has a broad discretionary power to admit a new ground, which it should exercise in accordance with the overriding objective in r.2 (*Bramley Ferry Supplies v HMRC* [2017] UKUT 214 (TCC)). In practice, the Administrative Appeals Chamber of the Upper Tribunal does not take a strict approach in social security cases, unless a very significant delay in raising a new point is liable to create unfairness towards the other party.

p.1767, *amendment to the Tribunal Procedure (Upper Tribunal) Rules 2008 (SI 2008/2698) ˙r.23 (Notice of appeal)*

4.052   With effect from July 23, 2017, rr.5 and 10 of the Tribunal Procedure (Amendment) Rules 2017 (SI 2017/723) amended r.23(1)(a) of the 2008 Rules by substituting ", 26B or 26C" for "or 26B".

pp.1768-1769, *annotation to the Tribunal Procedure (Upper Tribunal) Rules 2008 (SI 2008/2698) r.23 (Notice of appeal)*

4.053   Where the First-tier Tribunal has given permission to appeal on limited grounds, only those grounds may be advanced in the notice of appeal and, if it is wished to add other grounds, an application for permission to appeal on those additional grounds must be made to the Upper Tribunal. In other cases, the grounds of appeal need not be limited to the grounds put before the First-tier Tribunal. Once the notice of appeal has been lodged, the Upper Tribunal has a broad discretionary power to admit a new ground, which it should exercise in accordance with the overriding objective in r.2 (*Bramley Ferry Supplies v HMRC* [2017] UKUT 214 (TCC)). In practice, the Administrative Appeals Chamber of the Upper Tribunal does not take a strict approach in social security cases, unless a very significant delay in raising a new point is liable to in raising a new point is liable to create unfairness towards the other party.

p.1769, *amendment to the Tribunal Procedure (Upper Tribunal) Rules 2008 (SI 2008/2698) r.24 (Response to the notice of appeal)*

With effect from July 23, 2017, rr.5 and 11 of the Tribunal Procedure   4.054
(Amendment) Rules 2017 (SI 2017/723) amended r.24 of the 2008 Rules by substituting for para.(1):

"(1) This rule and rule 25 do not apply to—
  (a) a road transport case, in respect of which Schedule 1 makes alternative provision; or
  (b) a financial sanctions case in respect of which Schedule 4 makes alternative provision.".

For the meaning of "financial sanctions case", see, above, the supplementary annotation to r.1.

p.1772, *insertion of the Tribunal Procedure (Upper Tribunal) Rules 2008 (SI 2008/2698) r.26C (Financial sanctions cases)*

With effect from July 23, 2017, rr.5 and 12 of the Tribunal Procedure   4.055
(Amendment) Rules 2017 (SI 2017/723) inserted r.26C into the 2008 Rules. It merely provides: "Schedule 4 makes provision for financial sanctions cases." See, above, the supplementary annotation to r.1.

pp.1781-1782, *annotation to the Tribunal Procedure (Upper Tribunal) Rules 2008 (SI 2008/2698) r.34 (Decision with or without a hearing)*

See the annotation to r.27 of the Tribunal Procedure (First-tier Tribu-   4.056
nal) (Social Entitlement Chamber) Rules 2008, including the supplementary annotation above.

p.1784, *annotation to the Tribunal Procedure (Upper Tribunal) Rules 2008 (SI 2008/2698) r.37 (Public and private hearings)*

See, above, the supplementary annotation to r.30 of the Tribunal   4.057
Procedure (First-tier Tribunal) (Social Entitlement Chamber) Rules 2008.

p.1796, *insertion of the Tribunal Procedure (Upper Tribunal) Rules 2008 (SI 2008/2698) Sch.4 (Procedure in financial sanctions cases)*

4.058   With effect from July 23, 2017, rr.5 and 13 of the Tribunal Procedure (Amendment) Rules 2017 (SI 2017/723) inserted Sch.4 into the 2008 Rules. It makes provision for procedure in financial sanctions cases (see, above, the supplementary annotation to r.1) and therefore is not set out here.

PART V

UPDATING MATERIAL:
VOLUME IV

TAX CREDITS AND HMRC-
ADMINISTERED SOCIAL SECURITY
BENEFITS

Commentary by

Nick Wikeley

Edward Mitchell

p.69, *annotation to the Social Security Contributions and Benefits Act 1992 s.171ZC (Entitlement: general)*

Note that the claimant's notice to the employer must be in writing if so requested: see subs.(2) and *Sharfudeen v T J Morris Ltd t/a Home Bargains* [2017] UKEAT 272, where the notice to the employer was out of time in any event. 5.001

p.108, *annotation to the Social Security Contributions and Benefits Act 1992 Sch.11 para.2 (Circumstances in which periods of entitlement to statutory sick pay do not arise*

Add to the commentary on para.(2), where it lists the various exclusions, the following additional exclusion: 5.002

(6) employees who had entitlement to ESA in the previous 85 days (subs-para.(dd)).

p.128, *annotation to the Social Security Contributions (Transfer of Functions, etc.) Act 1999 s.9 (Regulations with respect to decisions)*

For one such (rare) case that went to appeal see for example *Flemington Care Home v Revenue and Customs* [2017] UKFTT 300 (TC), in which the FTT (Tax) dismissed the employer's appeal against the HMRC decision, taken after referral to doctors under s.9, that the appellant (who had a foot injury but had allegedly been seen dancing at a concert) was entitled to SSP. 5.003

p.146, *annotation to the Tax Credits Act 2002 s.3 (Claims)*

As the commentary notes, if one member of a married couple is ordinarily resident in the UK but the other is not, the resident spouse should make a claim as a single person. But see *HA v HRMC (TC)* [2015] UKUT 708 (AAC) where the claimant's husband had resided in the UK for several extended periods, had moved address with her, had worked until he had been made redundant (when he claimed JSA), had obtained indefinite leave to remain in the UK and was on the electoral roll in the UK. However, at the same time the claimant's husband also retained strong links in Ghana, where he had both an apartment and employment. In the Upper Tribunal, Judge Hemingway dismissed the claimant's appeal against the FTT decision that she was not entitled to claim tax credits as a single person for the 2011/12 tax year. In dismissing the claimant's further appeal, the Court of Appeal in *Arthur v HMRC* [2017] EWCA Civ 1756; [2018] AACR 10 held that the claimant's husband was a person who was "ordinarily resident" in the UK as at April 6, 2011 for the purposes of a joint tax credit claim under s.3(3) of the Tax Credits Act 2002. Accordingly, the claimant herself was not able to make claim tax credits as a single person. Newey LJ helpfully set out the relevant legal principles on ordinary residence at paragraph 16 of his judgment (see further the note to pp.707-709 below). 5.004

p.169, *annotation to the Tax Credits Act 2002 s.14 (Initial decisions)*

5.005   In *LS & RS v HMRC (TC)* [2017] UKUT 257 (AAC) a three-judge panel of the Upper Tribunal expressed the view that a s.18 decision (fixing entitlement for a tax year) would cause an appeal to the First-tier Tribunal against a s.14 decision to lapse. This cannot, however, apply to all s.14 decisions and appeals. If HMRC decide not to make an award of tax credit, there will be no subsequent s.18 decision (i.e. no lapsing event). A s.18 decision can only be given where a tax credit has been awarded for the whole or part of a tax year (since the preceding s.17 notice can only be issued in such circumstances).

p.171, *annotation to the Tax Credits Act 2002 s.15 (Revised decisions after notifications)*

5.006   In *LS & RS v HMRC (TC)* [2017] UKUT 257 (AAC) a three-judge panel of the Upper Tribunal expressed the view that a s.18 decision (fixing entitlement for a tax year) would cause an appeal to the First-tier Tribunal against a s.15 decision to lapse.

p.172, *annotation to the Tax Credits Act 2002 s.16 (Other revised decisions)*

5.007   Note that the power under subs.(2) is wider than the power to amend or terminate, and so accordingly, the giving of a subs. (2) notice is not a necessary precondition to the exercise of subs. (1) powers: *ME v HMRC (TC)* [2017] UKUT 227 (AAC).

p.173, *annotation to the Tax Credits Act 2002 s.16 (Other revised decisions)*

5.008   As authority for the proposition that HMRC cannot engage in a fishing expedition or random investigation under these powers, see *ME v HMRC (TC)* [2017] UKUT 227 (AAC).

p.174, *annotation to the Tax Credits Act 2002 s.16 (Other revised decisions)*

5.009   The role of the First-tier Tribunal on a s.16(1) appeal was further examined by Upper Tribunal Judge Wright in *ME v HMRC (TC)* [2017] UKUT 227 (AAC). HMRC's power to amend or terminate an award under s.16(1) arises where it has "reasonable grounds for believing" the rate of tax credit awarded is not the rate to which an individual is entitled or an individual is not entitled to any award. Does the FTT simply address whether, in its determination, those 'reasonable grounds' exist or does it squarely address actual entitlement? Judge Wright decided that the FTT is to 'stand in the shoes of the HMRC decision maker' and decide for itself whether there were reasonable grounds for believing any of the matters referred to in s.16(1). If the answer is yes, the Tribunal is to go on to decide whether to terminate or amend the award, as from the date of the HMRC decision under appeal. Note, the Tribunal is not required to amend or terminate, it simply has the power to do so.

p.175, *annotation to the Tax Credits Act 2002 s.16 (Other revised decisions)*

Note that in addition the three-judge panel in *LS and RS v HMRC* 5.010 [2017] UKUT 257 (AAC) decided that the Upper Tribunal, unlike the FTT, had jurisdiction to hear an appeal against a 'decision' of the FTT in a lapsed s.16 case. In the exercise of that jurisdiction, the Upper Tribunal has power to hear and decide an issue that has become academic as between the parties. The three-judge panel also decided that, following the introduction of the requirement for an Appellant to seek 'Mandatory Reconsideration' before exercising the right of appeal (s.38), it is no longer possible for the FTT to treat an extant s.16 appeal as continuing against the s.18 decision that has replaced the s.16 decision.

p.191, *amendment to the Tax Credits Act 2002 s.28 (Overpayments)*

With effect from September 25, 2017, art.6(2)(a) of the Tax Credits 5.011 (Exercise of Functions in relation to Northern Ireland and Notices for Recovery of Tax Credit Overpayments) Order 2017 (SI 2017/781) substituted "Commissioners may" for "Board may" in subs.(1), while art.6(2)(b) substituted for "repaid to the Board" the following new subparagraphs:

"—
(a) repaid to the Commissioners; or
(b) treated as if it were an amount recoverable by the Secretary of State under section 71ZB of the Administration Act(1) or (as the case may be) by the relevant Northern Ireland Department under section 69ZB of the Administration (Northern Ireland) Act".

With effect from the same date, art.6(2)(c) of the same Order substituted in subs.(3) for the words from "the amount" to the end the following words "to the Commissioners, the Secretary of State or (as the case may be) the relevant Northern Ireland Department, the amount which the Commissioners decide is to be repaid or treated as recoverable under subsection (1)(b)".

With effect from the same date, art.6(2)(d) of the same Order substituted in subs.(4) for the words from "the amount" to "is to repay" the following words "to the Commissioners, the Secretary of State or (as the case may be) the relevant Northern Ireland Department, the amount mentioned in subsection (3) unless the Commissioners decide that each is liable for'';

With effect from the same date, art.6(2)(e) of the same Order substituted "Commissioners" in subs.(5) and (6) for "Board" in each place it occurs.

With effect from the same date, art.6(2)(f) of the same Order inserted after subs.(6) the following new subsections:

"(7) In this section and in section 29—
"the Administration Act" means the Social Security Administration Act 1992;
"the Administration (Northern Ireland) Act" means the Social Security Administration (Northern Ireland) Act 1992;
"the relevant Northern Ireland Department" means the Department for Communities.
(8) In this section, "the Commissioners" means the Commissioners for Her Majesty's Revenue and Customs."

p.192, *annotation to the Tax Credits Act 2002 s.28 (Overpayments)*

5.012   Delete the fourth sentence in para.1.364 starting "Subsection (1) gives a power . . . " and replace with the following text: "Subsection (1) gives a power to (but does not impose a duty on) HMRC to require overpayments to be repaid to HMRC or, following the amendment made by SI 2017/781 treated as an amount recoverable by the Secretary of State for Work and Pensions under s.71ZB of the Social Security Administration Act 1992. Section 71ZB is the DWP's relatively new power to recover certain overpaid benefits, a power which is not conditional on a finding of misrepresentation or failure to disclose a material fact."

In the fifth sentence of the same annotation, delete "collect an overpayment" and replace with "require an overpayment to be repaid".

p.192, *amendment to the Tax Credits Act 2002 s.29 (Recovery of overpayments)*

5.013   With effect from September 25, 2017, art.6(3)(a) of the Tax Credits (Exercise of Functions in relation to Northern Ireland and Notices for Recovery of Tax Credit Overpayments) Order 2017 (SI 2017/781) inserted "or paid" after "repaid" in subs.(1) while art.6(3)(b) substituted for subs.(4) the following new subsection:

"(4) Where a notice states that this subsection applies in relation to an amount (or part of an amount), it may be recovered—
    (a) subject to provision made by regulations, by deduction from payments of any tax credit under an award made for any period to the person, or either or both of the persons, to whom the notice was given;
    (b) by the Secretary of State—
        (i) by deductions under section 71ZC of the Administration Act (deduction from benefit);
        (ii) by deductions under section 71ZD of that Act (deduction from earnings); or
        (iii) as set out in section 71ZE of that Act (court action etc); or
    (c) by the relevant Northern Ireland Department—

> (i) by deductions under section 69ZC of the Administration (Northern Ireland) Act (deduction from benefit);
> (ii) by deductions under section 69ZD of that Act (deduction from earnings); or
> (iii) as set out in section 69ZE of that Act (court action etc).".

p.193, *annotation to the Tax Credits Act 2002 s.29 (Recovery of overpayments)*

As regards the powers under subs.(4), note also that where the over-payment is treated as recoverable under s.71ZB of the Social Security Administration Act 1992 (see s.28), the Secretary of State may use the recovery mechanisms in ss.71ZC to 71ZD of the 1992 Act (deduction from benefit or earnings or court action). 5.014

p.193, *annotation to the Tax Credits Act 2002 s.31 (Incorrect statements, etc.)*

In *SP v HMRC (No.2)* [2017] UKUT 329 (AAC) Upper Tribunal 5.015 Judge Levenson decided that, in fixing the amount of a penalty, it is "necessary to mark the seriousness of the issue" but, for a first-time penalty involving only negligence, it is not necessary to create "additional hardship". The Judge allowed the Appellant's appeal and replaced a £500 penalty with a £100 penalty which was "more than a nominal penalty but not so great as to be disproportionate or create inappropriate additional hardship". In that case, the Appellant had 'guessed' that her annual income was £11,000 when in fact it was some £22,000.

p.214, *annotation to the Tax Credits Act 2002 s.38 (Appeals)*

Replace the penultimate paragraph in 1.399 starting "A further illus- 5.016 tration . . . " with the following annotation:

Worryingly, more recent cases suggest that HMRC's "formerly unsatisfactory approach to FTT submissions" has not been wholly remedied. One example is the decision of Upper Tribunal Judge Hemingway in *MD v HMRC* (TC) [2017] UKUT 106 (AAC). Another led to scathing criticisms by Upper Tribunal Judge Wikeley in *VO v HMRC* [2017] UKUT 343 (AAC), a decision which began with the following words:

"1. Well, here we go yet again.
2. I used the phrase 'Well, here we go again' with a sense of frustration, bordering on despair, to open my decision in *NI v HMRC* [2015] UKUT 160 (AAC), a case in which I criticised Her Majesty Revenue and Customs (HMRC) for both its decision making processes and its conduct of appeals in relation to tax credits claims. That phrase has been echoed in other tribunal jurisdictions where HMRC's conduct has come under similar critical scrutiny:

see e.g. *Pandey v Revenue and Customs (Income Tax/Corporation Tax: Penalty)* [2017] UKFTT 216 (TC).

3. So, yes, in short this is yet another sorry tale of HMRC institutional incompetence and inefficiency which could well have led to injustice, were it not for the persistence of the Appellant."

In *VO* HMRC's written response to the Appellant's appeal failed to mention or include all relevant documentary evidence. The possible existence of undisclosed material was clearly suggested by the material that was disclosed, for example the Appellant's statement that she had sent further information to HMRC and the HMRC's calculation of hours worked indicated some raw data applied by HMRC was absent from the appeal response. The First-tier Tribunal erred in law by failing to recognise these clear "alarm bells".

p.247, *correction to arrangement of selected sections for the Income Tax (Earnings and Pensions) Act 2003*

5.017   After the entry for s.318A insert:

318AZA. Meaning of "eligible employee"

p.271, *amendments to the Income Tax (Earnings and Pensions) Act 2003 s.318A (Childcare: limited exception for other care)*

5.018   In subs.(1), in the introductory words, delete "for a" and insert "for an eligible". In the concluding words of the same sub-section, and after the words "meaning of", insert ""eligible employee", see section 318AZA, and for the meaning of".

p.272, *amendments to the Income Tax (Earnings and Pensions) Act 2003 s.318A (Childcare: limited exception for other care)*

5.019   In subs.(5)(a) after "employer's" insert "eligible".

p.273, *amendment to the Income Tax (Earnings and Pensions) Act 2003 by insertion of new s.318AZA (Meaning of "eligible employee")*

5.020   Insert after s.318A and immediately before s.318AA the following new section:

"Meaning of "eligible employee"
318AZA.—(1) An employee is an eligible employee for the purposes of section 318A if conditions A to C are met in relation to the employee.
    (2) Condition A is that the employee—
        (a) was employed by the employer immediately before the relevant day, and
        (b) has not ceased to be employed by the employer on or after that day.
    (3) "The relevant day" means the day specified by the Treasury in regulations for the purposes of this section.

(4) Condition B is that there has not been a period of 52 tax weeks ending on or after the relevant day which has not included at least one qualifying week.

(5) In subsection (4)—

"qualifying week" means a tax week in which care for a child has been provided for the employee under the scheme by the employer in circumstances in which conditions A to D in section 318A are met, and

"tax week" has the meaning given by section 318A(7).

(6) Condition C is that the employee has not given the employer a childcare account notice.

(7) A "childcare account notice" is a written notice informing the employer that the employee wishes to leave the scheme in order to be able to open a childcare account under section 17 of the Childcare Payments Act 2014 or enable the employee's partner to do so.

(8) In subsection (7) "partner" is to be read in accordance with regulations made under section 3(5) of that Act.

(9) For the meaning of "care" and "child", see section 318B."

p.273, *amendment to the Income Tax (Earnings and Pensions) Act 2003 s.318B (Childcare: meaning of "care", "child" and "parental responsibility")*

In subs.(1), delete "and 318A" and replace with "to 318AZA". 5.021

p.296, *correction to the Income Tax (Earnings and Pensions) Act 2003 s.671 (Amounts in excess of taxable maximum)*

Delete the words "and relevant welfare supplementary payments" in the second place where they occur in subs.(1). 5.022

p.356, *amendments to the Income Tax (Trading and Other Income) Act 2005 s.31B (Relevant maximum)*

In subs.(3), after "greater than" insert "the higher of £300,000 or". In 5.023 subs.(4), after "greater than" insert "the higher of £300,000 or". In subs.(5)(a), before "the VAT threshold" insert "the higher of £150,000 or". In subs.(5)(b), after "tax year," insert "the higher of £300,000 or". In subs.(6) delete "the VAT threshold is" and replace with: "the amounts specified in subsections (3), (4) and (5) and the VAT threshold are".

p.497, *annotation to the Working Tax Credit (Entitlement and Maximum Rate) Regulations 2002 (SI 2002/2005) reg.2 (Interpretation)*

In *JF v HMRC* (TC) [2017] UKUT 334 (AAC) Upper Tribunal 5.024 Judge Wikeley decided that the new definition did not displace the long-standing principle that that, in the context of self-employment, remunerative work means work carried out with the desire, hope and intention of claiming a reward or profit (*R(FIS) 6/85*), nor did it require un-costed activities or non-remunerated hours to be discounted, "without due consideration". Judge Wikeley also noted that claimants seeking to establish self-employed status should not be expected to provide business plans of too exacting a standard:

> "31 . . . Empirical evidence demonstrates the heterogeneity of the many different forms of self-employment . . . Self-employed working tax credit claimants (typically) are not putting together business proposals of sufficient rigour to pass muster on a Masters of Business Administration course or to withstand scrutiny in an episode of Dragons' Den. Usually they are much more modest enterprises, as in the present case, and expectations about the documentary paper trail should be adjusted accordingly."

In *JF* Judge Wikeley rejected the argument that, under the new definition of "self-employed", time spent setting up a business and handing out leaflets door-to-door could not count. In *VO v HMRC (TC)* [2017] 343 (AAC) Judge Wikeley also decided that time spent on networking and promoting a business was not categorically excluded. These activities are potentially relevant in deciding whether a person is "self-employed" and in quantifying hours of work done in expectation of payment for the purposes of regulation 4.

p.504, *annotation to the Working Tax Credit (Entitlement and Maximum Rate) Regulations 2002 (SI 2002/2005) reg.4 (Entitlement to basic element of working tax credit: qualifying remunerative work)*

5.025 Note that CTC/2103/2006 was approved by Upper Tribunal Judge Wikeley in *VO v HMRC* (TC) [2017] UKUT 343 (AAC).

p.522, *amendments to the Working Tax Credit (Entitlement and Maximum Rate) Regulations 2002 (SI 2002/2005) reg.13 (Entitlement to child care element of working tax credit)*

5.026 The amendment regulations at footnote 4 should be 2008/1879, not 2009/1879.

p.523, *annotation to the Working Tax Credit (Entitlement and Maximum Rate) Regulations 2002 (SI 2002/2005) reg.13 (Entitlement to child care element of working tax credit)*

5.027 Delete the annotation under the heading "Incapacitated" and replace with the following:

Incapacitated
The definition of "incapacitated" is set out in paras.(5)-(12). The definition is referential in that it operates by reference to the award of some disability or incapacity-related benefit or a disability or incapacity-related adjustment to a benefit or war pension, or the provision of the NHS service referred to in para.(8). Save for the EU law point described below, this definition is exhaustive. Whether or not a person might generally be considered incapacitated is irrelevant (*AS v HMRC (TC)* [2017] UKUT 361 (AAC). The decision in *AS v HMRC (TC)*

involved a Dutch invalidity benefit whose British equivalent would fall within reg.13(6)(b). Upper Tribunal Judge Jacobs held that the regulation needed to be read as including the Dutch invalidity benefit. Otherwise, the appellant would be deprived of a social advantage contrary to Art.7(2) of Regulation (EU) 492/2011.

p.612, *annotation to the Child Tax Credit Regulations 2002 (SI 2002/2007) reg.5 (Maximum age and prescribed conditions for a qualifying young person)*

Delete the paragraph commencing "In *ML v HMRC (TC)* [2015] UKUT 166 (AAC)" and replace with: 5.028

An amendment to the definition of "approved training" in reg.1(3) of the Child Benefit (General) Regulations 2006 means that approved training no longer exists in England, only in Scotland and Wales. The amending instrument, the Child Benefit (General) (Amendment) Regulations 2015 (SI 2015/1512), omitted the definition of "approved training" in relation to England with effect from August 31, 2015.

p.646, *amendment to the Tax Credits (Claims and Notifications) Regulations 2002 (SI 2002/2014) reg.7A (Time limit for claims—the Childcare Payments Act 2014)*

With effect from May 17, 2017, reg.2(2) of the Tax Credits (Claims   5.029 and Notifications) (Amendment) Regulations 2017 (SI 2017/597) substituted "paragraphs (2A) to (4)" for "paragraphs (3) and (4)" in paras.(1) and (2). With effect from the same date, reg.2(3) of the same amending regulations inserted after para.(2) the following new paragraph:

"(2A) Where—
    (a) a claim for a tax credit is received by a relevant authority at an appropriate office and the person making the claim, or in the case of joint claimants either person, has made a valid declaration of eligibility under section 4(2) of the Childcare Payments Act 2014,
    (b) no payments under section 20(1)(a) of the Childcare Payments Act 2014 have been made out of any childcare account held by the person making the claim, or in the case of joint claimants either person, and
    (c) all the childcare accounts held by the person making the claim for tax credits, or in the case of joint claimants both persons, have been closed,
regulation 7 shall apply .".

pp.647-648, *annotation to the Tax Credits (Claims and Notifications) Regulations 2002 (SI 2002/2014) reg.7A(1) and (2) (Time limit for claims—the Childcare Payments Act 2014)*

In the last sentence to the annotation to para.(1), delete "paras (3) and   5.030 (4)" and replace with "paras (2A) to (4)". Likewise in the last sentence to the annotation to para.(2) delete "paras (3) and (4)" and replace with "paras (2A) to (4)".

p.648, *annotation to the Tax Credits (Claims and Notifications) Regulations 2002 (SI 2002/2014) reg.7A(2A) (Time limit for claims—the Childcare Payments Act 2014)*

5.031   Insert the following new annotation after para.2.306:

Paragraph (2A)
This applies the usual backdating rule in reg.7, rather than the rules in this regulation, where a claimant has made a valid declaration of eligibility under the Childcare Payments Act 2014 but the claimant's childcare account has been closed and no payments have been made out of the account.

p.701, *annotation to the Tax Credits (Immigration) Regulations 2003 (SI 2003/653) reg.3 (Exclusion of persons subject to immigration control from entitlement to tax credits)*

5.032   In the annotation to paras.(4)-(9), delete the fourth and fifth sentences in the first paragraph of 2.422 (starting "Any such retrospective claim . . . ") and replace with following commentary: 'Any such retrospective claim must be made within one month of notification from the IND (para.(5)).'

pp.707-709, *annotation to the Tax Credits (Residence) Regulations 2003 (SI 2003/654) reg.3 (Circumstances in which a person is treated as not being in the United Kingdom)*

5.033   In *HA v HRMC (TC)* [2015] UKUT 708 (AAC) the claimant's husband had resided in the UK for several extended periods, had moved address with her, had worked until he had been made redundant (when he claimed JSA), had obtained indefinite leave to remain in the UK and was on the electoral roll in the UK. However, at the same time the claimant's husband also retained strong links in Ghana, where he had both an apartment and employment. Judge Hemingway dismissed the claimant's appeal against the FTT decision that she was not entitled to claim tax credits as a single person for the 2011/12 tax year. In dismissing the claimant's further appeal, the Court of Appeal in *Arthur v HMRC* [2017] EWCA Civ 1756; [2018] AACR 10 held that the claimant's husband was a person who was "ordinarily resident" in the UK as at April 6, 2011 for the purposes of a joint tax credit claim under s.3(3) of the Tax Credits Act 2002. Accordingly, the claimant herself was not able to make claim tax credits as a single person. The Court of Appeal also concluded it was open to the FTT to consider events after April 6, 2011 in deciding whether the husband was ordinarily resident (applying *Levene v IRC* [1928] A.C. 217). Newey LJ helpfully set out the relevant legal principles as follows:

"16. Guidance on the meaning of "ordinarily resident" can be found in three decisions of the House of Lords: *Levene v Inland Revenue*

Commissioners [1928] AC 217, *Inland Revenue Commissioners v Lysaght* [1928] AC 234 and *R (Shah) v Barnet LBC* [1983] 2 AC 309. Those cases provide authority for the following propositions:

i) The expression "ordinary residence" "connotes residence in a place with some degree of continuity and apart from accidental or temporary absences" (*Levene*, at 225, per Viscount Cave LC);

ii) "[T]he converse to 'ordinarily' is 'extraordinarily' and . . . part of the regular order of a man's life, adopted voluntarily and for settled purposes, is not 'extraordinary'" (*Lysaght*, at 243, per Viscount Sumner). Consistently with this, "ordinarily resident" "refers to a man's abode in a particular place or country which he has adopted voluntarily and for settled purposes as part of the regular order of his life for the time being, whether of short or long duration" (*Shah*, at 343, per Lord Scarman);

iii) "Ordinary residence" differs little from "residence" (*Levene*, at 222, per Viscount Cave LC). "Ordinarily resident" means "no more than that the residence is not casual and uncertain but that the person held to reside does so in the ordinary course of his life" (*Lysaght*, at 248, per Lord Buckmaster);

iv) A person can be resident in a place even though "from time to time he leaves it for the purpose of business or pleasure" and, conversely, "a person who has his home abroad and visits the United Kingdom from time to time for temporary purposes without setting up an establishment in this country is not considered to be resident here" (*Levene*, at 222-223, per Viscount Cave LC);

v) A person can also be resident in a place even though he would prefer to be elsewhere. In *Lysaght*, Lord Buckmaster said (at 248):

'A man might well be compelled to reside here completely against his will; the exigencies of business often forbid the choice of residence, and though a man may make his home elsewhere and stay in this country only because business compels him, yet none the less, if the periods for which and the conditions under which he stays are such that they may be regarded as constituting residence, as in my opinion they were in this case, it is open to the Commissioners to find that in fact he does so reside";

vi) A person may reside in more than one place (*Levene*, at 223, per Viscount Cave LC);

vii) "Ordinary residence" is not synonymous with "domicile" or "permanent home" (*Shah*, at 342-343 and 345, per Lord Scarman);

viii) "Immigration status" "may or may not be a guide to a person's intention in establishing a residence in this country" (*Shah*, 348, per Lord Scarman); and

ix) "There are two, and no more than two, respects in which the mind of the 'propositus' is important in determining ordinary residence": "[t]he residence must be voluntarily adopted" and "there must be a degree of settled purpose", which could potentially be "a specific limited purpose" (*Shah*, at 344 and 348, per Lord Scarman). Lord Scarman explained in *Shah* (at 344):

'The purpose may be one; or there may be several. It may be specific or general. All that the law requires is that there is a settled purpose. This is not to say that the 'propositus' intends to stay where he is indefinitely; indeed his purpose, while settled, may be for a limited period. Education, business or profession, employment, health, family, or merely love of the place spring to mind as common reasons for a choice of regular abode. and there may well be many others. All that is necessary is that the purpose of living where one does has a sufficient degree of continuity to be properly described as settled.'"

p.743, *amendment to the Child Benefit (General) Regulations 2006 (SI 2006/223) reg.1(3) (Citation, commencement and interpretation)*

5.034   With effect from June 1, 2017, reg.2(2) of the Child Benefit (General) (Amendment) Regulations 2017 (SI 2017/607) amended the definition of "approved training" in reg. 1(3) by deleting subpara.(d) and substituting:

"(d) in relation to Northern Ireland, known as "PEACE IV Children and Young People 2.1" or "Training for Success".

p.1070, *amendment to the Child Trust Funds Regulations 2004 (SI 2004/1450) reg.10(3) (Statements for an account)*

5.035   With effect from October 1, 2017, reg.3 of the Child Trust Funds (Amendment No.2) Regulations 2017 (SI 2017/748) substituted for sub-para.(3)(c) the following new sub-paragraph:

"(c) where a person has been appointed by the Treasury or the Secretary of State by virtue of section 3(10) of the Act, to that person on behalf of the child, and".

p.1078, *amendment to the Child Trust Funds Regulations 2004 (SI 2004/1450) reg.13(7) (Conditions for application by responsible person or the child to open an account etc.)*

5.036   With effect from October 1, 2017, reg.4(a) of the Child Trust Funds (Amendment No.2) Regulations 2017 (SI 2017/748) substituted for sub-para.(7)(e) the following new sub-paragraph:

"(e) where a person is appointed by the Treasury or the Secretary of State by virtue of section 3(10) of the Act, or".

p.1079, *amendment to the Child Trust Funds Regulations 2004 (SI 2004/1450) reg.13(11) (Conditions for application by responsible person or the child to open an account etc.)*

5.037   With effect from October 1, 2017, reg.4(b) of the Child Trust Funds (Amendment No.2) Regulations 2017 (SI 2017/748) substituted for "the Official Solicitor or the Accountant of Court, he" in para.(11) the following phrase: "the person appointed by the Treasury or the Secretary of State by virtue of section 3(10) of the Act, that person.".

p.1099, *amendment to the Child Trust Funds Regulations 2004 (SI 2004/1450) reg.33A (The Official Solicitor or Accountant of Court to be the person who has the authority to manage an account)*

With effect from October 1, 2017, reg.5(a) of the Child Trust Funds (Amendment No.2) Regulations 2017 (SI 2017/748) substituted "The person appointed by the Treasury or the Secretary of State by virtue of section 3(10) of the Act" in the heading for "The Official Solicitor or Accountant of Court".   **5.038**

With effect from the same date, reg.5(b) of the same amending regulations substituted the following new paragraph for para.(1):

"(1) The person appointed by the Treasury or the Secretary of State by virtue of section 3(10) of the Act is to be the person who has the authority to manage a child's account for the purposes of section 3(6)(b) of the Act where the circumstances specified in paragraph (2) apply."

With effect from the same date, reg.5(c)(i) of the same amending regulations inserted before sub-para.(2)(a) the following new sub-paragraphs:

"(za) except in a case of a person who was a looked after child or a looked after and accommodated child on 30th September 2017, there is a continuous period of at least twelve months during which the circumstances under sub-paragraphs (a) and (b) apply,

(zb) in a case of a person who was a looked after child or a looked after and accommodated child on 30th September 2017, the circumstances under sub-paragraphs (a) and (b) apply,".

With effect from the same date, reg.5(c)(ii) of the same amending regulations substituted "a child" for "the child" in sub-para.(2)(a).

pp.1100–1101, *amendment to the Child Trust Funds Regulations 2004 (SI 2004/1450) reg.33A (The Official Solicitor or Accountant of Court to be the person who has the authority to manage an account)*

With effect from October 1, 2017, reg.5(d) of the Child Trust Funds (Amendment No.2) Regulations 2017 (SI 2017/748) omitted paras.(2A), (2B), (3) and (5).   **5.039**

With effect from the same date, reg.5(e) of the same amending regulations substituted "person appointed by the Treasury or the Secretary of State by virtue of section 3(10) of the Act" for "Official Solicitor or Accountant of Court" in each place the phrase appears in para.(4).

p.1102, *amendment to the Child Trust Funds Regulations 2004 (SI 2004/1450) reg.33A (The Official Solicitor or Accountant of Court to be the person who has the authority to manage an account)*

5.040 With effect from October 1, 2017, reg.5(f) of the Child Trust Funds (Amendment No.2) Regulations 2017 (SI 2017/748) omitted the definition of "return period" in para.(6) while reg.5(g) inserted after para.(6) the following new paragraph:

"(7) Where the appointment of a person ("original appointee") by the Treasury or the Secretary of State by virtue of section 3(10) of the Act ceases, the original appointee must provide any information held by that person in connection with the management of a child trust fund to the new person (if any) appointed instead.".

pp.1127-1128, *amendment to the Childcare Payments Eligibility Regulations 2015 (SI 2015/448) reg.9 (The requirement to be in qualifying paid work)*

5.041 With effect from December 7, 2017, reg.3(a)-(c) of the Childcare Payments (Eligibility) (Amendment) Regulations 2017 (SI 2017/1101) substituted "holds" for "hold" in para.(1); omitted "four times" in para.(1)(b)(ii); and inserted at the end of para.(1)(b)(ii) the following new sub-paragraph:

"; or
(c) the person is in paid work as an employed person and as a self-employed person and the person's expected income from the work in the period specified in paragraph (4) is greater than or equal to the relevant threshold.",

With effect from the same date, reg.3(d)-(e) of the same amending regulations substituted "paragraph (1) does" for "regulation 9(1) will" in para.(1A)(2); substituted "31" for "14" in paras.(2)(a)(ii) and (2)(b)(ii); and omitted "previous" in para.(5A).

p.1129, *amendment to the Childcare Payments Eligibility Regulations 2015 (SI 2015/448) reg.10 (Calculation of expected income)*

5.042 With effect from December 7, 2017, reg.4 of the Childcare Payments (Eligibility) (Amendment) Regulations 2017 (SI 2017/1101) omitted para.(5).

pp.1129-1130, *amendment to the Childcare Payments Eligibility Regulations 2015 (SI 2015/448) reg.10 (Self-employed persons: start-up periods)*

5.043 With effect from December 7, 2017, reg.5 of the Childcare Payments (Eligibility) (Amendment) Regulations 2017 (SI 2017/1101) inserted "or (c)" after "regulation 9(1)(b)" in paras.(1) and (4) and substituted "at least 48 months" for "4 calendar years" in para.(3).

pp.1129-1130, *amendment to the Childcare Payments Eligibility Regulations 2015 (SI 2015/448) reg.12 (Qualifying paid work: time off in connection with sickness or parenting)*

With effect from December 7, 2017, reg.6 of the Childcare Payments (Eligibility) (Amendment) Regulations 2017 (SI 2017/1101) omitted "ordinary or additional" in para.(1)(f); substituted "a" for "an ordinary" in para.(1)(g); omitted para.(1)(h); and substituted "31" for "14" in para.(4). 5.044

p.1132, *amendment to the Childcare Payments Eligibility Regulations 2015 (SI 2015/448) reg.13 (Qualifying paid work: caring, incapacity for work or limited capability for work)*

With effect from December 7, 2017, reg.7 of the Childcare Payments (Eligibility) (Amendment) Regulations 2017 (SI 2017/1101) substituted for para.(1)(b)(v) the following: 5.045

"(v) contributory employment and support allowance under section 1 of the Welfare Reform Act 2007 or section 1 of the Welfare Reform Act (Northern Ireland) 2007; or".

p.1140, *amendment to the Childcare Payments Regulations 2015 (SI 2015/522) reg.5 (Variation of entitlement periods)*

With effect from December 7, 2017, reg.3(a) of the Childcare Payments (Amendment) Regulations 2017 (SI 2017/1096) omitted "or" at the end of sub-para.(1)(b) and inserted at the end of sub-para.(1)(c) the following new sub-paragraph: 5.046

"; or
(d) in order to align the entitlement period of an account holder ("A") with the declaration period of A's partner under regulation 15 of the Childcare (Early Years Provision Free of Charge) (Extended Entitlement) Regulations 2016."

With effect from the same date, reg.3(b) of the same amending regulations inserted after para.(1) the following new paragraph:

"(1A) The length of the variation referred to in paragraph (1) shall not exceed two months.".

p.1148, *amendment to the Childcare Payments Regulations 2015 (SI 2015/522) reg.17 (Compensatory payments)*

With effect from December 7, 2017, reg.4 of the Childcare Payments (Amendment) Regulations 2017 (SI 2017/1096) substituted for para.(3A) the following: 5.047

"(3A) The circumstances specified in this paragraph are that—
(a) a person is unable to open a childcare account, or
(b) a person's childcare account fails to function effectively
for a continuous period of at least 14 days, due to a serious technical failure affecting HMRC or the account provider.".

PART VI

UPDATING MATERIAL: VOLUME V

UNIVERSAL CREDIT

Commentary by

John Mesher

Richard Poynter

Nick Wikeley

p.xxvii, *Table of Cases (entry for PL v Department for Social Development)*

This entry should be in the Table of Commissioners' Decisions on 6.001
p.xxix as a decision of a Northern Ireland Social Security Commissioner.

p.xxviii, *Table of Cases (entry for R (on the application of Reilly) v Secretary of State for Work and Pensions)*

This entry wrongly refers to this decision of the Supreme Court as 6.002
merely a variant of the Court of Appeal's decision in *SSWP v Reilly and Hewstone* and *SSWP v Jeffrey and Bevan*. The case references given are for the Court of Appeal decision only, which appears in paras 1.69, 1.102 and 2.282. The reference for the Supreme Court decision is [2013] UKSC 68; [2014] 1 A.C. 453 and it appears in paras 1.69, 1.92, 1.102, 1.103 and 2.282.

pp.54-60, *annotation to the Welfare Reform Act 2012 s.14 (Claimant commitment)*

Two appeals before the Upper Tribunal in Scotland may possibly 6.002.1
address the question of whether the current standard terms of claimant commitments, e.g. in the form of a provision like "I will attend and take part in appointments with my adviser when required" are sufficient in themselves to be a notification of the imposition of a work-related requirement (e.g. the work-focused interview requirement under s.15 of the WRA 2012) under s.24(4).

p.77, *annotation to the Welfare Reform Act 2012 s.24(4) (Imposition of requirements)*

Two appeals before the Upper Tribunal in Scotland may possibly 6.002.2
address the question of whether the current standard terms of claimant commitments, e.g. in the form of a provision like "I will attend and take part in appointments with my adviser when required" are sufficient in themselves to be a notification of the imposition of a work-related requirement (e.g. the work-focused interview requirement under s.15 of the WRA 2012) under s.24(4).

pp.79-80, *annotation to the Welfare Reform Act 2012 s.26 (Higher-level sanctions)*

S v SSWP (UC) [2017] UKUT 477 (AAC) actually decides only a 6.002.3
relatively short point about the meaning of "for no good reason" in ss.26 and 27 of the WRA 2012. The First-tier Tribunal had said that the claimant's professed ignorance of the effect of work (including part-time work) on his universal credit entitlement could not amount to a good reason for failing to undertake all reasonable work search action because ignorance of the law was no defence. On the claimant's appeal to the

Upper Tribunal the Secretary of State accepted that, by analogy with the well-established case law on good cause for a delay in claiming, ignorance of the law was capable of constituting a good reason. Judge Mitchell agreed that the tribunal had erred in law, but concluded that the error was not material because the only proper conclusion on the evidence was that the claimant could reasonably have been expected to raise with his work coach or other DWP official any concerns or confusions over the financial implications on his universal credit award of taking any of the sorts of work he had agreed to search for. Thus, even on the correct approach the claimant did not have a good reason for what the tribunal had concluded was a failure under s.27(2)(a).

On a more general point raised when permission to appeal to the Upper Tribunal was given, the judge decided in para.54 that there was no material difference in meaning between the phrases "for no good reason" and "without a good reason" and that both referred to the absence of a good reason. However, the point made in the main volume annotation about a possible difference in meaning may not yet have been conclusively rejected, as it is not clear that in the particular circumstances it would have mattered which was adopted.

It may also be that the analogy with good cause (indeed in para.57 the judge said that "good reason" expressed the same concept as "good cause" but in more modern language) is misleading or at least incomplete. That is because when considering good cause for a delay in claiming there is no difficulty in adopting the general meaning approved in *R(SB) 6/83* of some fact that, having regard to all the circumstances (including a claimant's state of health and the information that he had or might have obtained), would probably have caused a reasonable person of the same age and experience to act or fail to act as the claimant had done. It was in that context that the principle that a reasonable ignorance or mistaken belief as to rights could constitute good cause was established. But the question there is what a reasonable person could be expected to do to secure an advantage to them in the form of the benefit claimed late. In the context of universal credit sanctions, the notion of reasonableness carries a distinctly different force. So where the work search requirement under s.17(1)(a) of the WRA 2012 to take all reasonable action to obtain paid work is concerned, reasonableness must be based on what level of activity the community that funds universal credit is entitled to expect from a claimant as a condition of receipt of the benefit. Similar, although not necessarily identical, factors are present in relation to the other work-related requirements and the sanctions for voluntarily and for no good reason ceasing work or losing pay. Although all personal circumstances are relevant, the notion of a balance between those circumstances and the claimant's proper responsibilities is not captured by the traditional concept of "good cause". The better analogy would seem to be with "just cause" as used in unemployment benefit and in old style JSA before the 2012 amendments. The adoption of the "good cause" approach in relation to claimed ignorance of rights in *S* cannot be taken as excluding such an approach. The full meaning of "for no good reason" remains to be worked out.

pp.88-89, *annotation to the Welfare Reform Act 2012 s.27 (Other sanctions)*

See *S v SSWP (UC)* [2017] UKUT 477 (AAC), discussed in the entry   6.002.4
for pp.79-80, on the sanction under s.27(2)(a) and "for no good reason".

p.119, *annotation to the Welfare Reform and Work Act 2016, s18 (loans for mortgage interest etc.)*

Regulations have now been made under ss.18, 19 and 21: see the   6.003
Loans for Mortgage Interest Regulations 2017 (SI 2017/725) in the *New Legislation* section, above.

p.139, *annotation to the Universal Credit Regulations 2013 (SI 2013/376) reg.4 (When a person is responsible for a child or qualifying young person)*

On the meaning of "normally living with", see now *MC v SSWP (UC)*   6.003.1
[2018] UKUT 44 (AAC), holding that the term does not simply mean
living with one person for longer than with any other person.

pp.217-220, *annotation to the Universal Credit Regulations 2013 (SI 2013/376) reg.57 (Self-employed earnings)*

The Chartered Institute of Taxation published an interesting short   6.004
report from its Low Incomes Tax Reform Group in October 2017 (*Self-employed claimants of universal credit—lifting the burdens*), identifying many
practical problems arising from the present form of the legislation.
The current intention is that the Universal Credit (Surpluses and Self-employed Losses) (Digital Service) Amendment Regulations 2015 (SI
2015/345), whose implementation has twice been deferred, will be
brought into force in April 2018. Regulation 7 of the Universal Credit
(Miscellaneous Amendments, Saving and Transitional Provision) Regulations 2018 (SI 2018/65) changes the coming into force date for the
Regulations to April 11, 2018 and makes further amendments. The
Regulations will introduce complex rules for attributing surplus income
in periods of non-entitlement to universal credit to periods of entitlement that will interact with the rules on self-employed earnings, especially the minimum income floor (reg.62), with particular difficulty.
They will also allow some carrying forward of self-employed losses in any
one assessment period to future assessment periods, although subject
also to the minimum income floor.

pp.226-227, *annotation to the Universal Credit Regulations 2013 (SI 2013/376) reg.61 (Information for calculating earned income—real time information)*

SSWP v RW (rule 17) (UC) [2017] UKUT 347 (AAC) concerned   6.005
circumstances in which HMRC's real time earnings feed showed notification on two dates in February 2016 (February 1, 2016 and February

29, 2016) of the claimant having received earnings. Her assessment period ran from the first of each calendar month to the last day of that month. Both receipts were taken into account in relation to February 2016, resulting in a much reduced universal credit entitlement. The claimant's case on mandatory reconsideration and appeal was that her January 2016 earnings were received on Sunday January 31, 2016, but not reported by her employer until the next day (as apparently confirmed in HMRC documents). She had no control over when the earnings information was reported. The First-tier Tribunal, in allowing the claimant's appeal, rejected the Secretary of State's argument that para.(3) did not justify any departure from the basic rule in reg.61(2)(a) that, where the employer is a Real Time Information employer, the amount of a claimant's earnings for any assessment period is to be based on the information which is both reported to HMRC and received by the Secretary of State from HMRC in that assessment period. The tribunal relied on two alternative reasons: that under para.(3)(b)(i) no information had been received from HMRC in respect of the January assessment period and that under para.(3)(b)(ii) the information received in respect of the February 2016 assessment period failed to reflect the definition of employed earnings in reg.55 in some material respect. The Secretary of State appealed to the Upper Tribunal, but on receipt of detailed directions from Judge Wright, applied, without giving any reasons, to withdraw the appeal. The Secretary of State, on being directed to explain why the request was made, wrote that it had been concluded that the case could be brought within para.(3)(b)(i) on the basis that reporting a payment by an employer after the date on which it was actually made can be considered a failure by the employer (and drawing attention to the provisions of paras (4) and (5)). In the light of that explanation Judge Wright consented to the withdrawal of the appeal. He directed that his decision recording that, although it determined none of the issues involved, go onto the AAC website as the Secretary of State's reasoning might be relevant in other cases.

With respect to all involved in *RW*, it is submitted that the various approaches sketched in above are either wrong or not to the point. First, the reliance on para.(3)(b)(i) in relation to the January 2016 assessment, even if justified, appears to be a red herring. Paragraph (3)(b) applies in respect of a particular assessment period. If no information was received from HMRC because of a failure by the employer that could only have affected entitlement in the January 2016 assessment period and not entitlement in the February 2016 assessment period. It appears that the tribunal altered the amount of entitlement for the February 2016 assessment period and it not clear what, if any, adjustment was made in relation to the January 2016 assessment period. Further, it appears a more natural reading of para.(3)(b)(i) that it applies only where no information has been received from HMRC by the date on which a decision is made about a particular assessment period, not where information has been received by that date but involves some late recording of receipts. Thus the reason for the Secretary of State's support of the tribunal's decision appears flawed.

Second, the alternative basis adopted by the tribunal under para.

(3)(b)(ii) also appears flawed in so far as it relied on the information received from HMRC having failed to reflect the definition of employed earnings in reg.55. Regulation 55 is concerned with the nature of the categories of payments that count or do not count as such earnings and with allowable deductions, not with any rules as to the assessment period to which any payment is to be attributed. It is reg.54(1) that supplies the general principle that, unless otherwise provided in Chap.2 of the Regulations, the calculation of earned income in respect of any assessment period is to be based on the actual amounts received in that period. The information received from HMRC in *RW* did not fail to reflect any element of the definition in reg.55. It failed to reflect the fact that the claimant received a payment (which plainly fell within reg.55) on January 31, 2016, which is a different thing. The tribunal in its statement of reasons referred to reg.55(5) as indicating that the purpose of reg.55 was to find the employed earnings in an assessment period. It is true that reg.55(5), on deductions for national insurance, income tax and pension contributions, refers to those being for the purpose of calculating the amount of employed earnings in respect of an assessment period, but that merely sets the context and does not make the definition in reg.55 include any requirement that amounts be notified in the same assessment period as they were received in.

However, the tribunal's decision may be supported on a rather simpler and more straightforward basis. Why could it not have been concluded that the circumstances fell within reg.61(3)(b)(ii) because the information received from HMRC was incorrect in a material respect? The word "incorrect" is one that can legitimately be given a relatively broad interpretation. The information notified by HMRC on Monday February 1, 2016 was incorrect in the sense that, whether the delay in reporting over the preceding weekend was the employer's or HMRC's the dating of the notification on the first available working day created a materially misleading impression. The way would then be open, as reg.61(2) would not apply, to apply the ordinary rules in regs 54 and 55 to both assessment periods in accordance with reg.61(4) and (5).

pp.228-230, *annotation to the Universal Credit Regulations 2013 (SI 2013/376) reg.62 (Minimum income floor)*

The Chartered Institute of Taxation published an interesting short report from its Low Incomes Tax Reform Group in October 2017 (*Self-employed claimants of universal credit—lifting the burdens*), identifying many practical problems arising from the present form of the legislation, especially relating to the minimum income floor (MIF).   **6.006**

The current intention is that the Universal Credit (Surpluses and Self-employed Losses) (Digital Service) Amendment Regulations 2015 (SI 2015/345), whose implementation has twice been deferred, will be brought into force in April 2018. Regulation 7 of the Universal Credit (Miscellaneous Amendments, Saving and Transitional Provision) Regulations 2018 (SI 2018/65) changes the coming into force date for the Regulations to April 11, 2018 and makes further amendments. The Regulations will introduce complex rules for attributing surplus income in periods of non-entitlement to universal credit to periods of entitlement that will interact with the rules of self-employed earnings, especially the MIF, with particular difficulty. They will also allow some carrying forward of self-employed losses in any one assessment period to future assessment periods, although subject also to the MIF.

pp.231-232, *annotation to the Universal Credit Regulations 2013 (SI 2013/376) reg.64 (Meaning of "gainful self-employment")*

6.007   *JF v HMRC (TC)* [2017] UKUT 334 (AAC) concerned the definition of "self-employed" in reg.2(1) of the Working Tax Credit (Entitlement and Maximum Rate) Regulations 2002 as in force with effect from April 6, 2015, which includes a condition that the trade, profession or vocation be "organised and regular". Judge Wikeley gave guidance that, in assessing organisation and regularity for the purposes of WTC, HMRC should "get real" and adjust expectations about the documentary support to be expected for the modest enterprises often involved. Nor should the facts that a claimant did not have an accountant or a business plan necessarily mean that the condition was not met. However, by contrast with the position in WTC, self-employed universal credit claimants will no doubt be arguing that their business is not organised, developed and regular, so as to avoid the operation of the minimum income floor under reg.62, rather than the other way round, to qualify for WTC.

p.245, *amendment to the Universal Credit Regulations 2013 (SI 2013/376) reg.76(1)(a) (Special schemes for compensation etc.)*

6.008   With effect from June 19, 2017, reg.9(a) of the Social Security (Emergency Funds) (Amendment) Regulations 2017 (SI 2017/689) inserted the words "or support" after the word "compensation" in the introductory words. From the same date reg.9(b) omitted the word "or" at the end of sub-para.(iii). From the same date reg.9(c) inserted the following new sub-paragraphs:

"(iv) the terrorist attacks in London on 22nd March 2017 or 3rd June 2017,

(v) the bombing in Manchester on 22nd May 2017".

p.259, *amendment to the Universal Credit Regulations 2013 (SI 2013/376) reg.87 (References to paid work)*

6.009   With effect from November 6, 2017, reg.4(3) of the Social Security (Qualifying Young Persons Participating in Relevant Training Schemes) (Amendment) Regulations 2017 (SI 2017/987) substituted the words "better-paid work" for the words "better paid work". Bizarrely, this purely semantic amendment does not apply to universal credit awards unless they fall within reg.5(1)(a)-(d) of the Universal Credit (Digital Service) Amendment Regulations 2014 (SI 2014/2887) (reg.5 of the amending Regulations).

p.260, *amendment to the Universal Credit Regulations 2013 (SI 2013/376) reg.88 (Expected hours)*

With effect from April 3, 2017, reg.6 of the Employment and Support 6.010 Allowance and Universal Credit (Miscellaneous and Transitional and Savings Provisions) Regulations 2017 (SI 2017/204) inserted the words "(subject to the following sub-paragraphs)" after "responsible carer" in para.(2)(a)(i). From the same date it inserted a new sub-para.(aa) after sub-para.(a):

"(aa)   where the claimant is a responsible carer of a child who has not yet reached compulsory school age, the number of hours that the Secretary of State considers is compatible with those caring responsibilities;".

From the same date it inserted the words "who has reached compulsory school age but who is" after the words "a child" in para.(2)(b).

Those amendments were omitted in error from the main volume for 2017/18. The general note to reg.88 should be read subject to them. The effect is to create in para.(2)(aa) a new category of responsible carers of children under compulsory school age whose required hours are restricted to what is compatible with those caring responsibilities without the condition in para.(2)(a)(ii) that the claimant has reasonable prospects of obtaining paid work. Compulsory school age is reached at the beginning of the school term following 1 January, 1 April or 1 September, according to which date first follows the child's 5th birthday.

p.264, *amendment to the Universal Credit Regulations 2013 (SI 2013/376) reg.90(5) (Claimants subject to no work-related requirements—minimum income floor)*

With effect from November 26, 2014, reg.4(7) of the Universal Credit 6.010.1 and Miscellaneous Amendments (No.2) Regulations 2014 (SI 2014/2888) substituted the following for para.(5):

"(5) A claimant falls within section 19 of the Act if they are treated as having earned income in accordance with regulation 62 (minimum income floor)."

This amendment was omitted in error from the 2017/18 main volume and earlier editions. The annotations should be read subject to this change.

p.264, *annotation to the Universal Credit Regulations 2013 (SI 2013/376) reg.90 (Claimants subject to no work-related requirements—the earnings thresholds)*

See the entry for p.260 for the April 2017 amendments to reg.88 on 6.011 expected hours that were omitted in error from the main volume.

pp.269-270, *annotation to the Universal Credit Regulations 2013 (SI 2013/376) reg.95 (Work search requirement—all reasonable action)*

6.012   See the entry for p.260 for the April 2017 amendments to reg.88 on expected hours that were omitted in error from the main volume.

In *RR v SSWP (UC)* [2017] UKUT 459 (AAC), the First-tier Tribunal, in upholding two medium-level sanctions on the basis that the claimant had not taken work-search action for the 35 expected hours in two weeks, failed to consider whether there should be deductions from 35 hours under reg.95(2)(b) when there was evidence of circumstances (having to deal with the fall-out from divorce or other family proceedings) that could have amounted to a domestic emergency or other temporary circumstances. The tribunal appeared to think that the 35 hours were immutable, which was plainly an error of law. Alternatively, the claimant could have been taken to satisfy the condition in s.17(1)(a) through reg.95(1)(a)(ii), which applies even though the expected hours, less deductions, are not met. The decision-maker and the tribunal put some emphasis on the claimant having agreed in her claimant commitment to prepare and look for work for 35 hours a week. Judge Wikeley pointed out that the claimant commitment was only in terms of "normally" spending 35 hours a week, but in fact the number of hours specified in a claimant commitment cannot be directly relevant unless they establish a lesser number of hours under reg.88(2) or an agreement to a deduction of hours under reg.95(2). The test is in terms of the expected hours less deductions, which the claimant commitment merely records, or "all reasonable action" under reg.95(1)(a)(ii). It is worth noting that the claimant commitment specified 35 hours normally for a combination of work preparation (s.16(1) of the Welfare Reform Act 2012) and work search, so did incorporate an unquantified deduction under reg.95(2)(a).

The judge, in re-making the decision in the claimant's favour, did not expressly consider the condition that a deduction under para.(2) be agreed by the Secretary of State. He must either have regarded that condition as one on which a First-tier Tribunal was entitled to substitute its own agreement or have regarded he Secretary of State's support of the appeal in the Upper Tribunal and of the substitution of a decision as necessarily involving agreement to a deduction. Similarly, there was no express consideration of the overriding condition in reg.95(1)(b) that the action taken in a week gave the claimant the best prospects of obtaining work. That must be regarded as having been satisfied in the absence of it having been raised on behalf of the Secretary of State in the support of the appeal to the Upper Tribunal.

See also the entry for p.281 (reg.99(5)).

p.272, *annotation to the Universal Credit Regulations 2013 (SI 2013/376) reg.97(2) (Work search requirement and work availability requirement—limitations)*

6.013   See the entry for p.260 for the April 2017 amendments to reg.88 on expected hours that were omitted in error from the main volume.

p.281, *annotation to the Universal Credit Regulations 2013 (SI 2013/376) reg.99(5) (Circumstances in which requirements must not be imposed)*

See the entry for pp.269-270 and *RR v SSWP (UC)* [2017] UKUT   6.014
459 (AAC). The Upper Tribunal judge suggested that another way of looking at the case, rather than exploring deductions from 35 as the expected number of hours under reg.95(2), was to consider whether a work search requirement could not be imposed for the weeks in question on the basis that the claimant was dealing with a domestic emergency or other temporary circumstances (reg.99(5)(b)). The judge's suggestion that reg.99(2A) and (5) apply only when the circumstances are such that it is unreasonable to require the claimant to comply with any work search requirement at all, rather than merely to undertake more than reduced hours of work search action, appears right. The evidence in *RR* probably did not support such a conclusion.

p.282, *annotation to the Universal Credit Regulations 2013 (SI 2013/376) reg.99(6) and (6A) (Circumstances in which requirements must not be imposed)*

The Social Security Advisory Committee published an interesting   6.015
paper, *In-work progression and Universal Credit* (Occasional Paper No.19) in November 2017. The paper welcomes the DWP's adoption of a cautious "test and learn" approach and the current Randomised Control Trial, but recommends that the DWP should test a wider range of interventions and quickly develop a wider understanding of the variety of circumstances of working claimants who will fall within the ambit of universal credit. It also recommends tackling operational complexities that can be an obstacle to in-work progression and clarifying policy in a number of areas, such as where claimants are working part-time in order to study, re-train or pursue other interests.

p.338, *amendment to the Universal Credit Regulations 2013 (SI 2013/376) Sch.4 Pt.5 (Social Rented Sector other than Temporary Accommodation)*

With effect from April 30, 2017, reg.2(1) and (2) of the Universal   6.016
Credit (Tenant Incentive Scheme) Amendment Regulations 2017 (SI 2017/427) substituted the following for the italicised cross-heading above para.31:

"*Amount taken into account as the relevant payment*"

p.338, *amendment to the Universal Credit Regulations 2013 (SI 2013/376) Sch.4 Pt.5 (Social Rented Sector other than Temporary Accommodation)*

With effect from April 30, 2017, reg.2(1) and (3) of the Universal   6.017
Credit (Tenant Incentive Scheme) Amendment Regulations 2017 (SI 2017/427) inserted a new para.32A after para.32 as follows:

"Reduction under tenant incentive scheme

32A.—(1) Where a reduction in the rent or service charge payments for which a renter would otherwise have been liable is applied by a provider of social housing under an approved tenant incentive scheme, the amount of any relevant payment to be taken into account under paragraph 6 is to be determined as if no such reduction had been applied.

(2) In paragraph (1) "approved tenant incentive scheme" means a scheme which is—

(a) operated by a provider of social housing and designed to avoid rent arrears by allowing reductions in rent or service charges or other advantages in return for meeting specified conditions; and

(b) approved by the Secretary of State."

p.342, *annotation to the Universal Credit Regulations 2013 (SI 2013/376) Sch.4 Pt.3 paras.8-12 (Housing costs element for renters— General provisions about calculation of amount of housing costs element for renters—Room allocation)*

6.018   For a summary of the current law on what constitutes a "bedroom" for the purposes of paras 8-12, see *M v SSWP (UC)* [2017] UKUT 443 (AAC). On the facts of that case, the Upper Tribunal (Judge Mitchell) decided that the First-tier Tribunal had not erred in law in finding that, in the circumstances of that case, a room with an area of 43 sq. ft. was a bedroom.

p.343, *annotation to the Universal Credit Regulations 2013 (SI 2013/376) Sch.4 Pt.3 paras.8-12 (Housing costs element for renters— General provisions about calculation of amount of housing costs element for renters—Room allocation—Adult placement schemes and foster parents)*

6.019   In *SSWP v PE and Bolton MBC (HB)* [2017] UKUT 393 (AAC), the claimant had a "spare" bedroom that she sometimes used to accommodate disabled adults who were placed with her under an adult placement scheme for one-to-one support in respect of their disabilities. The First-tier Tribunal held that reg.B13 of the Housing Benefit Regulations (which contains provisions that are equivalent to paras 8-12) discriminated unlawfully against the claimant by reference to the more favourable treatment given to foster parents (who performed a similar service but for children rather than disabled adults). The Upper Tribunal (Judge Jacobs) held that the First-tier Tribunal's decision was not wrong in law. It is understood that the Upper Tribunal has refused the Secretary of State permission to appeal to the Court of Appeal.

p.365, *amendment to the Universal Credit Regulations 2013 (SI 2013/376) Sch.10 para.17(1)(a) (Capital to be disregarded)*

6.020   With effect from November 2, 2017, art.15 of the Social Services and Well-being (Wales) Act 2014 and the Regulation and Inspection of

Social Care (Wales) Act 2016 (Consequential Amendments) Order 2017 (SI 2017/901) amended para.17(1)(a) by substituting the words ", or section 29 or 30 of the Children (Scotland) Act 1995 or section 37, 38, 109, 110, 114 or 115 of the Social Services and Well-being (Wales) Act 2014 " for the words "or section 29 or 30 of the Children (Scotland) Act 1995".

p.408, *amendment to the Universal Credit (Transitional Provisions) Regulations 2014 (SI 2014/1230) reg.12 (Modification of tax credits legislation: overpayments and penalties)*

With effect from September 25, 2017, art.7(2) of the Tax Credits (Exercise of Functions in relation to Northern Ireland and Notices for Recovery of Tax Credit Overpayments) Order 2017 amended reg. by omitting sub-para.(3)(b) and substituting a new sub-para.(3)(a)(ii) as follows: 6.021

"(ii) in paragraph (b), for the words from "as if it were" to the end substitute "as an overpayment of universal credit".

With effect from the same date, art.7(3) of the same amending Order omitted para.(4).

pp.772-3, *amendment to Universal Credit, Personal Independence Payment, Jobseeker's Allowance and Employment and Support Allowance (Claims and Payments) Regulations 2013 (SI 2013/380) reg.41 (Evidence and information required from pension fund holders)*

With effect from November 16, 2017, reg.15 of the Social Security (Miscellaneous Amendments No. 4) Regulations 2017 (SI 2017/1015) amended reg.41(3)(b) to read as follows: 6.022

"(b) in the case of—
    (i) a personal pension scheme or occupational pension scheme where income withdrawal is available, the [rate of the annuity which may have been purchased with the funds held under the scheme]; or
    (ii) a personal pension scheme or occupational pension scheme where income withdrawal is not available, the [rate of the annuity which might have been purchased with the fund] if the fund were held under a personal pension scheme or occupational pension scheme where income withdrawal was available,

p.777, *commentary to Universal Credit, Personal Independence Payment, Jobseeker's Allowance and Employment and Support Allowance (Claims and Payments) Regulations 2013 (SI 2013/380) reg.47 (Payment of universal credit)*

With effect from October 4, 2017, the effect of reg.47(1) is modified in relation to Scotland by regs 2 and 3 of the Universal Credit (Claims   6.022.1

and Payments) (Scotland) Regulations 2017 (SSI 2017/227): see Part VII below.

p.785, *commentary to Universal Credit, Personal Independence Payment, Jobseeker's Allowance and Employment and Support Allowance (Claims and Payments) Regulations 2013 (SI 2013/380) reg.58 (Payment to another person on the claimant's behalf)*

6.022.2   With effect from October 4, 2017, the effect of reg.58(1) is supplemented in relation to Scotland by regs 4 and 5 of the Universal Credit (Claims and Payments) (Scotland) Regulations 2017 (SSI 2017/227): see Part VII below.

p.812, *amendment to the Universal Credit, Personal Independence Payment, Jobseeker's Allowance and Employment and Support Allowance (Decisions and Appeals) Regulations 2013 (SI 2013/381) reg.6 (Late application for a revision)*

6.023   With effect from November 16, 2017, reg.16 of the Social Security (Miscellaneous Amendments No. 4) Regulations 2017 (SI 2017/1015) amended reg.6(3) by substituting the number "12" for the number "13".

PART VII

SCOTLAND:
LEGISLATION CONCERNING
DEVOLVED MATTERS

Scotland Act 1998

Acts of the Scottish Parliament

28.—(1) Subject to section 29, the Parliament may make laws, to be known as Acts of the Scottish Parliament. 7.001

(2) Proposed Acts of the Scottish Parliament shall be known as Bills; and a Bill shall become an Act of the Scottish Parliament when it has been passed by the Parliament and has received Royal Assent.

(3) A Bill receives Royal Assent at the beginning of the day on which Letters Patent under the Scottish Seal signed with Her Majesty's own hand signifying Her Assent are recorded in the Register of the Great Seal.

(4) The date of Royal Assent shall be written on the Act of the Scottish Parliament by the Clerk, and shall form part of the Act.

(5) The validity of an Act of the Scottish Parliament is not affected by any invalidity in the proceedings of the Parliament leading to its enactment.

(6) Every Act of the Scottish Parliament shall be judicially noticed.

(7) This section does not affect the power of the Parliament of the United Kingdom to make laws for Scotland.

[[1] (8) But it is recognised that the Parliament of the United Kingdom will not normally legislate with regard to devolved matters without the consent of the Scottish Parliament.]

AMENDMENT

1. Scotland Act 2016 ss.2 and 72(7) (May 23, 2016).

GENERAL NOTE

This section empowers the Scottish Parliament to make legislation. It forms part of a series of provisions which deal with the legislative competence of the Scottish Parliament and the passing of legislation. Sections 29-36 make further provision in this regard. 7.002

Legislative competence

29.—(1) An Act of the Scottish Parliament is not law so far as any provision of the Act is outside the legislative competence of the Parliament. 7.003

(2) A provision is outside that competence so far as any of the following paragraphs apply—

(a) it would form part of the law of a country or territory other than Scotland, or confer or remove functions exercisable otherwise than in or as regards Scotland,

(b) it relates to reserved matters,

(c) it is in breach of the restrictions in Schedule 4,

(d) it is incompatible with any of the Convention rights or with [[1] EU] law,

(e) it would remove the Lord Advocate from his position as head of the systems of criminal prosecution and investigation of deaths in Scotland.

(3) For the purposes of this section, the question whether a provision of an Act of the Scottish Parliament relates to a reserved matter is to be determined, subject to subsection (4), by reference to the purpose of the provision, having regard (among other things) to its effect in all the circumstances.

(4) A provision which—

(a) would otherwise not relate to reserved matters, but

(b) makes modifications of Scots private law, or Scots criminal law, as it applies to reserved matters,

is to be treated as relating to reserved matters unless the purpose of the provision is to make the law in question apply consistently to reserved matters and otherwise.

[² (5) Subsection (1) is subject to section 30(6).]

AMENDMENTS

1. The Treaty of Lisbon (Changes in Terminology) Order 2011 (SI 2011/1043) arts. 3 and 6 (April 22, 2011).
2. Scotland Act 2012 ss.9(2) and 44(5) (July 3, 2012).

GENERAL NOTE

7.004   This section limits the competence of the Scottish Parliament to make laws. It provides that an Act of the Scottish Parliament (ASP) will not be law so far as any provision of it is outside the legislative competence of the Parliament. It further defines in subs.(2) what is meant by a provision of an ASP being outside the legislative competence of the Parliament. This includes legislation purportedly relating to reserved matters. Section 30 then introduces the list of reserved matters (which are set out in Schedule 5) and provides for the modification of Schedules 4 and 5 by subordinate legislation.

Legislative competence: supplementary

7.005   **30.**—(1) Schedule 5 (which defines reserved matters) shall have effect.

(2) Her Majesty may by Order in Council make any modifications of Schedule 4 or 5 which She considers necessary or expedient.

(3) Her Majesty may by Order in Council specify functions which are to be treated, for such purposes of this Act as may be specified, as being, or as not being, functions which are exercisable in or as regards Scotland.

(4) An Order in Council under this section may also make such modifications of—

(a) any enactment or prerogative instrument (including any enactment comprised in or made under this Act), or

(b) any other instrument or document,

as Her Majesty considers necessary or expedient in connection with other provision made by the Order.

[¹ (5) Subsection (6) applies where any alteration is made—

(a) to the matters which are reserved matters, or

(b) to Schedule 4,

(whether by virtue of the making, revocation or expiry of an Order in Council under this section or otherwise).

(6) Where the effect of the alteration is that a provision of an Act of the Scottish Parliament ceases to be within the legislative competence of the Parliament, the provision does not for that reason cease to have effect (unless an enactment provides otherwise).]

Amendment

1. Scotland Act 2012 ss. 9(1) and 44(5) (July 3, 2012).

General Note

This section introduces the list of reserved matters in Schedule 5. It also   7.006
provides power, by Order in Council, to modify Schedules 4 or 5 and to specify that functions should be treated as being, or not being, exercisable "in or as regards Scotland" for particular purposes. Section F1 of Part 2 of Schedule 5 reserves social security matters to the Westminster Parliament, but subject to certain exceptions. I should be noted that provisions in Part 3 of the Scotland Act 2016 make a series of important amendments to Section F1 of Part 2 of Schedule 5, not all of which are in force yet. These amendments will increase the devolved responsibility for welfare policy and delivery in Scotland through the devolution of welfare powers to the Scottish Parliament and/or the Scottish Ministers. For example, s.22 of the Scotland Act 2016, when fully in force, will amend Section F1 to give the Scottish Parliament legislative competence in relation to disability, industrial injuries and carers' benefits, which are currently reserved to Westminster. The Scottish Parliament will have the power to create additional benefits, replace existing benefits with new benefits or other payments and to determine the structure and value of such provision. Similarly, the amendments made by s.23, when fully in force, will give the Scottish Parliament legislative competence over provision of financial or other assistance for the purposes of meeting or reducing maternity expenses, funeral expenses and expenses for heating incurred due to cold weather. See further the paper by the Scottish Government, *A New Future for Social Security: Consultation on Social Security in Scotland* (July 2016) and the Social Security (Scotland) Bill 2017 (SP Bill 18), currently before the Scottish Parliament.

Schedule 5   7.007

PART II

SPECIFIC RESERVATIONS

Preliminary

1. The matters to which any of the Sections in this Part apply are reserved matters for the purposes of this Act.

2. A Section applies to any matter described or referred to in it when read with any illustrations, exceptions or interpretation provisions in that Section.

3. Any illustrations, exceptions or interpretation provisions in a Section relate only to that Section (so that an entry under the heading "exceptions" does not affect any other Section).

7.008   *[Heads A-E and F2-F4 and G-L omitted]*

Head F—Social Security

F1. Social security schemes

Section F1.

Schemes supported from central or local funds which provide assistance for social security purposes to or in respect of individuals by way of benefits.

Requiring persons to—

(a) establish and administer schemes providing assistance for social security purposes to or in respect of individuals, or

(b) make payments to or in respect of such schemes,

and to keep records and supply information in connection with such schemes.

The circumstances in which a person is liable to maintain himself or another for the purposes of the enactments relating to social security and the Child Support Acts 1991 and 1995.

The subject-matter of the Vaccine Damage Payment Scheme.

Illustrations

7.009   National Insurance; Social Fund; [¹ . . .] recovery of benefits for accident, injury or disease from persons paying damages; deductions from benefits for the purpose of meeting an individual's debts; sharing information between government departments for the purposes of the enactments relating to social security; making decisions for the purposes of schemes mentioned in the reservation and appeals against such decisions.

Exceptions

7.010   [⁸ **Exception 1**

Any of the following benefits—

(a) disability benefits, other than severe disablement benefit or industrial injuries benefits,

(b) severe disablement benefit, so far as payable in respect of a relevant person, and

(c) industrial injuries benefits, so far as relating to relevant employment or to participation in training for relevant employment;

but this exception does not except a benefit which is, or which is an element of, an excluded benefit.

Exception 2

Carer's benefits, other than a benefit which is, or which is an element of, an excluded benefit.]

[³ **Exception 3**]

The subject-matter of Part II of the Social Work (Scotland) Act 1968 (social welfare services), section 2 of the Chronically Sick and Disabled Persons Act 1970 (provision of welfare services), section 50 of the Children Act 1975 (payments towards maintenance of children), section 15 of the Enterprise and New Towns (Scotland) Act 1990 (industrial injuries benefit), and sections 22 (promotion of welfare of children in need), 29 and 30 (advice and assistance for young persons formerly looked after by local authorities) of the Children (Scotland) Act 1995.

[⁹ **Exception 4**

Providing financial or other assistance for the purposes of meeting or reducing—

(a) maternity expenses,

(b) funeral expenses, or

(c) expenses for heating in cold weather.]

[⁴ **Exception 5**

Providing financial assistance to an individual who—

(a) is entitled to a reserved benefit, and

(b) appears to require financial assistance, in addition to any amount the individual receives by way of reserved benefit, for the purpose, or one of the purposes, for which the benefit is being provided.

This exception does not except discretionary financial assistance in a reserved benefit.

This exception also does not except providing financial assistance to meet or help to meet housing costs (as to which, see exception 6).

This exception also does not except providing financial assistance where the requirement for it arises from reduction, non-payability or suspension of a reserved benefit as a result of an individual's conduct (for example, non-compliance with work-related requirements relating to the benefit) unless—

(a) the requirement for it also arises from some exceptional event or exceptional circumstances, and

(b) the requirement for it is immediate.

For the purposes of this exception "reserved benefit" means a benefit which is to any extent a reserved matter.]

[¹⁰ **Exception 6**   7.011

Providing financial assistance to an individual who—

(a) is entitled to—

(i) housing benefit, or

(ii) any other reserved benefit payable in respect of a liability to make rent payments, and

(b) appears to require financial assistance, in addition to any amount the individual receives by way of housing benefit or such other reserved benefit, to meet or help to meet housing costs.

This exception does not except discretionary financial assistance in a reserved benefit.

This exception also does not except providing financial assistance where the requirement for it arises from reduction, non-payability or suspension of a reserved benefit as a result of an individual's conduct (for example, non-compliance with work-related requirements relating to the benefit) unless—

(a) the requirement for it also arises from some exceptional event or exceptional circumstances, and

(b) the requirement for it is immediate.

For the purposes of this exception—

"rent payments"—

(a) has the meaning given from time to time by paragraph 2 of Schedule 1 to the Universal Credit Regulations 2013 (S.I. 2013/376) or any re-enactment of that paragraph, or

(b) if at any time universal credit ceases to be payable to anyone, has the meaning given by that paragraph or any re-enactment of that paragraph immediately before that time;

"reserved benefit" means a benefit which is to any extent a reserved matter.]

[⁵ Exception 7

Providing financial or other assistance to or in respect of individuals who appear to require it for the purposes of meeting, or helping to meet, a short-term need that requires to be met to avoid a risk to the well-being of an individual.

This exception does not except providing assistance where the requirement for it arises from reduction, non-payability or suspension of a benefit as a result of an individual's conduct (for example, non-compliance with work-related requirements relating to the benefit) unless—

(a) the requirement for it also arises from some exceptional event or exceptional circumstances, and

(b) the need is immediate as well as short-term.

Exception 8

Providing occasional financial or other assistance to or in respect of individuals who have been or might otherwise be—

(a) in prison, hospital, a residential care establishment or other institution, or

(b) homeless or otherwise living an unsettled way of life,

and who appear to require the assistance to establish or maintain a settled home.]

[⁶ Exception 10

Schemes which provide assistance for social security purposes to or in respect of individuals by way of benefits and which—

(a) are supported from sums paid out of the Scottish Consolidated Fund,

(b) do not fall within exceptions 1 to 9, and

(c) are not connected with reserved matters (other than matters reserved only by virtue of this Section).

This exception does not except providing assistance by way of pensions to or in respect of individuals who qualify by reason of old age.

This exception does not except providing assistance where the requirement for it arises from reduction, non-payability or suspension of a reserved benefit as a result of an individual's conduct (for example, non-compliance with work-related requirements relating to the benefit) unless—

(a) the requirement for it also arises from some exceptional event or exceptional circumstances, and

(b) the requirement for it is immediate.

For the purposes of this exception "reserved benefit" means a benefit which is to any extent a reserved matter.

In this exception the reference to schemes supported from sums paid out of the Scottish Consolidated Fund does not include schemes—

(a) in respect of which sums are at some time paid out of the Scottish Consolidated Fund, but

(b) which are directly supported from payments out of the Consolidated Fund, the National Insurance Fund or the Social Fund, or out of money provided by Parliament.]

[⁷ **Exclusions from exceptions 1 to 10**

Nothing in exceptions 1 to 10 is to be read as excepting—

(a) the National Insurance Fund,

(b) the Social Fund, or

(c) the provision by a Minister of the Crown of assistance by way of loan for the purpose of meeting, or helping to meet, an intermittent expense.]

Interpretation

"Benefits" includes pensions, allowances, grants, loans and any other form of financial assistance. 7.012

Providing assistance for social security purposes to or in respect of individuals includes (among other things) providing assistance to or in respect of individuals—

(a) who qualify by reason of old age, survivorship, disability, sickness, incapacity, injury, unemployment, maternity or the care of children or others needing care,(b) who qualify by reason of low income, or(c) in relation to their housing costs or liabilities for local taxes.

[² [¹¹ . . .]]

[¹² *"Disability benefit"* means a benefit which is normally payable in respect of—

(a) a significant adverse effect that impairment to a person's physical or mental condition has on his or her ability to carry out day-to-day activities (for example, looking after yourself, moving around or communicating), or

(b) a significant need (for example, for attention or for supervision to avoid substantial danger to anyone) arising from impairment to a person's physical or mental condition;

and for this purpose the adverse effect or need must not be short-term.

"Severe disablement benefit" means a benefit which is normally payable in respect of—

(a) a person's being incapable of work for a period of at least 28 weeks beginning not later than the person's 20th birthday, or

(b) a person's being incapable of work and disabled for a period of at least 28 weeks;

and *"relevant person"*, in relation to severe disablement benefit, means a person who is entitled to severe disablement allowance under section 68 of the Social Security Contributions and Benefits Act 1992 on the date on which section 22 of the Scotland Act 2016 comes into force as respects severe disablement benefit.

"Industrial injuries benefit" means a benefit which is normally payable in respect of—

(a) a person's having suffered personal injury caused by accident arising out of and in the course of his or her employment, or

(b) a person's having developed a disease or personal injury due to the nature of his or her employment;

and for this purpose *"employment"* includes participation in training for employment.

"Relevant employment", in relation to industrial injuries benefit, means employment which—

(a) is employed earner's employment for the purposes of section 94 of the Social Security Contributions and Benefits Act 1992 as at 28 May 2015 (the date of introduction into Parliament of the Bill for the Scotland Act 2016), or

(b) would be such employment but for—

(i) the contract purporting to govern the employment being void, or

(ii) the person concerned not being lawfully employed,

as a result of a contravention of, or non-compliance with, provision in or made by virtue of an enactment passed to protect employees.

"Carer's benefit" means a benefit which is normally payable in respect of the regular and substantial provision of care by a person to a disabled person; and for this purpose

"disabled person" means a person to whom a disability benefit is normally payable.

"Excluded benefit" means—

(a) a benefit, entitlement to which, or the amount of which, is normally determined to any extent by reference to a person's income or capital (for example, universal credit under Part 1 of the Welfare Reform Act 2012),

(b) a benefit which is payable out of the National Insurance Fund (for example, employment and support allowance under section 1(2)(a) of the Welfare Reform Act 2007), or

(c) a benefit payable by way of lump sum in respect of a person's having, or having had—

(i) pneumoconiosis,

(ii) byssinosis,

(iii) diffuse mesothelioma,

(iv) bilateral diffuse pleural thickening, or

(v) primary carcinoma of the lung where there is accompanying evidence of one or both of asbestosis and bilateral
diffuse pleural thickening.

"Employment" includes any trade, business, profession, office or vocation (and *"employed"* is to be read accordingly).]

AMENDMENTS

1. Welfare Reform Act 2012 Sch.14(1) para.1 (April 1, 2013).
2. Scotland Act 1998 (Modification of Schedule 5) (No.2) Order 2013 (SI
   2013/192) art.2(3) (April 1, 2013).
3. Scotland Act 2016 Pt 3 s.22(3) (September 5, 2016).
4. Scotland Act 2016 Pt 3 s.24 (September 5, 2016).
5. Scotland Act 2016 Pt 3 s.26 (September 5, 2016).
6. Scotland Act 2016 Pt 3 s.28(2) (September 5, 2016).
7. Scotland Act 2016 Pt 3 s.23(3) (September 5, 2016).
8. Scotland Act 2016 Pt 3 s.22(2) (May 17, 2017).
9. Scotland Act 2016 Pt 3 s.23(2) (May 17, 2017).
10. Scotland Act 2016 Pt 3 s.25 (April 1, 2017).
11. Scotland Act 2016 Pt 3 s.23(4) (May 17, 2017).
12. Scotland Act 2016 Pt 3 s.22(4) (May 17, 2017).

The Universal Credit (Claims and Payments) (Scotland) Regulations 2017

SI 2017/227

[In force October 4, 2017]

Made on June 27, 2017 by the Scottish Ministers in exercise of the powers conferred by section 5(1)(i) and (p) and section 189(4)(a), (5) and (6) of the Social Security Administration Act 1992 and all other powers enabling them to do so.

In accordance with sections 29(4) and 30(3) of the Scotland Act 2016, they have consulted the Secretary of State.

GENERAL NOTE

7.012.1   These Regulations modify the effect of the Universal Credit, Personal Independence Payment, Jobseeker's Allowance and Employment and Support Allowance (Claims and Payments) Regulations 2013 as they apply to a "Scottish UC applicant or recipient" as defined in reg.1(2).

Citation, commencement and interpretation

7.013   **1.**—(1) These Regulations may be cited as the Universal Credit (Claims and Payments) (Scotland) Regulations 2017 and come into force on 4th October 2017.

(2) In these Regulations—

"the 2013 Claims and Payments Regulations" means the Universal Credit, Personal Independence Payment, Jobseeker's Allowance and Employment and Support Allowance (Claims and Payments) Regulations 2013;

"housing costs element" has the meaning in regulation 25 of the Universal Credit Regulations 2013, but does not include a housing costs element calculated under schedule 5 of those Regulations (housing costs element for owner-occupiers);

"Scottish UC applicant or recipient" means a person applying for universal credit, or awarded universal credit, who resides in Scotland (and any one of the members of a couple living in Scotland who jointly make a claim for, or have been awarded, universal credit).

Persons to be able to request twice-monthly payments

7.014   **2.**—(1) Despite regulation 47(1) of the 2013 Claims and Payments Regulations (universal credit generally to be paid monthly in arrears), a Scottish UC applicant or recipient may request at any time to receive future payments of universal credit twice-monthly in arrears, where that is more frequent than the payments that would otherwise be made.

(2) A person who has made the request referred to in paragraph (1) may at any time—

(a) request that the Secretary of State cancel it; or

(b) make a further such request.

(3) The Secretary of State must agree to a request made under paragraph (1) or (2), unless the Secretary of State considers it to be

unreasonable to implement the request, in which case the Secretary of State must advise the person who made it of the reasons for its refusal.

(4) Nothing in this regulation restricts the ability of the Secretary of State to arrange for payments of universal credit to be made twice-monthly, or more or less frequently than twice-monthly, in any case or class of case.

GENERAL NOTE

Regulation 47(1) of the Universal Credit, Personal Independence Payment, Jobseeker's Allowance and Employment and Support Allowance (Claims and Payments) Regulations 2013 provides that universal credit is payable monthly in arrears in respect of each assessment period: see para.4.57 of Vol.V of the main work. However, this regulation allows a Scottish UC applicant or recipient to request that future payments of universal credit should be made twice-monthly in arrears. Under para.(3), the Secretary of State must agree to that request unless it is considered unreasonable to implement it, in which case reasons must be given for the refusal.

The general principle in reg.47(1) is subject to a general power for the Secretary of State to make other arrangements for the payment of universal credit in any case or class of case. Para.(4) provides that reg.2 does not limit that power.

7.015

Persons to be advised that they can request twice-monthly payments

3.—(1) Every person entitled to request twice-monthly payments under regulation 2(1) must be advised that he or she can so request and be given information about the implications of that choice.

(2) Paragraph (1) does not apply where the Secretary of State is arranging, or has arranged, for payments of universal credit to be made twice-monthly, or more frequently than twice-monthly.

7.016

GENERAL NOTE

Unless universal credit is already being paid twice-monthly (or more frequently), those who are entitled to request twice-monthly payments of universal credit must be advised that they can do so and be given information about the implications of that choice.

7.017

Tenants to be able to request direct payments for rent and services

4.—(1) A Scottish UC applicant or recipient whose award of universal credit will include, or includes, a housing costs element in respect of a rent payment or service charge payment may request at any time to have an amount of universal credit paid directly to the person to whom those payments are due.

(2) In paragraph (1)—
(a) "rent payment" has the meaning given by paragraph 2 of schedule 1 of the Universal Credit Regulations 2013; and
(b) "service charge payment" has the meaning given by paragraph 7 of that schedule.

7.018

(3) A person who has made the request referred to in paragraph (1) may at any time—

(a) request that the Secretary of State cancel it; or

(b) make a further such request.

(4) The Secretary of State must agree to a request made under paragraph (1) or (3), unless the Secretary of State considers it to be unreasonable to implement the request, in which case the Secretary of State must advise the person who made it of the reasons for its refusal.

(5) The amount of an award of universal credit to be paid in accordance with paragraph (1) is the amount of the housing costs element of the award that relates to liability to make rent payments and service charge payments or, if less, the amount of the award.

(6) Nothing in this regulation restricts the ability of the Secretary of State to direct that payments of universal credit be made to a person other than a claimant under regulation 58 of the 2013 Claims and Payments Regulations (payment to another person on the claimant's behalf) or to make deductions and payments in accordance with the provisions of schedule 6 of those Regulations.

GENERAL NOTE

7.019 Under reg.58 of the Universal Credit, Personal Independence Payment, Jobseeker's Allowance and Employment and Support Allowance (Claims and Payments) Regulations 2013, (para.4.69 of Vol.V of the main work) the Secretary of State may direct that universal credit be paid to another person (*e.g.*, a landlord) if appears to him to be necessary to protect the interests the interests of the claimant(s) or a member of their family. Reg.60, and Sch.6 para.7, (para.4.102 of Vol.V of the main work) allow the Secretary of State to make deductions from universal credit and pay them to a landlord, where a claimant is in arrears of rent or service charges. However, in England and Wales, there is no general power to pay the housing costs element of universal credit to anyone other than the claimant.

However, reg.4 allows Scottish UC applicants or recipients whose universal credit includes the housing costs element in respect of rent or service charges to request to have that element paid directly to their landlords. Under para.(4), the Secretary of State must agree to that request unless it is considered unreasonable to implement it, in which case reasons must be given for the refusal.

Para.(5) provides that reg.4 does not limit the Secretary of State's powers under reg.58 and Sch.6 para.7.

Tenants to be advised that they can request direct payments for rent and services

7.020 **5.**—(1) Every person entitled to request direct payments under regulation 4(1) must be advised that he or she can request to have an amount of universal credit paid directly, as described in that regulation.

(2) Paragraph (1) does not apply where the Secretary of State is arranging, or has arranged, for universal credit to be paid directly.

GENERAL NOTE

Unless the housing costs element of universal credit is already being paid directly to the landlord, those who are entitled to request direct payments must be advised that they can do so. In contrast to reg.3, there is no requirement that they should also be given information about the implications of that choice.

Applications for, and awards of, universal credit to which these Regulations do not apply

6.—(1) These Regulations have no effect in relation to—   7.021

(a) an award of universal credit which has been made before 4th October 2017;

(b) an application made before that date for such an award or an award made as a result of such an application;

(c) an award of universal credit which is not administered on the digital service computer system operated by the Secretary of State in digital service areas;

(d) an application for such an award which will not be administered on that system if granted;

(e) an award of universal credit which is administered on that system only as a result of a decision of the Secretary of State to transfer the administration of that award to that system from another system operated by the Secretary of State.

(2) For the purpose of paragraph (1)(c), "digital service area" has the meaning given in regulation 5(3) of the Universal Credit (Digital Service) Amendment Regulations 2014.

GENERAL NOTE

These regulations do not apply to Scottish UC applicants or recipients who are   7.022
in "live service" areas or in respect of awards made before October 4, 2017, or in respect of claims for such an award.

PART VIII

FORTHCOMING CHANGES AND UP-RATINGS OF BENEFITS

FORTHCOMING CHANGES

Universal Credit

There are a number of impending changes to the universal credit **8.001**
regime. Following the Autumn Budget statement for 2017, the Secretary
of State for Work and Pensions announced on November 23, 2017 a
number of adjustments to the planned roll-out of universal credit (see
the DWP press release at https://www.gov.uk/government/news/more-
detail-on-15-billion-package-of-support-for-universal-credit). The most
significant of these changes is the abolition of the 7-day waiting period
with effect from February 14, 2018 (see Universal Credit (Miscellaneous
Amendments, Saving and Transitional Provision) Regulations 2018(SI
2018/65), reg.3(3), omitting reg.19A of the Universal Credit Regulations 2013 (SI 2013/376), as previously amended). Other reforms
include extending the repayment of advances of universal credit from 6
to 12 months, and allowing claimants to receive 100% of their payment
upfront from January 2018 (those who made a claim in December 2017
can get a 50% advance, and then in January can ask for a top up to
100%). These, other minor February 2018 amendments and more
extensive amendments coming into force in April 2018 will be included
in the 2018/19 main volumes. As part of this wider process the DWP is
also changing the rate of Universal Credit full service rollout for 3
months from February 2018 to 10 jobcentres a month, increasing to 41
in May 2018. However, the Secretary of State also announced that:

> "To help to ensure a smooth transition to full service, we have also
> decided to close new claims to our prototype universal credit live
> service. That will not affect any existing claims. In addition, currently
> any new UC claim from a family with three or more children will be
> routed back to tax credits until November 2018. With the extension to
> the roll-out plan that will now shift to the end of January 2019."

As a result, potential new claimants in live service areas are to be
directed to claim housing benefit or other legacy benefits (see DWP, *HB
Urgent Bulletin 4/2017*). These changes have been effected by the Secretary of State making a determination in the exercise of his discretionary
powers under regulation 4(1) of the Universal Credit (Transitional Provisions) Regulations 2014 (SI 2014/1230). Existing claims in the areas in

question will not be affected. See further DWP, *ADM Memo 1/18*. The revised roll-out programme is detailed in *Transition Rollout Schedule —November 2017 to December 2018*: https://www.gov.uk/government/uploads/system/uploads/attachment_data/file/664591/universal-credit-transition-rollout-schedule.pdf

Note also that in Scotland and as from January 31, 2018, the Universal Credit (Claims and Payments) (Scotland) Amendment Regulations 2017 (SSI/2017/436) amend the Universal Credit (Claims and Payments) (Scotland) Regulations 2017 (SSI/2017/227). These amendments permit greater flexibility in the payment of universal credit to claimants in Scotland—i.e. twice-monthly payments and payments direct to a landlord. These will be available to all claimants whose awards are being, or will be, administered on the digital service computer system, whereas before they were only available to full service claims made on or after October 4, 2017.

The Loans for Mortgage Interest Regulations 2017

8.002   As a result of the Loans for Mortgage Interest Regulations 2017 (SI 2017/725), support for mortgage interest (SMI) will no longer exist as a component of benefit for new or existing claimants as from April 6, 2018. Claimants will instead be invited to apply for a loan if they want to continue to be supported. Loans will berepaid upon the sale of a claimant's house or on aclaimant's return to work, if the borrower can afford it. As the 2017 Regulations came into effect earlier for certain purposes, they have been included in Part I above (New Legislation); see the General Note there.

NEW BENEFIT RATES FROM APRIL 2018

NEW BENEFIT RATES FROM APRIL 2018

(Benefits covered in Volume I)

	April 2017	April 2018
	£ pw	£ pw
Disability benefits		
Attendance allowance		
higher rate	83.10	85.60
lower rate	55.65	57.30
Disability living allowance		
care component		
highest rate	83.10	85.60
middle rate	55.65	57.30
lowest rate	22.00	22.65
mobility component		
higher rate	58.00	59.75
lower rate	22.00	22.65
Personal independence payment		
daily living component		
enhanced rate	83.10	83.60
standard rate	55.65	57.30
mobility component		
enhanced rate	58.00	59.75
standard rate	22.00	22.65
Carer's allowance	62.70	64.60
Severe disablement allowance		
basic rate	75.40	77.65
age related addition—higher rate	11.25	11.60
age related addition—middle rate	6.25	6.45
age related addition—lower rate	6.25	6.45

	April 2017	April 2018
	£ pw	£ pw

Maternity benefits

Maternity allowance
standard rate — 140.98 — 145.18

Bereavement benefits and retirement pensions

Widowed parent's allowance or widowed mother's allowance — 113.70 — 117.10

Bereavement allowance or widow's pension
standard rate — 113.70 — 117.10

Retirement pension

	April 2017	April 2018
Category A	122.30	125.95
Category B (higher)	122.30	125.95
Category B (lower)	73.30	75.50
Category C	73.30	75.50
Category D	73.30	75.50

New state pension — 159.55 — 164.35

Incapacity benefit

Long-term incapacity benefit

	April 2017	April 2018
basic rate	106.40	109.60
increase for age—higher rate	11.25	11.60
increase for age—lower rate	6.25	6.45
invalidity allowance—higher rate	11.25	11.60
invalidity allowance—middle rate	6.25	6.45
invalidity allowance—lower rate	6.25	6.45

Short-term incapacity benefit

	April 2017	April 2018
under pension age—higher rate	95.00	97.85
under pension age—lower rate	80.25	82.65
over pension age—higher rate	106.40	109.60
over pension age—lower rate	102.10	105.15

Dependency increases

Adult

	April 2017	April 2018
carer's allowance	36.90	38.00
severe disablement allowance	37.10	38.20
retirement pension (Category A)	66.35	68.35
retirement pension (Category C)	39.70	40.90
long-term incapacity benefit	61.80	63.65
short-term incapacity benefit under pension age	48.15	49.60
short-term incapacity benefit over pension age	59.50	61.30

Child — 11.35[1] — 11.35[1]

	April 2017	April 2018
	£ pw	£ pw

Industrial injuries benefits

Disablement benefit

100%	169.70	174.80
90%	152.73	157.32
80%	135.76	139.84
70%	118.79	122.36
60%	101.82	104.88
50%	84.85	87.40
40%	67.88	69.92
30%	50.91	52.44
20%	33.94	34.96

unemployability supplement

basic rate	104.90	108.05
increase for adult dependant	62.70	64.60
increase for child dependant	11.35[1]	11.35[1]
increase for early incapacity—higher rate	21.70	22.35
increase for early incapacity—middle rate	14.00	14.40
increase for early incapacity—lower rate	7.00	7.20

constant attendance allowance

exceptional rate	135.80	139.80
intermediate rate	101.85	104.85
normal maximum rate	67.90	69.90
part-time rate	33.95	34.95

exceptionally severe disablement allowance	67.90	69.90

Reduced earnings allowance

maximum rate	67.88	69.92

Death benefit
widow's pension

higher rate	122.30	125.95
lower rate	36.69	37.79
widower's pension	122.30	125.95

Notes

1. These sums payable in respect of children are reduced if payable in respect of the only, elder or eldest child for whom child benefit is being paid (see reg.8 of the Social Security (Overlapping Benefits) Regulations 1979 on p.619 of Vol.1 of the main work).

	April 2017	April 2018
	£ pw	£ pw

Employment and support allowance

Contribution-based personal rates

assessment phase—*aged under 25*	57.90	57.90
aged 25 or over	73.10	73.10
main phase	73.10	73.10

Components

work-related activity	29.05	29.05
support	36.55	37.65

Income-based personal allowances

single person—*aged under 25*	57.90	57.90
aged 25 or over	73.10	73.10
lone parent—*aged under 18*	57.90	57.90
aged 18 or over	73.10	73.10
couple—*both aged under 18*	57.90	57.90
both aged under 18, with a child	87.50	87.50
both aged under 18, (main phase)	73.10	73.10
both aged under 18, with a child (main phase)	114.85	114.85
one aged under 18, one aged 18 or over	114.85	114.85
both aged 18 or over	114.85	114.85

Premiums

pensioner—*single person with no component*	86.25	89.90
couple with no component	128.40	133.95
enhanced disability—*single person*	15.90	16.40
couple	22.85	23.55
severe disability—*single person*	62.45	64.30
couple (one qualifies)	62.45	64.30
couple (both qualify)	124.90	128.60
carer	34.95	36.00

NEW BENEFIT RATES FROM APRIL 2018

(Benefits covered in Volume II)

	April 2017	April 2018
	£ pw	£ pw

Contribution-based jobseeker's allowance

personal rates—*aged under 25*	57.90	57.90
aged 25 or over	73.10	73.10

Income support and income-based jobseeker's allowance

personal allowances		
single person—*aged under 25*	57.90	57.90
aged 25 or over	73.10	73.10
lone parent—*aged under 18*	57.90	57.90
aged 18 or over	73.10	73.10
couple—*both aged under 18*	57.90	57.90
both aged under 18, with a child	87.50	87.50
one aged under 18, one aged under 25	57.90	57.90
one aged under 18, one aged 25 or over	73.10	73.10
both aged 18 or over	114.85	114.85
child	66.90	66.90
premiums		
family—*ordinary*	17.45	17.45
lone parent	17.45	17.45
pensioner—*single person (JSA only)*	86.25	89.90
couple	128.40	133.95
disability—*single person*	32.55	33.55
couple	46.40	47.80
enhanced disability—*single person*	15.90	16.40
couple	22.85	23.55
disabled child	24.78	25.48
severe disability—*single person*	62.45	64.30
couple (one qualifies)	62.45	64.30
couple (both qualify)	124.90	128.60
disabled child	60.90	62.86
carer	34.95	36.00

Pension credit

Standard minimum guarantee		
single person	159.35	163.00
couple	243.25	248.80

New Benefit Rates from April 2018

	April 2017	April 2018
	£ pw	£ pw
Additional amount for severe disability		
single person	62.45	64.30
couple (one qualifies)	62.45	64.30
couple (both qualify)	124.90	128.60
Additional amount for carers	34.95	36.00
Savings credit threshold		
single person	137.35	140.67
couple	218.42	223.82
Maximum savings credit		
single person	13.20	13.40
couple	14.90	14.99

NEW TAX CREDIT AND BENEFIT RATES 2018–2019

(Benefits covered in Volume IV)

	2017–18	2018–19
	£ pw	£ pw
Benefits in respect of children		
Child benefit		
only, elder or eldest child (couple)	20.70	20.70
each subsequent child	13.70	13.70
Guardian's allowance	16.70	17.20
Employer-paid benefits		
Standard rates		
Statutory sick pay	89.35	92.05
Statutory maternity pay, Statutory paternity pay	140.98	145.18
Statutory shared parental pay	140.98	145.18
Statutory adoption pay	140.98	145.18
Income threshold	113.00	116.00

	2017–18	2018–19
	£ pa	£ pa
Working tax credit		
Basic element	1,960	1,960
Couple and lone parent element	2,010	2,010
30 hour element	810	810
Disabled worker element	3,000	3,090
Severe disability element	1,290	1,330
Child care element		
maximum eligible cost for one child	*175 pw*	*175 pw*
maximum eligible cost for two or more		
children	*300 pw*	*300 pw*
per cent of eligible costs covered	*70%*	*70%*
Child tax credit		
Family element	545	545
Child element	2,780	2,780
Disabled child element	3,175	3,275
Severely disabled child element	4,465	4,600
Tax credit income thresholds		
Income rise disregard	2,500	2,500
Income fall disregard	2,500	2,500
Income threshold	6,420	6,420
Income threshold for those entitled to child tax		
credit only	16,105	16,105
Withdrawal rate	*41%*	*41%*

NEW UNIVERSAL CREDIT RATES FROM APRIL 2018

(Benefits covered in Volume V)

	April 2017	April 2018
	£ pm	£ pm
Standard allowances		
Single claimant—*aged under 25*	251.77	251.77
aged 25 or over	317.82	317.82
Joint claimant—*both aged under 25*	395.20	395.20
one or both aged 25 or over	498.89	498.89
Child element—*first child*	277.08	277.08
second/ subsequent child	231.67	231.67
Disabled child addition—*lower rate*	126.11	126.11
higher rate	372.30	383.86
Limited Capability for Work element	126.11	126.11
Limited Capability for Work and Work-Related Activity element	318.76	328.32
Carer element	151.89	156.45
Childcare element—*maximum for one child*	646.35	646.35
maximum for two or more children	1,108.04	1,108.04
Non-dependants' housing cost contributions	70.06	72.16
Work allowances		
Higher work allowance (no housing element)		
one or more children	397.00	397.00
limited capability for work	397.00	397.00
Lower work allowance		
one or more children	192.00	192.00
limited capability for work	192.00	192.00